)N INFORMATION SYSTEMS

Video training courses are available on the subjects
James Martin ADVANCED TECHNOLOGY LIBRARY of over 300 tapes and disks,
from Applied Learning, 1751 West Diehl Road, Naperville, IL 60540 (tel: 312-369-3000).

Database	Telecommunications	Networks and Data Communications	Society
AN END USER'S GUIDE TO DATABASE	TELECOMMUNICATIONS AND THE COMPUTER (third edition)	PRINCIPLES OF DATA COMMUNICATION	THE COMPUTERIZED SOCIETY
PRINCIPLES OF DATABASE MANAGEMENT (second edition)	FUTURE DEVELOPMENTS IN TELECOMMUNICATIONS (third edition)	TELEPROCESSING NETWORK ORGANIZATION	TELEMATIC SOCIETY: A CHALLENGE FOR TOMORROW
COMPUTER DATABASE ORGANIZATION (third edition)	COMMUNICATIONS SATELLITE SYSTEMS	SYSTEMS ANALYSIS FOR DATA TRANSMISSION	TECHNOLOGY'S CRUCIBLE
MANAGING THE DATABASE ENVIRONMENT (second edition)	ISDN	DATA COMMUNICATION TECHNOLOGY	VIEWDATA AND THE INFORMATION SOCIETY
DATABASE ANALYSIS AND DESIGN	**Distributed Processing**	DATA COMMUNICATION DESIGN TECHNIQUES	TELEVISION AND THE COMPUTER
VSAM: ACCESS METHOD SERVICES AND PROGRAMMING TECHNIQUES	COMPUTER NETWORKS AND DISTRIBUTED PROCESSING	SNA: IBM's NETWORKING SOLUTION	THE WORLD INFORMATION ECONOMY
DB2: CONCEPTS, DESIGN, AND PROGRAMMING	DESIGN AND STRATEGY FOR DISTRIBUTED DATA PROCESSING	ISDN	**Systems In General**
IDMS/R: CONCEPTS, DESIGN, AND PROGRAMMING	**Office Automation**	LOCAL AREA NETWORKS: ARCHITECTURES AND IMPLEMENTATIONS	A BREAKTHROUGH IN MAKING COMPUTERS FRIENDLY: THE MACINTOSH COMPUTER
SQL	IBM OFFICE SYSTEMS: ARCHITECTURES AND IMPLEMENTATIONS	OFFICE AUTOMATION STANDARDS	SAA: IBM's SYSTEMS APPLICATION ARCHITECTURE
Security	OFFICE AUTOMATION STANDARDS	DATA COMMUNICATION STANDARDS	
SECURITY, ACCURACY, AND PRIVACY IN COMPUTER SYSTEMS		CORPORATE COMMUNICATIONS STRATEGY	
SECURITY AND PRIVACY IN COMPUTER SYSTEMS		COMPUTER NETWORKS AND DISTRIBUTED PROCESSING: SOFTWARE, TECHNIQUES, AND ARCHITECTURE	

SNA

A ~~*James Martin*~~ **BOOK**

THE JAMES MARTIN BOOKS

- Application Development Without Programmers
- Communications Satellite Systems
- Computer Data-Base Organization, Second Edition
- Computer Networks and Distributed Processing: Software, Techniques, and Architecture
- Design and Strategy of Distributed Data Processing
- Design of Man-Computer Dialogues
- Design of Real Time Computer Systems
- An End User's Guide to Data Base
- Fourth-Generation Languages, Volume I: Principles
- Future Developments in Telecommunications, Second Edition
- Information Engineering
- An Information Systems Manifesto
- Introduction to Teleprocessing
- Managing the Data-Base Environment
- Principles of Data-Base Management
- Programming Real-Time Computer Systems
- Recommended Diagramming Standards for Analysts and Programmers
- Security, Accuracy, and Privacy in Computer Systems
- Strategic Data Planning Methodologies
- Systems Analysis for Data Transmission
- System Design from Provably Correct Constructs
- Technology's Crucible
- Telecommunications and the Computer, Second Edition
- Telematic Society: A Challenge for Tomorrow

- Teleprocessing Network Organization
- Viewdata and the Information Society

with Carma McClure

- Action Diagrams: Clearly Structured Program Design
- Diagramming Techniques for Analysts and Programmers
- Software Maintenance: The Problem and Its Solutions
- Structured Techniques: The Basis for Case, Revised Edition

with The ARBEN Group, Inc.

- A Breakthrough in Making Computers Friendly: The Macintosh Computer
- Data Communication Technology
- Fourth-Generation Languages, Volume II: Representative Fourth-Generation Languages
- Fourth-Generation Languages, Volume III: 4GLs from IBM
- Principles of Data Communications
- SNA: IBM's Networking Solution
- VSAM: Access Method Services and Programming Techniques

with Adrian Norman

- The Computerized Society

with Oxman

- Building Expert Systems

SNA

IBM's Networking Solution

JAMES MARTIN

with

Kathleen Kavanagh Chapman
The ARBEN Group, Inc.

PRENTICE-HALL, INC., Englewood Cliffs, New Jersey 07632

Library of Congress Cataloging-in-Publication Data

MARTIN, JAMES (date)
    SNA: IBM's networking solution.

    Includes index.
    1. SNA (Computer network architecture)
2. Computer network architectures. I. Chapman,
Kathleen Kavanagh. II. Title.
TK5105.5.M368 1987   004.6'5   86–30446
ISBN 0-13-815143-1

Editorial/production supervision: *Kathryn Gollin Marshak*
Jacket design: Bruce Kenselaar
Manufacturing buyer: *S. Gordon Obsourne*

SNA: IBM's Networking Solution
James Martin, with Kathleen Kavanagh Chapman

Printed in the United States of America

10   9   8   7   6   5

ISBN 0-13-815143-1   025

PRENTICE-HALL INTERNATIONAL (UK) LIMITED, *London*
PRENTICE-HALL OF AUSTRALIA PTY. LIMITED, *Sydney*
PRENTICE-HALL CANADA INC., *Toronto*
PRENTICE-HALL HISPANOAMERICANA, S.A., *Mexico*
PRENTICE-HALL OF INDIA PRIVATE LIMITED, *New Delhi*
PRENTICE-HALL OF JAPAN, INC., *Tokyo*
PRENTICE-HALL OF SOUTHEAST ASIA PTE. LTD., *Singapore*
EDITORA PRENTICE-HALL DO BRASIL, LTDA., *Rio de Janeiro*

TO JOHN AND MY PARENTS

—KKC

CONTENTS

PART V   NAUs: FUNCTION MANAGEMENT

PREFACE

Networks are being built at a rapidly increasing rate, and these networks are of increasing complexity and diversity. Intelligent terminals, minicomputers, desktop workstations, and programmable devices that control groups of terminals are spreading rapidly, and as the cost of microelectronic devices continues to drop, this spread will continue to gain momentum. This proliferation of devices, however, can cause substantial compatibility problems.

During the mid-1970s, several of the major computer manufacturers perceived that a large part of their future market was to come from distributed data processing. A wide range of machines would be hooked together into all manner of configurations. A user or application program at one machine would want to employ the facilities, data, or processing power of another, easily and inexpensively. For widely varying devices to be linked together, the hardware and software of these devices would have to be compatible; if compatibility was not achieved, complex interfaces would have to be built for meaningful communication to take place. In order to facilitate this compatibility, hardware manufacturers developed *network architectures* that allow complex networks to be built using a variety of equipment. The most widely used of these manufacturers' architectures, IBM's *Systems Network Architecture* (SNA), is the subject of this book.

In this book, we present a detailed explanation of the concepts, protocols, functions, and capabilities that constitute SNA as an architecture. We also describe several classes of SNA-compatible hardware and software products. Although a detailed description of the way in which the enormous number of SNA hardware and software products implement SNA is beyond the scope of this book, we do provide a context within which the capabilities, functions, and operations of specific products can be understood.

James Martin
Kathy Chapman

PART **I** CONCEPTS

1 NETWORK ARCHITECTURES

A network architecture defines protocols, standards, and message formats to which different machines and software packages must conform in order to achieve given goals. When new products are created that conform to the architecture, they will then be compatible, and they can be interlinked to share data, resources, and programs that already exist.

The goals and standards of an architecture are important to both the customers and the developer of the architecture. The architecture must provide customers with a variety of choices in the configuration of network machines, and it must allow them to change a configuration with relative ease as their systems evolve. It should provide the precise cooperation between distant intelligent machines required if the advantages of distributed data processing are to be realized.

Architectures should permit mass production of hardware or software building blocks that can be used in a variety of different machines. They also provide standards and definitions that allow development laboratories to create new machines and software that will be compatible with existing machines. These new products can then be integrated into existing distributed systems without the need for costly interfaces and program modifications.

THE NATURE OF ARCHITECTURE

Although architectures provide rules for the development of new products, these rules can change. This is because the term *architecture* in the computer industry often implies an overall scheme or plan that has not necessarily yet been fully implemented. It is the goal toward which its implementers strive. Thus architectures are bound to evolve and change as new hardware, software, and techniques are developed.

The term *architecture* is often used to describe database management systems, operating systems, and other highly complex software and hardware mechanisms. Architecture is a particularly important concept in describing distributed processing and computer network systems, because in these systems so many potentially incompatible hardware devices and software packages must fit together to form an easily used and easily modified whole.

With much complex software there is an *architectural definition* stating the eventual requirements. For database systems, for example, CODASYL (the committee that developed COBOL) has defined a long-range database architecture and has specified in great detail some of the protocols involved in that architecture. As with network architectures, individual implementations often provide only some of the functions defined in the complete architecture.

A good architecture ought to relate primarily to the needs of the end users rather than to enthusiasms for particular techniques. A well-architected house, for example, is one that reflects the desired life style of its owners rather than one that is designed to exploit a building technique that is currently in vogue. Fred Brooks, author of *The Mythical Man-Month,* defined *architecture* in a way that makes a clear distinction between architecture and engineering:

> Computer architecture, like other architecture, is the art of determining the needs of the user of a structure and then designing to meet those needs as effectively as possible within economic and technological constraints. Architecture must include engineering considerations, so that the design will be economical and feasible; but the emphasis in architecture is upon the needs of the user, whereas in engineering the emphasis is upon the needs of the fabricator.

Because SNA is an *architecture,* it is independent of any particular hardware or software product. For example, the *Virtual Telecommunications Access Method* (VTAM) is an IBM software product that conforms to and uses the SNA architecture. But an SNA network is not required to use VTAM, nor is it required to implement SNA functions in the same way that VTAM does.

DEVELOPERS OF ARCHITECTURES

Because of the importance of network architectures, several different types of organizations have gotten involved in standards and architecture development. These organizations can be categorized into three classes: *standards organizations, common carriers* (or the teleprocessing administrations that are their international counterparts), and *computer manufacturers.* Architectures designed by standards organizations, common carriers, and computer manufacturers have many characteristics in common. They all define the rules of a network and how the components of a network can interact. But there are also major differences.

Standards Organizations

The *International Telegraph and Telephone Consultative Committee* (CCITT) is an international standards organization based in Geneva, Switzerland. This organization has developed a complex and sophisticated architecture for computer networks that is described in a series of recommendations with names like X.3, X.25, X.28, and X.29. Many of these standards will be touched upon in this book. The International Organization for Standardization (ISO) has also published the description of a comprehensive architecture for computer networks called the Open Systems Interconnect (OSI) Reference Model. The OSI Reference Model is the subject of Chapter 6 of this book. However, the CCITT and ISO organizations are empowered only to describe or recommend the use of these standards. They can't implement the architectures or build the machines they describe. This must be handled either by computer manufacturers or by common carriers or teleprocessing administrations.

Common Carriers

A common carrier, like AT&T or Western Union, is a company that furnishes communications services to the general public. For communication between teleprocessing equipment, common carriers may employ protocols devised by standards organizations like the CCITT or ISO. But several common carriers offer advanced features like electronic mail that go far beyond simply transporting raw data back and forth between user machines. In essence, a common carrier network is the data processing equivalent of the telephone network. It allows machines to send data to one another, and it usually provides only a standard set of features. When an organization uses a common carrier network, it doesn't own that network, any more than a telephone user owns the telephone network.

Computer Manufacturers

Computer manufacturers' architectures, however, are specifically designed for distributed data processing systems that are used by individual organizations. And since an individual organization often owns and implements its own network, this type of network can be designed to meet the user's specific needs. However, while the network architecture defined by a computer manufacturer may facilitate interconnectability between the machines marketed by that manufacturer, they can make it difficult to interconnect machines offered by other competing vendors. The protocols used by communicating machines are often highly complex and are often completely different from one manufacturer to another. It may be relatively easy to hook a dumb terminal from one manufacturer to a computer from another. It is quite difficult, however, to connect a computing system that conforms to Digital Equipment Corporation's DECNET architecture to a network that conforms to IBM's SNA. (Many computer manufacturers do, however, provide gateway facilities to allow such connections to be made.)

PUBLIC NETWORKS VERSUS USER NETWORKS

In a general sense, a network consists of various hardware and software components that are interconnected in a way that allows information to be passed easily from one point to another. The actual transmission of data may be accomplished in a number of ways. For example, data transmission may take place across computer channels, telephone lines, satellite links, fiber-optic cables, or microwave connections. Common carriers and their international counterparts offer transmission facilities to the public, and these are often used to construct user networks. A distinction can then be made between the user-owned and -operated portion of a network and the parts that are owned and operated by a common carrier. In this book, we will be focusing on the user-owned portions of networks that conform to SNA.

One of the advantages of using an architecture like SNA is that the logical organization of the network is independent of its physical implementation. This means that changes can be made in the methods that are used to transmit data or the specific devices and transmission facilities that make up the network without having to change the logical organization of the network or the applications that use it.

OBJECTIVES OF SNA

Box 1.1 lists the major objectives that the architects of SNA defined. The objectives of SNA, while appearing at first glance simple and straightforward, are difficult to achieve. Meeting them requires a high level of technology. SNA defines an overall communication system that is user-independent. An SNA network relieves the network user of many network control and resource management functions that in earlier systems were the user's responsibility. To achieve this goal, SNA has defined a modular communication system that can be modified without having to modify the application programs that make use of the transmission facilities provided by the network. An SNA system is able to respond to new application demands and can accommodate the relatively unpredictable growth of new systems.

SIGNIFICANCE OF SNA

As can be seen by the list in Box 1.1, SNA has a variety of objectives that set it apart from earlier telecommunications systems. But it may not be clear at

BOX 1.1   Objectives of SNA

- **Versatility.** SNA formats and protocols must permit diverse hardware and software products to be interconnected to form unified systems.

- **Ease of Use.** SNA must provide a general solution to program-to-program communication through a network, while appearing like an extension of the operating system. SNA must also free users and application programmers from concerns about the network structure. Networks must be able to evolve without affecting users.

- **Distributed Processing Orientation.** SNA must provide an architecture that encourages the creation of distributed processing applications that employ distributed files.

- **Ease of Modification.** SNA must employ software that is divided into independent layers so that each layer can evolve independently without affecting other layers.

- **Reliability.** SNA must employ sophisticated high-level recovery procedures.

- **Use of Current Technology.** SNA hardware must use state-of-the-art technology, such as microprocessors in terminals and other network devices.

- **Modularity.** SNA must permit the use of a relatively small set of mass-produced, general-purpose building blocks in a wide diversity of network devices.

- **Ease of Implementation.** SNA must provide migration paths so that existing installed systems can make use of new network facilities without having to change existing application programs.

- **Unification.** SNA must unify IBM's teleprocessing product line so that all products employ a standard set of protocols. All future hardware and software products must be interconnectable at all levels.

first what is the significance of these objectives, and of SNA as a whole, to management, to application developers, and to users of systems that employ SNA hardware and software. Although the operations of the SNA network are meant to be transparent to users and to application developers, all data processing staff members must have a basic knowledge of SNA concepts and terminology in order to interface with data communications specialists and to deal with special conditions and circumstances. Technical managers, systems programmers, and network designers must have a much deeper understanding of SNA concepts in order to be in a position to select appropriate hardware and software products, make decisions about distributing data and processing power, interface SNA networks with other types of networks, and take full advantage of the services offered by SNA.

PREVIEW   SNA is like a complex machine or organism, and different perspectives will yield different views of it. End users of a network, for example, do not really want to know how the network operates. Like car owners, they simply want something that is easy to start and easy to use. The data processing personnel who design, implement, and work on a network, however, have a very different perspective. They must be concerned with a variety of large and small hardware and software conceptual issues. To understand SNA we must be able to synthesize these views.

We will begin our investigation of SNA in the next chapter by presenting the concepts that underlie SNA and by introducing basic SNA terminology. In the remaining chapters in Part I we will look at the various elements of SNA in more detail. The chapters in Part II examine some of the more advanced facilities that are provided by SNA hardware and software systems. Parts III and IV then look, in detail, at the functions performed by the various software layers that are defined by SNA.

SUMMARY   Network architectures are designed to provide compatibility among a wide variety of hardware and software products so that they can be used to build complex networks. A network architecture defines protocols, standards, and message formats to which different hardware and software products must conform. The term *architecture* in the computer industry often implies an overall scheme or plan that has not necessarily yet been fully implemented. It is the goal toward which its implementers strive. Thus architectures evolve and change as new hardware, software, and techniques are developed. Network architectures have been developed by standards organizations like the CCITT and ISO, by common carriers and teleprocessing administrations, and by computer manufacturers. The most widely used computer manufacturer's network architecture is IBM's Systems Network Architecture (SNA).

2 SNA CONCEPTS

This chapter introduces the basic concepts and explains the terminology associated with SNA. These concepts and terms include the components of an SNA network, SNA network configurations, SNA paths and network addresses, SNA communication links, and SNA sessions. We begin this discussion of SNA concepts and terminology by introducing the term *SNA user*.

NETWORK USERS

user, is either a person or an application program that uses the SNA network in order to communicate with some other user. *People* use networks to send or receive information, and thus the person interacting with the network through a terminal is considered to be a user of the network. Often, however, a person does not interact directly with the network but rather works through or with an *application program*. Application programs that use an SNA network are also considered users of the network. These application programs may be located at different points within the network; for example, they may be located in a terminal, in a terminal controller, or in a host computer. These application programs may, in turn, provide services either to people or to other application programs; but whenever they draw on the services of the SNA network, they are considered SNA users. Figure 2.1 illustrates this concept, with the dotted line representing logical interconnections that are implemented by the network between various network users. It is important to realize that SNA users are not themselves known to the network; SNA users are defined outside the architectural definition of SNA itself.

LOGICAL UNITS

An important purpose of an SNA network is to implement a *virtual* or *logical* path between users so

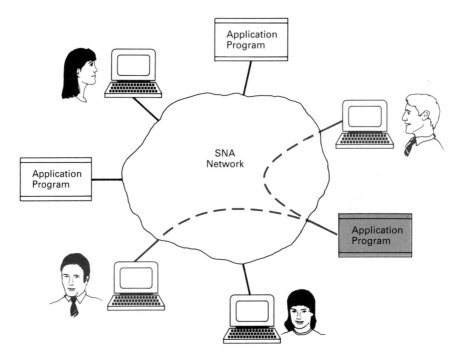

Figure 2.1   Network users.

that they can communicate with one another easily. This path is called *virtual* or *logical* because, although information appears to travel in a point-to-point fashion from one user to another, it may actually pass through several intermediate points on its way through the network. As the data pass through these intermediate devices in the network, operations may be performed that enable the data to travel more efficiently through the network. In some cases the data may even be converted from one form to another as they move through the network. All these functions, of course, are *transparent* to the users of the SNA network.

In discussing complex systems, it is important to have a clear understanding of the meanings of the term *transparent* and the terms *virtual* and *logical*. A *transparent* facility is one that actually exists but appears not to exist. The complex components and communication links that make up an SNA network do in fact exist, but they appear not to exist—they are transparent to the user. A *virtual* facility, in contrast, is one that appears to exist but in fact does not; the term *logical* is often used in place of *virtual* and means essentially the same thing. When two SNA users are communicating, it appears as if a simple virtual connection exists between them, when in fact the connection does not really exist but is implemented in a much more complex manner than it appears.

To establish a virtual or logical connection with another user, each user must gain access to the SNA network. SNA defines *logical units* (LUs) that provide points of access through which users interact with the SNA network. At the risk of oversimplifying a bit, a logical unit can be thought of as a *port* or *socket* into which a user plugs. An LU is not a *physical* port or plug but a *logical* one. SNA defines several logical unit types; each one provides *transmission capabilities* and a set of *services* that are related to a particular type of user. Logical units are implemented in the form of software or microcode and reside in the various devices that make up an SNA network. Logical unit types are identified by a number. Currently, seven major LU types are supported; they are identified by the numbers 0 through 7 (there is currently no type 5 logical unit). The logical unit of type 2, for example, is designated as LU type 2, or simply LU 2. As the functions performed by the various logical units evolve, new versions of the supporting software are often released. For example, the capabilities of LU 6 have been enhanced over time, and its latest version is now known as LU 6.2. LU 6.2 is the logical unit type that currently has the most comprehensive set of defined capabilities. LU 6.2 is used to implement a comprehensive set of functions collectively called Advanced Program-to-Program Communication (APPC). The various types of logical units that are defined by SNA and the capabilities of APPC are discussed in Chapters 8 and 9.

Figure 2.2 shows the relationship of network users to logical units. Logical

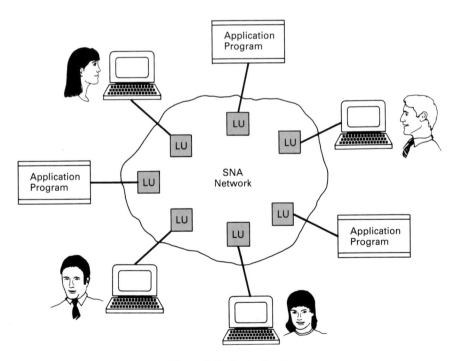

Figure 2.2 Logical units.

units provide one user with the ability to communicate with another user without the two users having to know detailed information about each other's characteristics. For example, one type of logical unit appears to the user as a logical terminal that has a set of characteristics that are defined independently of any specific piece of hardware. The characteristics of the logical terminal remain the same no matter what type of physical device the user happens to be using to access the network. If the physical terminal changes, the logical unit converts the information it receives from the new device in order to simulate the logical terminal that the logical unit represents. Thus users can communicate in a standard way, and both the users and the network are isolated from hardware changes.

PHYSICAL UNITS   An SNA network consists physically of various types of devices and the communication links that connect them. The devices that typically make up a network are computing systems, various types of controllers, and terminal devices. Just as SNA users (people or programs) that use the network are not part of the architectural definition of SNA, neither are the actual devices and communication links that are used to implement the network. Instead SNA uses *physical units* (PUs) to *represent* actual devices to the SNA network. A physical unit provides the services needed to manage and use a particular type of device and to handle any physical resources, such as communications links, that may be associated with it. A physical unit is implemented with some combination of hardware, software, and microcode within the particular device that the physical unit represents.

SYSTEM SERVICE CONTROL POINTS   In addition to logical units and physical units, an SNA network also has entities called *system service control points* (SSCPs). A system service control point provides the services needed to *manage* an SNA network (or some portion of a complex network) and to establish and control the interconnections that are necessary to allow network users to communicate with one another. Thus an SSCP has a broader function than a logical unit, which represents a single user, or a physical unit, which represents a physical device and its associated resources. Many of the functions that are performed by an SSCP are listed in Box 2.1.

SNA COMPONENTS   The components that make up an SNA network can be divided into two major categories, each of which consist of hardware, software, and microcode contained within the devices that make up the network. Figure 2.3 shows the relationships between these two major categories.

BOX 2.1　System Service Control Point (SSCP) functions

- Coordinating the interconnection of logical and physical units required to effect communication between network users
- Managing the bringing up and shutting down of the network
- Managing network resources
- Managing the recovery of communication without the loss of data when failures occur on the network
- Interacting with the network operating personnel and executing their commands
- Converting symbolic names employed by network users to internal network addresses
- Collecting measurement data on the usage of the network
- Acting on physical components of the network when necessary to establish interconnection—e.g., causing a telephone number to be dialed

- **Network Addressable Units.** NAUs consist of all the logical units, physical units, and system service control points, together with the communication links that connect them. They provide the services necessary to move information through the network from one user to another and to allow the network to be controlled and managed. Each network addressable unit has a *network address* that identifies it to the other NAUs in the network.

- **Path Control Network.** The path control network consists of lower-level components that control the routing and the flow of data through the network and handle the physical transmission of data from one *SNA node* in the network to another.

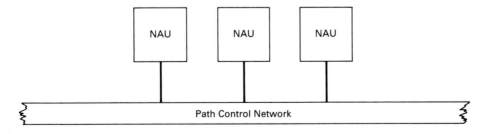

Figure 2.3　NAUs and the path control network.

SNA NODES

An *SNA node* is defined as a physical point in the SNA network that contains one or more network components. Each node contains both network addressable units and path control network components. An SNA node corresponds to a physical device and thus contains an SNA physical unit to represent that device to the network. If the node has application programs or terminal devices that offer users access to the network, the node also contains one or more logical units corresponding to the capabilities of those programs or terminals. One or more SNA nodes in the network must contain an SSCP. If a node does not contain an SSCP, it contains a *physical unit control point* (PUCP). A PUCP implements a subset of SSCP functions that are needed to activate or deactivate that particular node. Each node also contains path control network components that provide the services needed to enable the node to link to and communicate with other nodes. Figure 2.4 shows the relationship between SNA nodes and the various SNA components.

Each terminal, controller, or computing system that conforms to SNA specifications and contains SNA components can be a node in an SNA network. These nodes, along with the transmission links that connect them and any peripheral devices attached to them, are the *physical building blocks* of SNA. They contain the network service and control capabilities required both to operate the network and to handle information exchange between network users.

Technically speaking, an SNA node is contained within a device and consists only of the portion of the hardware, software, and microcode that specifically implements SNA functions. It is possible for a single physical device to contain multiple SNA nodes. However, for simplicity, if a device *contains* an SNA node, we will speak of the device itself as *being* the node. An SNA network can contain several different types of nodes. One way to distinguish between the various node types is to divide them into two major categories: *peripheral nodes* and *subarea nodes*. Figure 2.5 shows these two major node types.

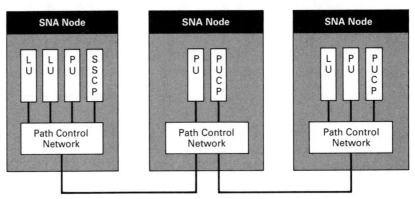

Figure 2.4 SNA nodes and components.

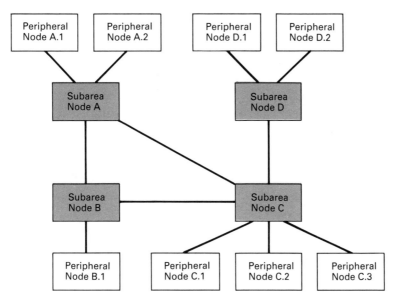

Figure 2.5   Subarea and peripheral nodes.

Peripheral Nodes

A peripheral node communicates directly only with the subarea node to which it is attached. For example, the two peripheral nodes attached to subarea node A cannot communicate directly with one another or directly with other subarea or peripheral nodes in the network; they exchange data only with subarea node A. In order for a peripheral node to exchange data with other nodes in the network, it must do so through its subarea node. Peripheral nodes are often called *cluster controllers,* and they are implemented in a wide variety of systems and terminals, including the IBM 3270 family, 5250 workstations, and 3730 distributed office systems. There are two types of peripheral nodes:

- **Type 2 Nodes.** Type 2 nodes have greater processing capabilities than type 1 nodes and are typically user-programmable. Most of IBM's newer terminal systems are type 2 nodes.
- **Type 1 Nodes.** Type 1 nodes have fewer capabilities than type 2 nodes and are typically not user-programmable. Type 1 nodes are generally implemented in older and less powerful terminals and controllers such as the IBM 6670, 3767, 5250, and 3790.

Subarea Nodes

A subarea node is a node that can communicate with its own peripheral nodes and also with other subarea nodes in the network. For example, in Fig. 2.5, subarea node A can communicate directly with subarea nodes B and C. It can also communicate with subarea node D by going through subarea node C. Subarea nodes are also of two types:

- **Type 5 Nodes.** A type 5 node is a subarea node that contains an SSCP. A type 5 node is typically contained within a general-purpose computing system, such as an IBM 30XX, 4300, 8100, System/36, or System/38, and is often called a *host node*.

- **Type 4 Nodes.** A type 4 node is a subarea node that does not contain an SSCP. A type 4 node is typically contained within a communications controller such as an IBM 3705 or 3725 and is often called a *communications controller node*.

Physical Unit Type

An SNA node always contains one physical unit, which represents the device and its resources to the network. A physical unit is given the same *type designation* as its corresponding node type. Thus each physical unit in the network is one of four possible types:

- Physical unit type 5 (PU type 5, or PU 5)
- Physical unit type 4 (PU type 4, or PU 4)
- Physical unit type 2 (PU type 2, or PU 2)
- Physical unit type 1 (PU type 1, or PU 1)

The original development work that led to the formal architectural description of SNA allowed for a type 3 node, possibly to function as a mid-network switch. However, enhancements to the capabilities of type 4 subarea nodes and type 2 peripheral nodes have now obviated the need for a type 3 SNA node and its corresponding PU type 3. Type 3 nodes and type 3 physical units are not referenced in any of the current SNA documentation.

The architectural definitions of the various physical unit types have been enhanced as SNA has evolved. The version of the type 2 physical unit that implements the most comprehensive set of functions is now known as PU type 2.1, or PU 2.1. This is the physical unit that is used in conjunction with LU 6.2 in implementing Advanced Program-to-Program Communication (APPC) facilities.

A SIMPLE SNA NETWORK

Figure 2.6 shows a configuration of nodes that makes up a simple SNA network. At the top of the figure is a host node (type 5) that manages the network. Connected to the host node is a communications controller node (type 4). There are three peripheral nodes (type 2) attached to the communications controller. Two of the peripheral nodes have various terminal devices attached to them; the other

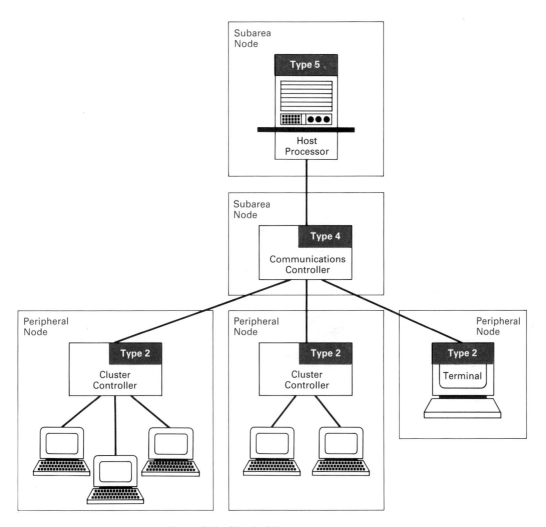

Figure 2.6 Simple SNA network.

peripheral node has a terminal integrated within it. Each of the nodes in the network contains the hardware, software, and microcode necessary to perform its required functions within the SNA network.

Figure 2.7 shows the various NAUs that might be contained in the network from Fig. 2.6. The host node contains the SSCP, which provides network management and user interconnection functions. Each of the nodes contains a physical unit (PU), which represents the device and its resources to the network. Some of the nodes also contain logical units (LUs) that provide users with access to the network. Users of this network include the terminal users shown at the bottom of the diagram and the application program running in the host node.

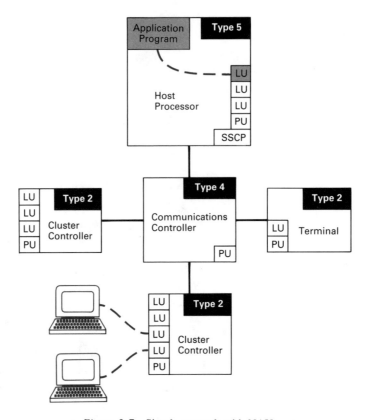

Figure 2.7   Simple network with NAUs.

As indicated in the diagram, some nodes are capable of supporting multiple concurrent users and thus will contain multiple logical units.

DOMAINS AND SUBAREAS

Figure 2.8 shows the structure of a somewhat more complex SNA network. In this network there are a single host node, two communications controller nodes, and six peripheral nodes. All the devices and nodes (with their resident NAUs) shown in Fig. 2.8 constitute a single *domain* that is managed by the system service control point (SSCP) in the host node. A domain is defined as *the set of SNA resources known to and managed by an SSCP*. This includes physical resources (the devices and the transmission links that tie them together) and software and microcode resources (operating systems, control programs, etc.) used to implement SNA components. A domain typically consists of multiple *subareas*. A subarea is defined as one subarea node and all the resources

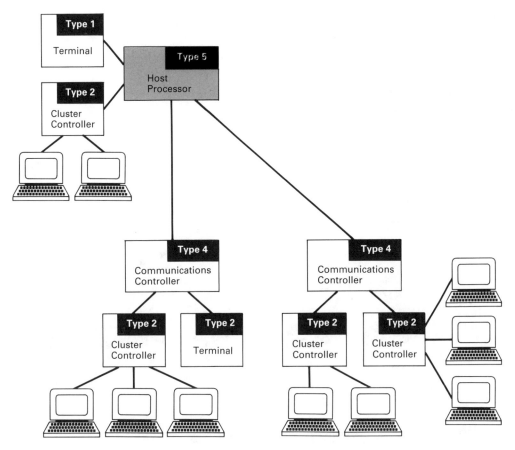

Figure 2.8 An SNA domain.

it controls, including the peripheral nodes attached to it. Figure 2.9 shows the
three subareas that make up the domain from Fig. 2.8.

**MULTIPLE-DOMAIN
NETWORKS**
The simplest SNA networks have only one domain
and consequently only one host node with its SSCP.
But this is not the case for all, or even the majority,
of currently implemented SNA networks; many SNA networks contain several
domains. The network shown in Fig. 2.10, for example, has seven domains,
each of which is managed by a type 5 host node having its own SSCP. Notice
that domains C, D, E, and G do not have communications controllers, and
domain C consists of a host node with no subordinate nodes.

When an SNA network consists of multiple domains, a terminal attached

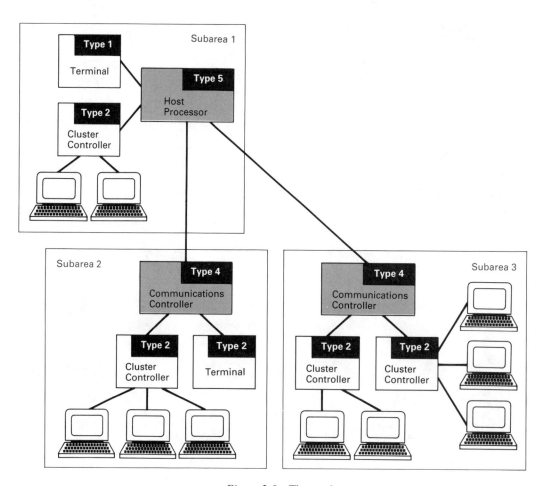

Figure 2.9 Three subareas.

to one host processor is able to communicate with an application program running in some other host processor in the network. For example, a terminal in domain A could communicate with an application program running in the host processor in domain C. The host processor in domain A is involved only in establishing a connection between the terminal and the host node. Once the connection is established, the terminal is free to communicate with the program running in the host processor in domain C without any further involvement of the host processor in domain A.

In a multiple-domain network, each SSCP uses a set of software called a *cross-domain resource manager* (CDRM). The CDRM uses a table that describes all the resources that are available in other domains. This table allows the SSCP to work with the communications controller in setting up sessions that

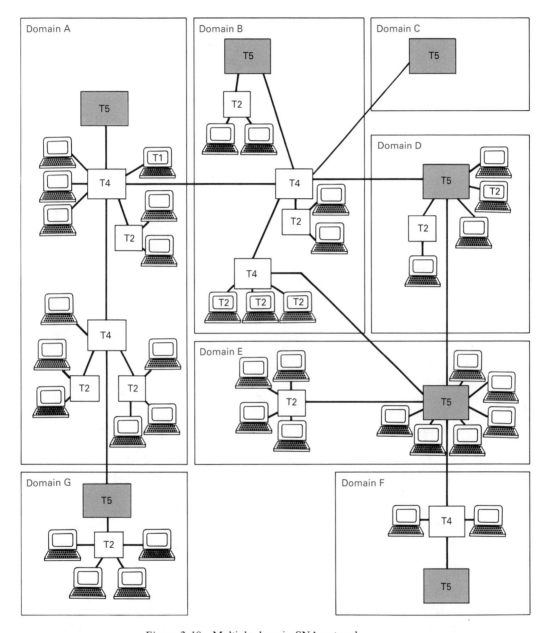

Figure 2.10 Multiple-domain SNA network.

span more than one domain. Once a connection is established, communication between domains is handled by the communications controller nodes. If a domain does not contain a communications controller node, cross-domain communication is handled by the host node.

PATHS

In order for two logical units to communicate, a path must be established between them. A path consists of the series of nodes and communication links over which data need to travel in getting from one logical unit to another. Often a number of possible paths can be established between a given pair of logical units. Figure 2.11 shows an example of this. If a logical unit in subarea A.2 wants to communicate with a logical unit in subarea E.1, two possible paths could be used: one through subarea nodes A.2, B.2, D.1, and E.1, the other through subarea nodes A.2, B.2, B.3, and E.1.

NETWORK ADDRESSES

The SNA software uses a system of network addresses in establishing paths between logical units and in transmitting messages across those paths. Each network addressable unit—physical unit, logical unit, or SSCP—has a *network address* that uniquely identifies it within the network. In addition, each network addressable unit has a *network name*. Typically, network users refer to NAUs by their network names rather than by their network addresses. The SSCP then translates each network name into its corresponding network address using a facility called the *network directory service*. The use of network names helps to shield users from changes that might occur in the physical or logical structure of the network. If the network is changed and a logical unit is assigned a new network address, network directory services is updated to reflect the change. This allows network users to continue to use the same network name to refer to the logical unit and thus not be affected by the change.

Each network address consists of two parts: a *subarea address* and an *element address*. The subarea address of a network addressable unit uniquely identifies the particular subarea in which the NAU resides. The element address uniquely identifies the NAU within its subarea.

Subarea Address

Each subarea node has access to a routing table that lists all the communication links and peripheral nodes that are attached to that node, as well as all subareas that can be reached from it. The table specifies, for each subarea, the particular link that should be used and the next node to which a message should be transmitted so as eventually to reach the destination subarea. The subarea address portion of a message's destination address is used along with the routing tables

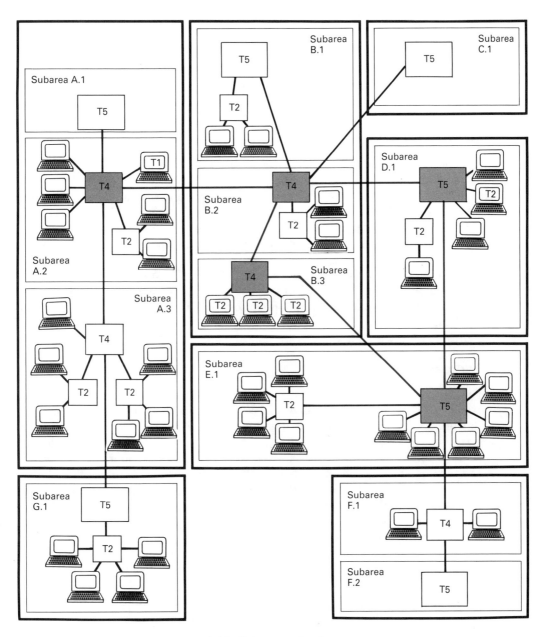

Figure 2.11   Subareas and paths.

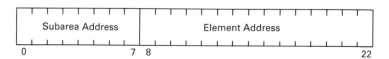

Figure 2.12   23-bit extended network address.

as the message is passed from one subarea node to the next in routing the message to its destination subarea.

Element Address

Once a message reaches its destination subarea, the element address portion of the destination address identifies the particular NAU that is to receive the message. A table called the *element routing table* is used to determine where to pass the message within that subarea. If the ultimate destination of the message is within a peripheral node, the subarea node converts the address to a local address that is meaningful to the appropriate peripheral node. This conversion is performed by a *boundary function* component in the subarea node. Peripheral nodes do not deal with complete network addresses; instead, they operate only with local addresses. Again, this makes it easier to change the network configuration. If a network reconfiguration causes the links between subarea nodes to be changed, only the subarea node routing tables need to be updated; the local addresses used within a subarea are not affected and need not be changed.

Address Structure

The structure of a network address depends on whether or not a feature called *extended network addressing* is used. With extended network addressing, each network address has a fixed format and is 23 bits in length (see Fig. 2.12). The first 8 bits of the address identify a subarea; the last 15 bits of the address identify an element within that subarea. Extended network addresses allow for 256 subareas and 32,768 elements in each subarea. If extended network addressing is not used, each network address is 16 bits in length, and its format can vary from network to network. The subarea portion of the address uses from 0 to 8 bits of the address, and the element address uses the remaining bits. The division of the address between the subarea portion and the element portion is known as the *address split*. For example, a 7/9 address split might be used in a particular network, as shown in Fig. 2.13. In this case, 7 bits are used for the

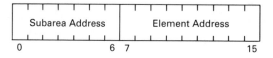

Figure 2.13   16-bit network address with 7/9 split.

subarea address and 9 bits for the element address. This allows for 128 subareas and 512 elements in each subarea. Other address splits can be used instead of a 7/9 split to suit the needs of the individual network.

SNA COMMUNICATION LINKS

As we have seen, messages are passed from one node to the next across a *communication link* that connects those two nodes. Basically, two types of communication links can connect nodes. For nodes that are in close physical proximity (in the same room or same building), the link can be implemented by a cable that is connected to one of the computing system's I/O channels. SNA includes protocols that can be used to control data transmission over a standard channel. If the nodes are not close enough for a direct cable connection using an I/O channel, conventional data communication facilities, such as a telephone line, are used to implement the link. The data communication link can take the form of either a point-to-point or a multipoint connection, and it can be either switched (temporary) or nonswitched (permanent). Regardless of the form taken, transmission over any communication link that is not implemented by a standard I/O channel connection is controlled by the Synchronous Data Link Control (SDLC) protocols that are defined as part of SNA. (Although SDLC is the standard SNA data link protocol, other protocols, such as the older binary-synchronous protocol, are supported in certain situations.) Figure 2.14 illustrates the various types of communication links that might be implemented in an SNA network.

I/O channel connections provide a very high rate of data transmission. Various types of SDLC links can be implemented, and they vary in the rate at which they can carry data. An SNA network can be constructed by using various communication link facilities in different combinations, and the performance of the network will depend on the particular facilities used. However, from a logical standpoint, the organization of an SNA network is independent of the of the physical transmission facilities that are used to implement it. Again, this independence makes it easier for the network to be modified. The specific physical transmission facility used for a particular link can be changed without the rest of the network being affected and without users being aware of the change.

Parallel Links

In many cases, two subarea nodes will be connected by a single communication link. It is possible, however, to implement multiple SDLC links between the same two subarea nodes. These links, which operate concurrently, are called *parallel links,* shown in Fig. 2.15. Data moving through the network are distributed among parallel links based on various routing considerations. Parallel links can be used to increase the efficiency of the network and also to increase its capacity.

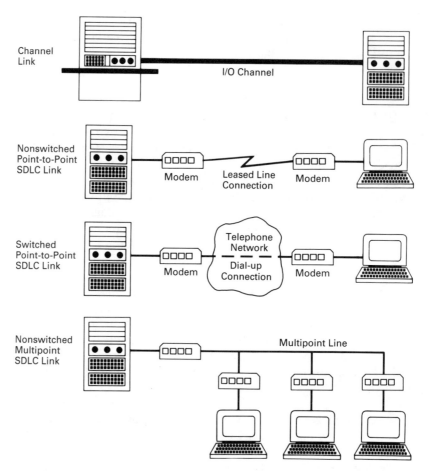

Figure 2.14 SNA links.

Transmission Groups

When subarea nodes are connected by parallel links, each link belongs to a *transmission group* (see Fig. 2.16). A transmission group is a set of parallel SDLC links with similar characteristics. They form a single logical link that has a higher capacity than each of the individual links in the group. In addition to providing higher capacity, a transmission group can also provide better availability. As long as any one of the links in the group is operating, the transmission group can be used. If one of the individual links fails, data flow will automatically be reassigned to the other links in the group; communication that is in progress between two network users is not disrupted by the failure.

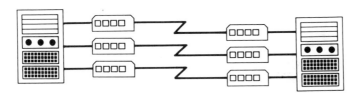

Figure 2.15   Parallel links.

SESSIONS

A fundamental concept of SNA is that no communication takes place between network addressable units until a *session* is established between them. A session is defined as follows:

> A session is a logical state that exists between two network addressable units
> to support a succession of transmissions between them to achieve a given
> purpose.

Some types of sessions are permanent and are automatically established when the network is brought into operation; they remain established as long as the network is operational. Other types of sessions are dynamic; they are established as required and broken when they are no longer needed. At any given moment on an SNA network, it is likely that many concurrent sessions will be established. Many of these separate sessions may share the same physical devices and communications links. For example, a logical unit in a host processor or in a cluster controller might be involved in several sessions at one time. A logical unit located in a terminal device, however, normally participates in only one session at a time with another logical unit.

The most fundamental type of session is one established between two logical units; this type of session allows the network users they represent to communicate with each other by means of the network. Figure 2.17 demonstrates this concept, with the dotted line representing the session that has been established between the terminal user and the application program. In addition to

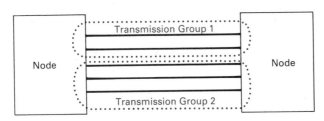

Figure 2.16   Transmission groups.

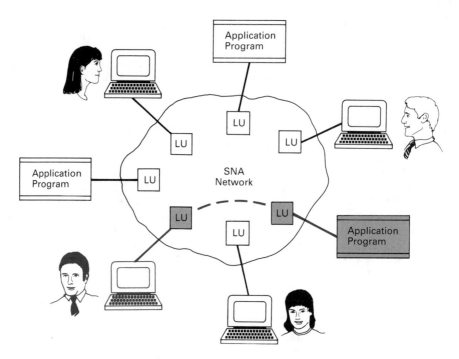

Figure 2.17   LU-to-LU session.

sessions between logical units, there are four other types of sessions that can be in operation in the network. Box 2.2 describes the five types of SNA sessions.

An LU-to-LU session is logically similar to a telephone call between two people. To set up a telephone call between me and you, all I need to know is your telephone number. Assuming that we are both SNA users and have logical units that represent us in the network, all I need to know in order to set up an SNA session with you is the network name of your logical unit. In neither case does either of us have to know where the other party is physically located. Nor do we have to know how the communication is taking place. The user of an SNA network is no more aware of the complexities of the computer network than a telephone user is aware of the complexities of the telephone system; the network is transparent to the user. SNA provides all required management and control functions, and also achieves this transparency, by employing a system of functional layers of control. These functional layers are the subject of the next chapter.

SUMMARY

A network user is a person or application program that uses the network to communicate. There are two primary components of an SNA network: network addressable units (NAUs) and

BOX 2.2   SNA session types

- **LU-to-LU Sessions.** These sessions fulfill the primary purpose of the network. An LU-to-LU session allows users of the network to communicate with one another. LU-to-LU sessions are typically established dynamically as given pairs of users have the need to communicate.

- **SSCP-to-SSCP Sessions.** These sessions involve only SNA networks that consist of multiple domains. All required SSCP-to-SSCP sessions are normally established automatically when the network is initialized and remain established as long as cross-domain communication between LUs is allowed. SSCP-to-SSCP sessions allow control information to be exchanged between the various SSCPs in the network.

- **SSCP-to-PU Sessions.** An SSCP must be permanently in session with each of the PUs in its domain, and these sessions are normally established automatically when the network is initialized. The network administrator can make a particular PU temporarily unavailable by terminating its SSCP-to-PU session. SSCP-to-PU sessions allow control information to be exchanged between the SSCP and the PUs in its domain.

- **SSCP-to-LU Sessions.** An SSCP must also be permanently in session with each of the LUs in its domain. An SSCP-to-LU session must be established before an LU can be accessed by a network user. In most cases, an SSCP-to-LU session is established for each LU when the network is initialized. As with PUs, the network administrator can make an LU temporarily inactive by terminating a particular SSCP-to-LU session.

- **PU-to-PU Sessions.** No specific session types are defined for communication between PUs; however, adjacent PUs may need to exchange network control information. This may need to be done, for example, to transfer a control program from a host processor to a cluster controller or to perform certain activation, deactivation, or testing functions.

the path control network. Network addressable units include logical units (LUs), physical units (PUs), and system service control points (SSCPs). A logical unit is a point of access through which a user interacts with the SNA network and also represents the user in the network. A physical unit represents a particular physical device that contains an SNA node and provides the services needed to manage that device in the network. An SSCP provides the services needed to manage an SNA network, or a particular portion of it, and establishes and controls the interconnections necessary for network users to communicate. The path control network supports the NAUs by controlling the routing and the flow of data as they are transmitted from one NAU to another.

An SNA node can be either a peripheral node or a subarea node. A peripheral node can communicate only with the subarea node to which it is attached. A subarea node can communicate with any other subarea node in the network. A subarea node with an SSCP is a type 5 node, often called a host node, and the portion of a network managed by a particular SSCP is called a domain. A subarea node without an SSCP is a type 4 node, often called a communications controller node. The portion of a network managed by a particular subarea node is called a subarea. Peripheral nodes are often called cluster controllers and are implemented in either type 2 or type 1 nodes; type 2 nodes have greater processing capabilities than type 1 nodes.

Every network addressable unit has a network name and a network address. The network address is divided into a subarea address and an element address. The boundary function component of a subarea node translates network addresses to and from local addresses used by attached peripheral nodes.

There are two types of communication links used to connect SNA nodes: computing system I/O channels and Synchronous Data Link Control (SDLC) data links. There may be parallel SDLC data links between two nodes, and a set of parallel links, each of which has the same data transmission capability, is called a transmission group. A session is a logical state that exists between two network addressable units to support a succession of transmissions between them. LU-to-LU sessions allow network users to communicate with one another. SSCP-to-SSCP, SSCP-to-LU, SSCP-to-PU, and PU-to-PU sessions are used for purposes of management and control.

3 SNA FUNCTIONAL LAYERS

A basic concept underlying all communication network architectures is the division of network functions into well-defined functional layers. As with any network architecture, the functions of SNA are broken into layers, with each layer providing a different group of services. Figure 3.1 illustrates the five major SNA functional layers. This chapter discusses the functions that are performed by each of the five major SNA layers.

DATA LINK CONTROL The lowest layer is the *data link control* layer. This layer is responsible for the transmission of data between two nodes over a particular physical link. A primary function of the data link control layer is to detect and recover from the transmission errors that inevitably occur.

Operating below SNA's lowest layer, as shown in Fig. 3.2, is a still lower-level layer generally called the *physical control* layer. The physical control layer addresses the transmission of bit streams over a physical circuit. The physical control layer does not assign any significance to the bits being transmitted. For example, it has no concern with how many bits make up each unit of data, nor

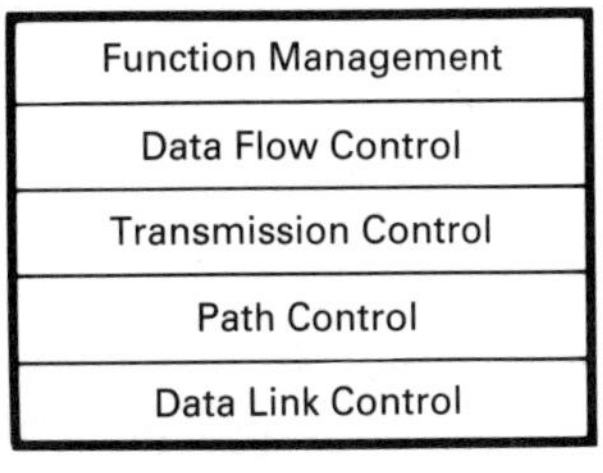

Function Management
Data Flow Control
Transmission Control
Path Control
Data Link Control

Figure 3.1 Major SNA functional layers.

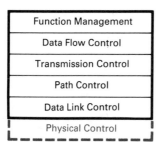

Figure 3.2   The Physical Control layer.

does it have any concern with the meaning of the data being transmitted. It is important to point out that the SNA architecture itself does not define the functions that are performed in the physical control layer, and specific methods of transmitting bits are not defined by SNA. Various methods of physical transmission can be employed in an SNA network, including computer channels, telephone lines, satellite links, and microwave transmission. The techniques used for physical transmission, though important, are defined outside the SNA architecture.

PATH CONTROL

The second major SNA layer is the *path control* layer. The path control layer is concerned with routing data from one node in the network to the next in the path that a message takes through the network. In a complex network, this path often passes over many separate data links through several nodes and may cross numerous domains.

TRANSMISSION CONTROL

The third functional layer, the *transmission control* layer, keeps track of the status of sessions that are in progress, controls the pacing of data flow within a session, and sees that the units of data that make up a message are sent and received in the proper sequence. The transmission control layer also provides an optional data encryption/decryption facility.

DATA FLOW CONTROL

The *data flow control* layer, the fourth major layer, is concerned with the overall integrity of the flow of data during a session between two network addressable units. This can involve determining the mode of sending and receiving, managing groups of related messages, and determining what type of response mode to use.

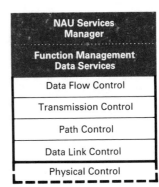

Figure 3.3   Function Management sublayers.

FUNCTION MANAGEMENT

The uppermost SNA functional layer is called the *function management* layer. The function management layer is highly complex and can be thought of as being divided into two sublayers: a function management data services sublayer and a NAU services manager sublayer, as shown in Fig. 3.3.

Function Management Data Services

The *function management data services* sublayer provides high-level SNA services and has the following two primary functions:

- Coordinating the interface between the network user and the network and the presentation of information to the user
- Controlling and coordinating the activities of the network as a whole and of all the sessions that are active

NAU Services Manager

The *NAU services manager* sublayer provides services to the function management data services sublayer below it and also to the data flow control and transmission control layers below the function management layer.

APPLICATION LAYER

We can think of a still higher-level layer, generally called the *application* layer, operating above the function management layer of SNA. This is shown in Fig. 3.4. The application layer represents the users—the application programs and the people that interface with the SNA network. As with the physical control layer, the application layer is not defined by the SNA architecture. Although this layer is important, it is defined outside the architecture of SNA itself.

This layered structure allows the SNA architecture to evolve much more

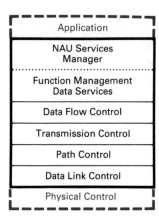

Figure 3.4 The Application layer.

easily than might otherwise be possible. If a way is found to make one layer operate more efficiently or if new technology becomes available that can provide more function in a layer, that layer can be changed with little or no effect on adjacent layers. It is somewhat like changing one module of a properly designed structured program; the efficiency or usability of the program as a whole can often be improved by replacing a single module without requiring modifications to the other modules of the program.

**SNA LAYERS
AND NETWORK
COMPONENTS**

Figure 3.5 shows how the SNA functional layers relate to the two major SNA components—the network addressable units (NAUs) and the path control network. The NAUs are implemented in the top three layers: function management, data flow control, and transmission control. The services of these layers are primarily concerned with enabling network users to send and receive data through the network and with assisting network operators with controlling and managing the network. The path control network component encompasses the bottom two layers: the path control layer and the data link control layer. These layers are concerned with controlling the routing and flow of data through the network and with the transmission of data from one node to another.

**COMMUNICATION
BETWEEN LAYERS**

The layered approach to network architectures makes it necessary to discuss two different types of communication that can take place between functional layers. The first type of communication is the physical communication that occurs between adjacent layers in the same node; the second type is the logical

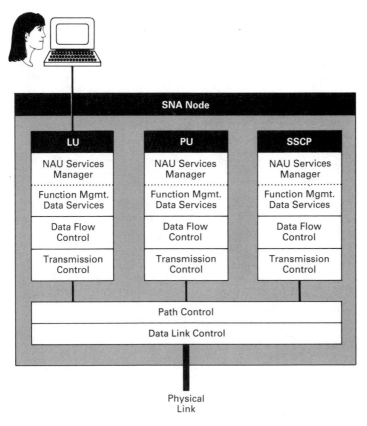

Figure 3.5   SNA layers and network organization.

communication that occurs between functionally paired layers in two communicating nodes.

Communication Between Adjacent Layers

SNA defines the manner in which communication takes place between adjacent layers in a single node. This is done by specifying which functions belong to each layer and what information must be exchanged between adjacent layers. For example, when user A at node 1 in Fig. 3.6 needs to transmit a message to user B at node 2, user A passes the message to the function management layer residing in node 1. Function management passes the message down to the data flow control layer, and so on. Each layer performs its functions and passes the data down to the next lowest layer until the data reach the physical control layer, at which point they are transmitted across a physical circuit to node 2. At node

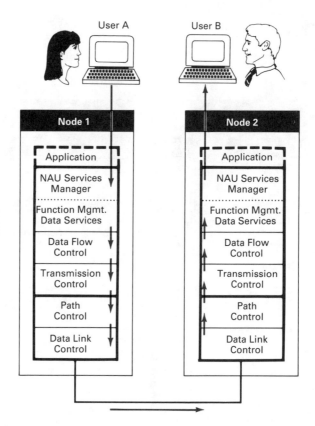

Figure 3.6 Communication between layers.

2, the information travels up through the functional layers until it is finally passed to user B.

Figure 3.7 shows the process when the message must traverse several data links to reach its location. All five major SNA functional layers are present in the intermediate nodes. However, the message passes up and down through only the two path control network SNA layers in the intermediate node.

As a message passes down through the functional layers of SNA, each layer performs a set of functions and may add control information to the message. This control information takes the form of message headers that are appended to the message, as shown in Fig. 3.8. Finally, when the message passes up through a complementary set of functional layers in the destination node, each of the headers is acted upon and stripped off by the appropriate layer (see Fig. 3.9). When the message reaches the destination user, all headers have been stripped off, and the message is received in its original form.

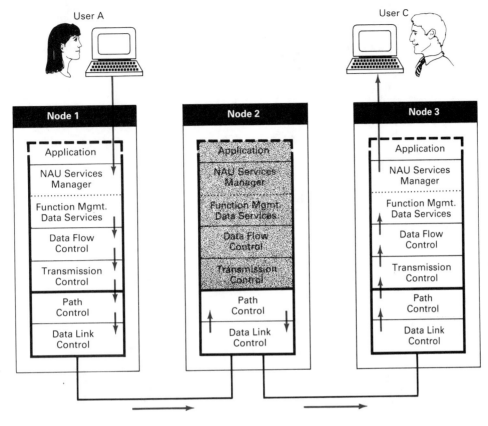

Figure 3.7 Multiple nodes.

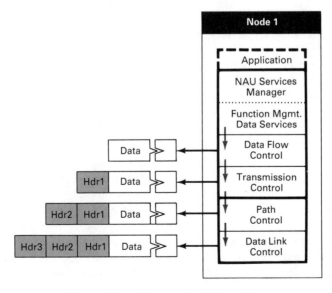

Figure 3.8 Adding control information.

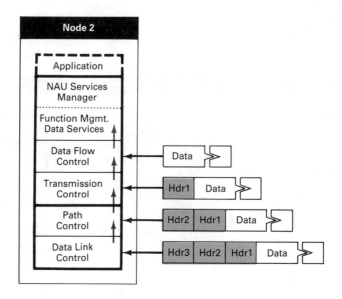

Figure 3.9   Stripping off control information.

Peer-to-Peer Communication

As just described, data are passed up and down through the various SNA functional layers as they are relayed from one adjacent node to another. While this physical communication is taking place, another type of communication is also logically taking place, as shown in Fig. 3.10. This diagram shows that although the message is physically passing down and then back up through the various SNA layers in making its way from user A to user B, the trip is transparent to the users. It appears as though the message is being transmitted directly between two peers, from user A to user B, at the application level. By the same token, a message can be thought of as passing from any layer in the sending node to the complementary layer in the receiving node, as shown in Fig. 3.11. At any given layer, the functions that are performed and the control information that is added to the message by all lower-level layers are transparent; it appears to that layer as if a direct virtual connection exists between the nodes at that level.

This logical communication that takes place between complementary layers is called *peer-to-peer communication*. SNA defines peer-to-peer communication very precisely, and the formats of the various message headers that are added at each layer are specified as part of the SNA architecture. Also, SNA protocols define how the complementary layers in separate nodes are to interact. Peer protocols define the meaning of the parameters that are included in headers and the actions that result from them. In this way an SNA node implemented using one set of hardware and software products can communicate with a node

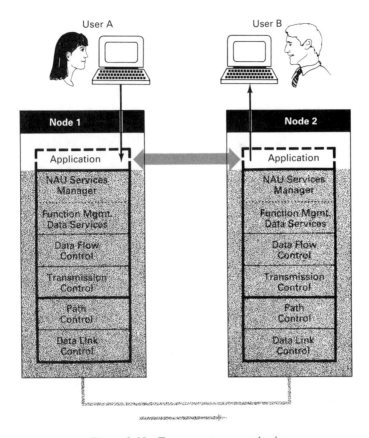

Figure 3.10   Transparent communication.

using a very different set of products as long as both nodes conform to the SNA formats and protocols. This allows SNA to encompass networks containing a wide diversity of hardware and software products. It also allows the products in use at one node to be changed without affecting other nodes in the network.

SUMMARY   SNA functions are assigned to well-defined functional layers. The data link control layer is responsible for the transmission of data between two nodes over a particular physical link. The data link control layer uses the services of a physical control layer that is defined outside the SNA architecture. The path control layer routes data from one node to the next. The transmission control layer tracks session status, controls the pacing of data flow, and sees that data units are properly sequenced. The data flow control layer manages the overall integrity of data flow during a

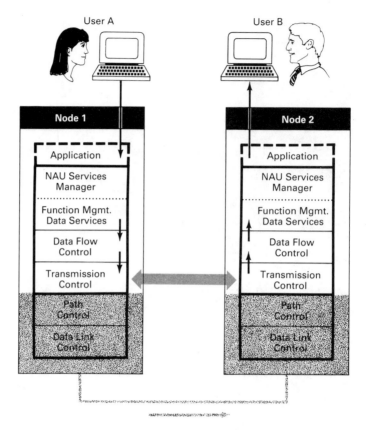

Figure 3.11   Peer to peer communication.

session. The function management layer is divided into two sublayers—function management data services and NAU services manager. The function management data services sublayer controls the interface with the network user and manages the activities of the network as a whole. The NAU services manager sublayer provides services to lower-level layers.

Two types of communication occur as data are transmitted through an SNA network. Communication between adjacent layers takes place as data pass from one layer to the next. Data are physically passed down through the various functional layers in the sending node, across over physical circuits, and back up through the functional layers in the receiving node. Control information is added and then stripped off by the various functional layers. Peer-to-peer communication is communication that logically takes place between the complementary layers in the sending and receiving nodes. The SNA architecture defines protocols that specify how equivalent layers in different nodes are to interact and defines the formats for headers that are added to messages by the various functional layers.

4 ROUTING AND DATA FLOW

So far we have examined general network architecture concepts and introduced the concepts and terminology associated with SNA. Here we take a closer look at the SNA network, seeing how data are routed through the system and how data flow is controlled. One of the functions of the path control network layers of SNA is to control the routing of data through the network. The routing is based on the path that is selected when a session is established between two logical units. A path defines the nodes through which a message travels as it passes from the sending logical unit to the receiving logical unit. Figure 4.1 shows a simple path over which data pass through one intermediate subarea node in going between the originating and the receiving subarea nodes.

EXPLICIT ROUTE AND ROUTE EXTENSION

The portion of a path from the originating subarea node to the receiving subarea node is called an *explicit route*. If peripheral nodes are involved in the transmission at either end, the portion of the path from the subarea node to the peripheral node is known as a *route extension*. A route extension consists of boundary function in the subarea node, which translates between full network addresses and local addresses, and the link between the subarea node and the peripheral node. This link is called a *peripheral link*. An explicit route and a route extension are shown in Fig. 4.2.

MULTIPLE EXPLICIT ROUTES

It is possible for more than one explicit route to exist between subarea nodes. Figure 4.3 shows four explicit routes that connect node B and node H. When a session is established between node B and node H, a particular explicit route is chosen from among the four available routes, and that route is used for all

41

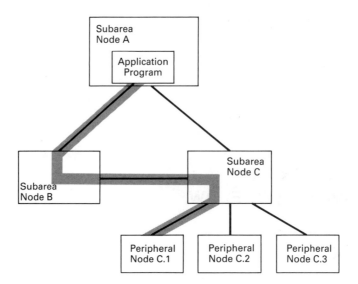

Figure 4.1 A path.

data transmission for the duration of the session. However, if a problem occurs with an explicit route, it is possible for the session to be reestablished using a different route. Multiple routes are useful for balancing transmission workloads; for example, if several sessions are established between two nodes, different sessions might use different routes. Different routes can also offer different transmission characteristics in terms of transmission rate, level of security, or response time.

Where parallel links exist between two nodes, different explicit routes can be defined using different transmission groups. For example, in Fig. 4.3, explicit routes 2, 3, and 4 could each use a different transmission group when transmitting data between node G and node H. Again, this provides greater reliability and flexibility. A given session uses the same transmission group for all its data transmission. Typically, links with the same transmission characteristics are assigned to the same transmission group. This allows each session to be assigned to a transmission group based on its transmission requirements. Transmission requirements can include such considerations as transmission rate,

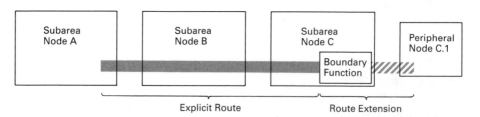

Figure 4.2 Explicit route and route extension.

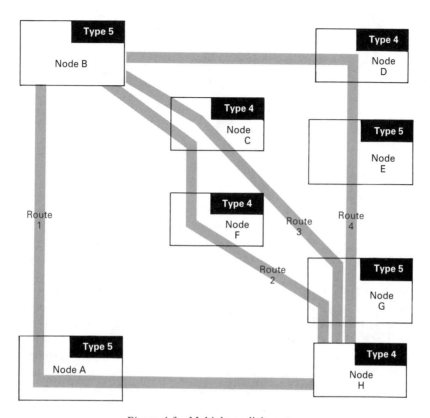

Figure 4.3   Multiple explicit routes.

reliability, and sensitivity to the high propagation delays that are experienced on satellite links.

VIRTUAL ROUTES   SNA routing functions also involve the use of *virtual routes*. A virtual route is a logical connection that appears to exist between subarea nodes. Each virtual route is assigned to an explicit route, and it is possible for several virtual routes to use the same explicit route (see Fig. 4.4). Each virtual route has a transmission priority of *high, medium,* or *low* associated with it. When several messages are waiting to be transmitted from one node to another, their respective transmission priorities are used to determine the sequence in which the messages are transmitted. Messages using a virtual route with a high priority are sent ahead of messages that are using a virtual route having a medium or low priority. As with explicit routes, a session uses a particular virtual route for the duration of a session. Assigning an appropriate virtual route to each session can help assure that an application that needs a fast response time can receive priority over other applications, even though the same explicit route is being shared.

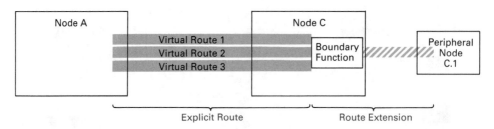

Figure 4.4   Virtual routes.

**CLASS OF
SERVICE**

When initiating a session, a network user can specify that a particular *class of service* be assigned to the session. This can be specified either directly at the time the session is initiated or indirectly in the form of a *logon mode* that is supplied when logging on to the network. If the user specifies a logon mode name when logging on, that name is translated to a particular class-of-service name as part of session initiation. The class of service corresponds to various requirements, such as the level of response time, security, or reliability that is required. Each class-of-service name is associated with a list of virtual routes that the network administrator has decided will meet the desired requirements. From that list, an available virtual route is chosen. The virtual route chosen determines the explicit route to be used and the transmission priority.

DATA FLOW

We will next see how data flow along the path, or route, that is established between two network users participating in a session. In Chapter 3 we described SNA organization as consisting of two collections of components: network addressable units and the path control network. Figure 4.5 shows a typical message flow. Message flow begins when a message passes from a network user to a network addressable unit and from there to the path control network element in that node. Then the message passes from node to node via the path control network until the destination node is reached. There it is passed back up to a network addressable unit and then to the receiving network user.

As we have seen in Chapter 3, when a message is passed between two network users, it is passed down and then back up through the various functional layers as it passes from node to node. First it travels downward through the layers of the transmitting node. If the message must pass through an intermediate node, it will also be processed by the two path control network layers of that node. Finally, it passes upward through all the layers of the receiving node.

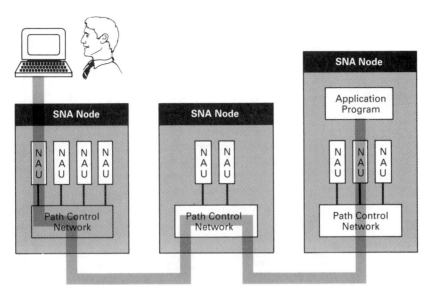

Figure 4.5   Message flow.

REQUEST/RESPONSE UNITS

All information exchanged between network addressable units takes the form of *requests* and *responses* to these requests. The messages that are exchanged in an SNA network are called *request units* and *response units*. A general term that is used to refer to either a request unit or a response unit is *request/response unit* (RU). As an RU passes through the layers of a sending node, control information is appended to the original RU.

BASIC INFORMATION UNITS

When a network user sends a request/response unit into the network, the function management layer passes the RU, along with a set of control parameters, down through the data flow control layer to the transmission control layer. The parameters supplied by the function management layer indicate the message type, the type of response expected, and the function management protocols that are in use. Information required by the data flow control layer to control the pacing of the transmissions is also included in these parameters.

Note that the data pass from function management through data flow control to the transmission control layer. The data flow control layer does not add information to an RU passed from function management. The data flow control layer does, however, create RUs of its own, also with parameters associated

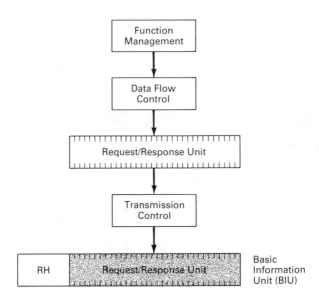

Figure 4.6   Basic Information Unit (BIU).

with them, that it passes directly to transmission control. The RUs created by the data flow control layer are used for control purposes—for example, to control the pacing of the RUs passed down from function management.

When the transmission control layer receives an RU along with its associated parameters, it uses these parameters to create a *request/response header* (RH) and appends it to the beginning of the RU (see Fig. 4.6). The unit of information made up of an RH and its associated RU is called a *basic information unit* (BIU). The RH stays attached to the request/response unit until the RU reaches its final destination. The transmission control layer in the destination node strips off the request/response header, acts on the information contained in it, and then passes the RU up through the data flow control layer to the function management layer.

BASIC TRANSMISSION UNITS

When the BIU is passed by the transmission control layer down to the path control layer, path control adds another header to the BIU to form a message unit called a *basic transmission unit* (BTU; see Fig. 4.7). This header, called the *transmission header* (TH), is used in guiding the BTU through the various data links that make up the selected path. For example, the transmission header contains the address of the final destination of the message, the address of the originating node, and additional path control information. It also contains information required to reassemble a message that may

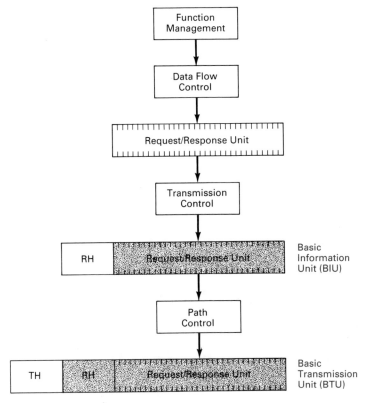

Figure 4.7   Basic Transmission Unit (BTU).

have been sliced up into smaller units, each of which is contained in its own BTU, or to separate messages that may have been blocked together in the same BTU. Information that makes recovery possible after a network failure can also be included in the transmission header. The transmission header also remains attached to the RU until it reaches the destination node. Intermediate nodes use information in the transmission header to determine which node is next in the path.

SDLC FRAMES   The path control layer passes each BTU down to the data link control layer for transmission over a physical circuit. The data link control layer takes each BTU, which consists of a request unit, a request/response header, and a transmission header, and adds yet another header and a trailer to create an *SDLC frame*. This is shown in Fig. 4.8. The data carried in the SDLC header and trailer are used to control physical transmission between two nodes and to detect transmission errors.

BOX 4.1 SNA request/response unit transmission

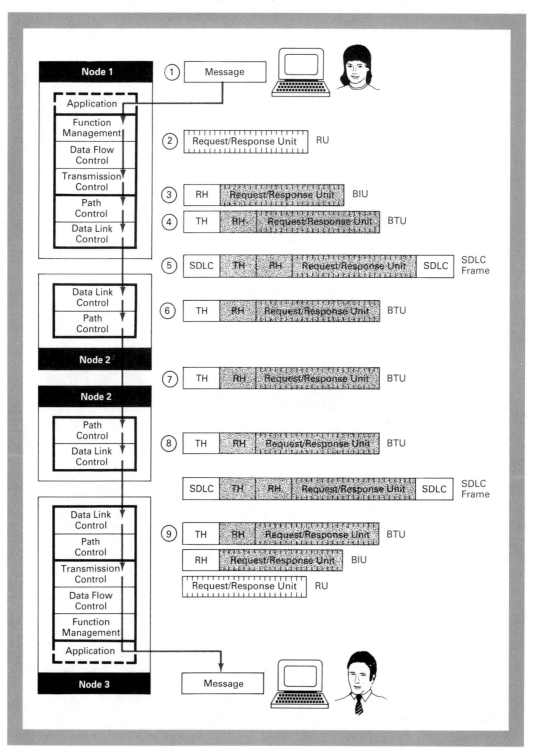

BOX 4.1   *(Continued)*

1. A user operating at the application layer formulates a message and passes it to the function management layer of SNA.

2. Function management constructs a *request/response unit* (RU) from the message and passes it down through the data flow control layer to transmission control.

3. Transmission control adds a *request/response header* (RH) to the RU, creating a *basic information unit* (BIU), and passes it to the path control layer.

4. Path control adds a *transmission header* (TH) to the BIU, creating a *basic transmission unit* (BTU). The TH contains the address of the first intermediate node to which the RU is to be sent. Path control then passes the BTU to data link control.

5. Data link control adds an *SDLC header and trailer* to the BTU, creating an *SDLC frame*. The frame is then transmitted over a physical link to the first intermediate node on the message's path.

6. At the intermediate node, data link control strips off the SDLC header and trailer and uses the information contained in them to check for transmission errors. It then passes the resulting BTU up to path control.

7. Path control uses information in the transmission header to determine the next node to which the RU must be passed.

8. The BTU is then passed back down to the data link control layer, where new SDLC headers and trailers are added, and the RU is sent to the next node.

9. At the message's final destination, the RU is passed up through the various layers, all headers and the trailer are removed, and the original message is passed to the receiving user operating at the destination node.

TRANSMISSION EXAMPLE   Box 4.1 shows the steps that are performed as a message passes through the network. The example shows how headers are added and stripped off in a transmission that originates at one node, passes through one intermediate node, and terminates at another node.

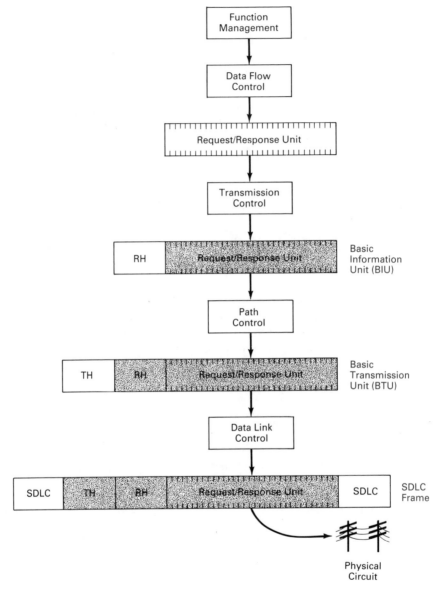

Figure 4.8   SDLC frame.

The use of so much control information at first may appear to be overly cumbersome. However, by using separate parameters and headers for the different layers, two very important results are achieved: independence of one layer from another and consistency within a single layer from one node to another. Generally, a layer concerns itself only with the control information that was added to the RU in the corresponding layer in another node. As long as the appropriate information is exchanged as a message is passed from one layer to the next, one layer is not affected by the processing done in another, and changes can be made at one layer without affecting other layers or other nodes.

SUMMARY   A path consists of a series of nodes through which a message passes in going from a sending logical unit to a receiving logical unit. The portion of the path from the originating subarea node to the receiving subarea node is the explicit route. The portion of the path from a subarea node to a peripheral node is a route extension. A virtual route is a logical connection between subarea nodes. Each virtual route is assigned to an explicit route, and several virtual routes can be assigned to the same explicit route. Based on the class of service requested by the user, a particular virtual route is selected for a session. The virtual route selected determines the explicit route used and the transmission priority that is assigned. A logon mode name may be used to specify the class of service.

All information exchanged between network addressable units is composed of request/response units (RUs). Transmission control adds a request/response header (RH) to each RU, forming a basic information unit (BIU). Path control adds a transmission header (TH) to each BIU, forming a basic transmission unit (BTU). Data link control adds an SDLC header and trailer to the BTU, forming a frame. Frames are then transmitted over a data link.

5 SNA SERVICES

In this chapter we examine the various services that are performed by an SNA network. We will categorize services in two ways. We will first show how services are related to the sessions that are in operation in the network. After that, we will show how those SNA services are distributed among the various SNA functional layers.

SESSION MANAGEMENT SERVICES

Of the various types of sessions, the one of most interest is the LU-to-LU session; as we have already mentioned, LU-to-LU is the only session type that a network user is aware of. All other session types are concerned with controlling the network and are transparent to network users. When a session is established between logical units, one of the LUs is designated the *primary* unit, and the other is designated the *secondary* unit. Often the primary unit is in a host processor, and the secondary unit is in a machine having less processing power. The primary unit implements more protocol features than the secondary unit and is responsible for recovery in the event of a failure. It is possible that the same logical unit might operate as the primary unit in one session and the secondary unit in another. The assignment of primary and secondary roles to logical units takes place at the time the session is initiated in a process called *binding*.

The primary services provided relative to LU-to-LU sessions are those needed to perform binding functions during session initiation, to control data flow while the session is in operation, and to terminate the session when it is no longer required.

- **Session Initiation.** The facilities used by different logical units vary enormously, since many different types of hardware and software can employ SNA

BOX 5.1   Session initiation functions

- **Protocol Establishment.** Establishing the operating protocols that the two logical units will use during the session
- **Facility Verification.** Ensuring that both logical units have the facilities, services, and software that will be required for the session
- **Resource Allocation.** Allocating necessary resources for the session
- **Data Structure Agreement.** Establishing an agreement between the LUs on the structure of the data to be interchanged
- **Recovery Protocol Establishment.** Establishing protocols to be used in recovering should a failure occur
- **Address Conversion.** Converting between network names and network addresses
- **Routing.** Establishing the route over which data will flow based on the class of service that has been requested

for different purposes. When a session is established, it is necessary to ensure that the parties involved have the resources they need to communicate and that they use complementary or matching facilities. Network names, which are symbolic references to resources, must also be converted into network addresses. These processes take place during the binding process. Binding is one of the primary session initiation functions of the SSCP; Box 5.1 lists some of the functions the SSCP performs during the session initiation.

- **Session Data Flow Control.** While a session is in progress, services are required to monitor and control the flow of data between the two LUs. Controlling the flow of data has several aspects, many of which are listed in Box 5.2.
- **Session Termination.** When data exchange is completed, the session is terminated, and any resources assigned to it are made available for use by other sessions. A session may also be deactivated because of a problem within the network or due to intervention by a network operator. SNA provides services that help determine if data exchange has been successfully completed at the time the session is terminated.

NETWORK MANAGEMENT

In addition to providing services related to managing individual sessions, SNA includes services aimed at the overall management of the network and its resources. Network management services perform the following functions:

- **Activation and Deactivation of SNA Resources.** These functions include checking that any needed physical resources are allocated and then assigning and releasing logical resources as required. An SNA network includes both logical resources, such as network addressable units, and the underlying physical resources, including processors, communications controllers, cluster controllers, terminals, and communication links.

- **Resource Sharing.** In a multiple-domain network, it is possible for different SSCPs to share the control of certain resources. Sometimes the sharing is serial, which means that only one SSCP can control the resource at one time. Other resources can be shared concurrently, up to a share limit that specifies the maximum number of SSCPs that can share a particular resource. Services are provided to support this sharing of resources.

- **Virtual Route Pacing.** The traffic resulting from all the concurrent sessions that are in operation over a particular route must be monitored and the data flow controlled so that the route and its underlying facilities are not overloaded. Several sessions may run concurrently using the same explicit routes and sometimes even the same virtual routes. Virtual route pacing controls the number of

BOX 5.2   Session data flow control functions

- **Session Level Pacing.** Monitoring data flow during a session to ensure that responses are received and the flow of data does not overload the receiving node. In a session, LUs alternate in sending and receiving data. Periodically, the sending LU must receive a response from the receiving LU indicating that messages have been correctly received. So as not to exceed the capacity of queues and buffers in the receiving LU, there is a limit to the amount of data that can be transmitted before a response is received. This limit is established as part of the session binding process.

- **Message Unit Sequencing.** Checking to see that message segments and message blocks are received in the same sequence in which they were sent. A logical message is not always transmitted through the network in a single RU. Large messages are sometimes broken into segments, and small messages may be combined into blocks. Part of controlling the flow of data involves the initial segmenting or blocking and the subsequent reconstruction of logical messages.

- **Cryptography.** Encrypting data before they are transmitted and then decrypting them when they have been received

- **Error Detection and Recovery.** Detecting errors that occur as data flow through the network, and if possible, recovering from them. If recovery is not possible, appropriate notification is sent to network users.

messages that an LU can send before receiving a response based on the total traffic on the route. (Session-level pacing controls the number of messages based on the capacity of the receiving node.)

- **Configuring the Network.** The configuration of an SNA network rarely remains static. Physical devices are added and removed, software is changed, and routes are changed to improve performance. Problems that occur in the network may require certain nodes or links to be bypassed. Configuration functions allow scheduled and unscheduled changes to be made to network configurations and make it possible for changes to be implemented with a minimum effect on network operations.

SNA FUNCTIONAL LAYERS

We will next see how the various SNA session services that have just been described, and other services supplied by the network, are distributed across the functional layers of SNA. Figure 5.1 shows the functional layers of SNA and some of the classes of service that are associated with them. When we look at the network from the viewpoint of the five major SNA functional layers, SNA services can be divided into two major categories:

- **NAU Services.** These comprise services that are associated with NAUs and the three functional layers implemented within them.
- **Path Control Network Services.** These are services that are associated with the two SNA layers that make up the path control network.

We will begin by looking at the NAU services that are supplied by each of the topmost three layers of SNA, beginning with the function management layer. We will then look at the services supplied by the two path control network layers.

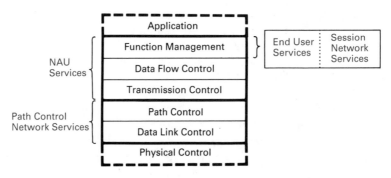

Figure 5.1 Function Management services.

FUNCTION MANAGEMENT SERVICES

As discussed in Chapter 3, the function management layer includes the NAU services manager and function management data services. These two function management sublayers provide two types of services: *end-user services* and *session network services*.

End-User Services

End-user services are concerned with the exchange of data between two logical units and are used in implementing LU-to-LU sessions. These services can be further subdivided into *session presentation services* and *application-to-application services*. The functions that are performed by both categories of end-user services are summarized here and are described in more detail in Box 5.3.

- **Session Presentation Services.** Session presentation services relate to the formatting and display of data.

- **Application-to-Application Services.** These include services that are used to implement LU-to-LU sessions that involve two application programs that communicate with each other.

The synchronization services that are a part of end-user services are especially important when LU-to-LU sessions are used for program-to-program communication. When application programs communicate, it may be necessary to take a series of actions that might involve transmitting a series of messages before a particular logical operation is completed. For example, an inventory update operation might involve updating inventory records in two locations. SNA allows the application program to reserve control over the required records or other resources until all the necessary processing has been completed. The logical operation is then considered to be *committed,* and the changes are considered completed. SNA provides services that allow the application programs to ensure that the logically related changes are synchronized. If a problem occurs during some part of the update operation and all the actions cannot be successfully completed, any changes that may already have been made are backed out, and all the records are restored to their previous form.

Session Network Services

In addition to end-user services, function management provides a set of session network services. These services primarily involve the SSCP and deal with the coordination of network activities. There are four types of session network serv-

58

BOX 5.3 Function management end-user services

Session Presentation Services

- **Data Formatting.** Formatting of data streams for particular terminal types, such as display screens and printers
- **Compression and Compaction.** Compressing and compacting data to make transmission more efficient
- **Screen Formatting.** Formatting data at the terminal using predefined screen formats

Application-to-Application Services

- **Network Transparency.** Allowing the two application programs to communicate without having to be aware of the structure of the network or the network protocols that are being used
- **Database Transparency.** Allowing a database to be accessed without having to specify in the application program where the database is located
- **Synchronization.** Synchronizing the related actions that application programs perform

ices: *session services, configuration services, maintenance and management services,* and *network operator services.* The functions that are performed by the four categories of session network services are summarized here and are described in detail in Box 5.4.

- **Session Services.** Session services support the activation and deactivation of sessions and are used in implementing all SSCP-to-LU and LU-to-LU sessions. It is possible for a logical unit to participate in more than one session at a time. If it does, session services ensures that it does not participate in more concurrent sessions than it has the resources to support.
- **Configuration Services.** Configuration services are concerned with the physical configuration of the network and with the various resources that are part of it. They are used in implementing SSCP-to-PU sessions.
- **Maintenance and Management Services.** Maintenance and management services are concerned with errors and failures in the network. They are used by both SSCP-to-LU and SSCP-to-PU sessions.
- **Network Operator Services.** Network operator services support communication between SSCPs and network operators.

BOX 5.4   Function management session network services

Session Services

- **Verification.** Verifying that the LUs have the proper authority to establish a session
- **Address Conversion.** Converting between network names and network addresses
- **Protocol Choice.** Determining the appropriate protocols and rules to be used during the session, including the request/response mode
- **Virtual Route Choice.** Determining the virtual route to be used, based on the requested class of service
- **Request Queuing.** Queuing activation requests that cannot be acted on immediately

Configuration Services

- **Address Table Maintenance.** Maintaining tables of network names and network addresses
- **Status Monitoring.** Monitoring the status of the NAUs and communication links that make up the network
- **Network Startup and Shutdown.** Starting up the network by activating nodes and links and shutting it down when it is no longer required
- **Link Activation and Deactivation.** Activating and deactivating links between nodes
- **Configuration Alteration.** Altering the configuration of the network, including restarting parts of the network that may have failed
- **Program Loading and Dumping.** Loading programs into nodes and dumping the contents of nodes

Maintenance and Management Services

- **Failure Testing.** Performing tests to determine whether a link or a node has failed
- **Failure Determination.** Determining the causes of failures
- **Statistics Gathering.** Collecting test results and error statistics

Network Operator Services

- **Statistics Gathering.** Gathering error statistics
- **Resource Activation and Deactivation.** Activating and deactivating network resources
- **Network Startup and Shutdown.** Starting and stopping the network itself

DATA FLOW CONTROL SERVICES

The services associated with the data flow control layer provide functions that help in maintaining the integrity of data flow within a particular session. Functions performed in the data flow control layer include these:

- **Flow Direction.** This function determines whether, for a given session, messages can be transmitted in both directions concurrently or in only one direction at a time.

- **Chaining.** Requests that are traveling in the same direction are sometimes grouped together into a larger unit called a *chain*.

- **Bracketing.** In some cases, a sequence of related messages that flow back and forth between two logical units and that constitute a single logical unit of work are grouped together into *brackets*.

- **Interchange Control.** This function controls the interchange of request and response units according to the mode selected at the time the session was activated.

- **Interruption.** A network user can, at any time during a session, request that the flow of data be interrupted.

TRANSMISSION CONTROL SERVICES

The services performed by the transmission control layer involve assuring that message units are sent and received in the proper sequence, keeping the flow of data within a session paced properly, and monitoring the status of the session. Among the functions provided are these:

- **Session-Level Pacing.** This function ensures that the sending unit does not transmit more message units than the receiving unit can handle.

- **Header Construction.** Transmission control constructs the request/response header using parameters passed down from higher levels and, on the receiving end, removes the header and passes appropriate parameters up to higher layers.

- **Sequence Checking.** Sequence numbers are checked to ensure that request and response units are received in the right sequence.

- **Encryption and Decryption.** Data can be encrypting before they are transmitted and decrypted after they are received. This function can be used in situations where security is an issue.

PATH CONTROL SERVICES

Up to this point we have been considering NAU services—services provided by the functional layers contained within network addressable units. Next we will look at the services that are part of the path control network. These services are primarily concerned with routing data from node to node, controlling the overall flow of data, and transmitting data across specific links. The path control layer within the path control network is concerned with the following functions:

- **Routing.** This function determines the next node to which a message unit should travel and the transmission group over which it should be transmitted.

- **Header Construction.** Path control creates a transmission header for each message unit before it is passed to data link control and, on the receiving end, processes and removes the transmission header.

- **Boundary Function.** A local address is translated into a full network address when a message unit passes from a peripheral node to a subarea node; the opposite translation takes place on the receiving end.

- **Segmenting and Blocking.** Large messages are sometimes broken into segments, and small messages are sometimes combined into larger blocks, where this will increase transmission efficiency; the opposite functions are then performed at the receiving node.

- **Message Unit Sequencing.** When a series of message units is transmitted over the same transmission group, different message units may use different links. If delays are encountered on a particular link, the message units may arrive out of sequence. Sequence numbers are used to ensure that message units reach the final receiving node in the same sequence in which they were transmitted from the sending node.

- **Virtual Route Pacing.** The traffic flowing from all sessions sharing a particular virtual route must be regulated. Path control services are used to detect congestion and to control the rate at which message units are transmitted along a virtual route.

DATA LINK CONTROL SERVICES

Data link control services are concerned with the transmission of data across a specific physical circuit. Functions performed in supplying these services include the following:

- **Header and Trailer Construction.** Data link control constructs data link headers and trailers prior to transmission and then checks and removes them after transmission.

- **Data Transfer.** This function involves transferring frames of data over a data link.

- **Error Detection.** Frames are checked for transmission errors after each frame is received.

- **Retransmission.** Frames that are found to be in error are automatically retransmitted.

SUMMARY   SNA services associated with SNA sessions can be divided into two categories: session management services and network management services. Session management services are used to initiate, control, and terminate sessions. Network management services are used to activate and deactivate SNA resources, to control the sharing of resources, to control the pacing of data transmitted over virtual routes, and to control the network configuration.

SNA services can also be classified according to the specific SNA functional layer that performs the service. Function management services include end-user services and session network services. End-user services are divided into session presentation services, which are concerned with the formatting and display of data across the network-user interface, and application-to-application services, which allow application programs to communicate with one another. Session network services fall into four categories. Session services support the initiation and termination of sessions. Configuration services help control the physical configuration of the network. Maintenance and management services support error detection and analysis. Network operator services support communication between SSCPs and network operators. Data flow control services maintain the integrity of data flow within a particular session. This includes determining send/receive mode, creating chains and brackets, controlling responses, and interrupting the flow of data on request. Transmission control services include session-level pacing, sequencing of message units, creation of the request/response header (RH), and encryption. Path control services include determining the next node to which a message should travel, choosing the transmission group to use, creating the transmission header (TH), performing boundary function address translation, segmenting and blocking messages, sequencing message units, and handling virtual route pacing. Data link control services include creating SDLC headers and trailers, transferring data over a link, and identifying and recovering from transmission errors.

6 SNA AND THE OSI MODEL

The International Organization for Standardization (ISO), in Geneva, Switzerland, is actively developing a generalized model of system interconnection, called the *Open Systems Interconnection Reference Model* (OSI model). Because of the increasing importance of the OSI model in international markets and in the United States, the differences between the SNA architecture and the OSI model are of great interest to IBM installations. This chapter will show how SNA relates to the OSI architecture.

The primary purpose of the OSI model is to provide a basis for coordinating the development of standards that relate to the flexible interconnection of systems using data communication facilities. In OSI terminology, a *system* is defined as follows:

> A set of one or more computers, the associated software, peripherals, terminals, human operators, physical processes, transfer means, etc., that forms an autonomous whole capable of performing information processing and/or information transfer.

The OSI model is concerned with the *interconnection of systems*—the way they exchange information—and not the *internal functions* that are performed by a given system. The OSI model provides a generalized view of a layered architecture. Under the broad definition that has been given for a system, the architecture can apply to a very simple system, such as the connection of a terminal to a computer, or to a very complex system, such as the interconnection of two entire computer networks. It also can be used as a model for a network architecture, which is how we will view it here. The development of the OSI model is still in progress. For some areas specific standards have been defined in support of the model; in other areas standards still need to be developed.

OSI LAYERS   The OSI model uses a layered approach, with sets of functions allocated to the various layers. Figure 6.1 shows the layers that have been defined as part of the OSI model. We will look at each of these layers in detail. But first, some basic concepts that underlie the layered architecture of the OSI model need to be defined. An *entity* is an active element within a layer. Two entities within the same layer are called *peer entities*. Entities in one layer provide services to entities in the layer above them and, in turn, receive services from entities in the layer below them. For example, entities in the presentation layer provide services to the application layer and receive services from the session layer. A key part, then, of the definition of a layer is the services it provides. In addition, each layer performs a set of functions in providing its services. We will also discuss the functions that a layer performs in providing its services to the next higher layer. We will now look at each of the OSI layers, from the bottom up.

SERVICE DATA   The units of data that are handled by the various lay-
UNITS   ers are defined by the OSI model as *service data units* that are preceded by the names of the layers with which they are associated. Thus the service data units handled by the physical layer are called *physical service data units,* the service data units handled by the data link layer are called *data link service data units,* and so on. The data units handled by the lower-level layers have come to have informal names that are often referenced in the literature. For example, data link service data units are often called *frames,* and network service data units are typically called *packets.*

PHYSICAL LAYER   The *physical layer* is responsible for the transmission of physical service data units, more often called *bits,* across a particular physical transmission medium that connects two or more data link entities. It involves a connection between two machines that allows electrical signals to be exchanged between them. Typically, the hardware consists of

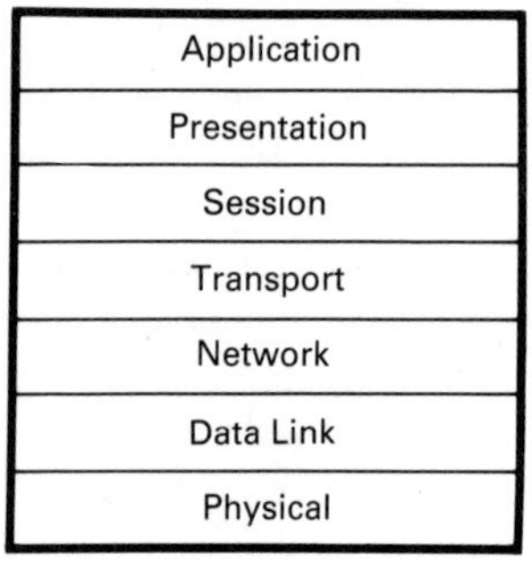

| Application |
| Presentation |
| Session |
| Transport |
| Network |
| Data Link |
| Physical |

Figure 6.1   OSI layers.

a cable, appropriate connectors, and two communicating devices, which are capable of both generating and detecting voltages on the connecting cables. Software consists of firmware, permanently installed in the devices, that controls the generation and detection of these voltages. Box 6.1 lists the services that the physical layer provides to the data link layer and describes some of the functions that the physical layer performs.

Protocols for the physical layer involve mechanical, electrical, functional, and procedural means for activating, maintaining, and deactivating physical connections. This includes the specification of physical connectors, cables, and electrical signals. At this level, hardware standards are extremely important. A

BOX 6.1　OSI physical layer

Services to the Data Link Layer

- **Physical Connections.** Transparent transmission of bit streams across physical connections

- **Physical Service Data Units.** Definition of the unit of data that is handled by the physical layer (*one bit* for serial transmission and *n bits* for parallel transmission)

- **Physical Connection End Points.** Definition of identifiers that are used by the data link layer to refer to physical connection end points

- **Data Circuit Identification.** Definition of identifiers that are used by the data link layer to refer to physical circuits

- **Sequencing.** Delivery of bits in the same order in which they were transmitted

- **Fault Condition Notification.** Notification of the data link layer when fault conditions occur

- **Quality-of-Service Parameters.** Definition of parameters that define quality of service, including error rate, service availability, transmission rate, and transit delay

Physical Layer Functions

- Activating and deactivating physical connections upon request from the data link layer

- Transmitting bits over a physical connection in a synchronous or asynchronous fashion

- Handling physical-layer management activities, including activation and error control computer must be equipped with an appropriate connector to which the cable can be connected. The cable must have an appropriate connector attached to each end. A terminal must also have an appropriate connector. Also, the computer and the terminal must agree on the voltage levels that will be used to transmit signals between the two devices. Standards are also important for the simple software, or firmware, that runs in the physical layer. For example, the firmware that runs in the computer and the firmware that runs in the terminal must agree as to how long in duration each bit should be and how to tell the difference between a one bit and a zero bit. The physical layer must deliver bits in the same sequence they are submitted and must notify the next higher layer of any faults that are detected. A physical connection might involve the interconnection of a series of data circuits. The transmission alternatives addressed by the physical layer include these:

- Duplex or half-duplex links
- Point-to-point or multipoint connections
- Synchronous or asynchronous transmission

Several standards have been defined for this layer, including CCITT Recommendation X.21. X.21 describes the interface that allows a terminal to operate in synchronous mode over a public data network.

DATA LINK LAYER
The *data link layer* is responsible for providing reliable data transmission from one network entity, or physical node, to another and for shielding higher layers from any concerns about the physical transmission medium. It is concerned with the error-free transmission of data link service data units, or *frames,* of data. Box 6.2 lists the services that the data link layer provides to the network layer and describes some of the functions the data link layer performs in providing those services.

A standard protocol that has been developed for the data link layer is high-level data link control (HDLC). HDLC is a bit-oriented, synchronous protocol for transmitting data. The SDLC protocol, which is the standard data link protocol defined by SNA, is effectively a subset of the HDLC protocol. SDLC is covered in Part III of this book. Most of the discussion of SDLC in Part III also applies to the HDLC protocol.

NETWORK LAYER
The *network layer* is concerned with transferring network service data units, more often called *packets,* of data from one transport entity to another. It is responsible for establishing, maintaining, and terminating the network connection between two transport entities and for transferring data along it in a way that keeps any higher layer from

BOX 6.2   OSI data link layer

Services to the Network Layer

- **Data Link Connection.** Establishment of a data link connection between two or more entities defined by the network layer (Data link connections are established and released dynamically.)

- **Data Link Service Data Units.** Definition of the unit of data handled by the data link layer (generally called a *frame,* consisting of a sequence of bits)

- **Data Link Connection End Point Identifiers.** Definition of identifiers that are used by the network layer to refer to data link connection end points

- **Sequencing.** Delivery of frames in the same order in which they were transmitted

- **Error Notification.** Notification of the network layer when unrecoverable errors occur

- **Flow Control.** Dynamic control over the rate at which a network entity receives frames from a data link connection

- **Quality-of-Service Parameters.** Definition of parameters that define quality of service, including mean time between unrecoverable errors, residual error rate, service availability, throughput, and transit delay

Data Link Layer Functions

- Establishing and releasing data link connections for use by the network layer

- Building a data link connection using one or more physical connections

- Delimiting data so that they can be sent as frames over a physical connection

- Synchronizing the receipt of data that have been split over several physical connections

- Maintaining the sequential order of frames that are transmitted over a data link connection

- Detecting and correcting transmission errors, with retransmission of frames if necessary

- Providing flow control, including dynamically altering the rate at which data units are accepted, and temporarily stopping transmission to a particular receiving entity upon request being concerned about, or aware of, the nature of that connection. At any given time there can be only one network connection between two given entities, although there can be several possible routes from which to choose when a particular connection is established.

The network layer handles routing of data through any intermediate nodes that are necessary. If the route involves more than one network, the network layer shields higher layers from dealing with any differences in transmission facilities, quality of service, or implementation technologies between the networks. The services provided by the network layer to the transport layer and many of the functions performed in providing those services are listed in Box 6.3.

A standard that has been developed for the network layer is CCITT Recommendation X.25 Level 3. Recommendation X.25 has three levels, each of

BOX 6.3   OSI network layer

Services to the Transport Layer

- **Network Addresses.** Definition of network addresses to be used in identifying entities defined by the transport layer

- **Network Connections.** Transfer of data between transport entities that are identified by network addresses (Each network connection is point to point, and multiple network connections can exist between transport entities.)

- **Network Connection End Point Identifiers.** Definition of unique end point identifiers that are associated with the network addresses used by the transport layer

- **Network Service Data Unit Transfer.** Definition of the unit of data that is handled by the network layer (generally called a *packet*, on which no maximum size limit is imposed by the architecture)

- **Quality-of-Service Parameters.** Definition of parameters that define quality of service, including residual error rate, service availability, throughput, transit delay, and connection-establishment delay. A selected quality of service is maintained for the duration of the network connection.

- **Error Notification.** Notification of the transport layer when unrecoverable errors occur (Error notification may or may not lead to network disconnection.)

- **Sequencing.** Delivery of frames in the same order in which they were transmitted if requested by the transport layer

BOX 6.3 *(Continued)*

- **Flow Control.** Provision for stopping the transfer of packets upon request by the transport entity that is receiving packets
- **Expedited Network Service Data Unit Transfer.** An optional expedited service for handling information exchange over a network connection
- **Reset.** An optional service that, when requested by a transport entity, causes the network layer to discard all packets currently in transit and to notify the transport entity at the other end of the connection that a reset has occurred
- **Release.** Release of a network connection upon request by a transport entity

Network Layer Functions

- Determining an optimum routing over the possible network connections that can exist between two network addresses and then relaying packets over the various point-to-point connections that make up that route
- Providing a network connection between two transport entities and transferring data over the network connection in a transparent fashion
- Multiplexing multiple network connections onto a single data link connection in order to optimize their use
- Segmenting and/or blocking packets for the purposes of facilitating the transfer of packets over network connections
- Detecting errors and recovering from them
- Selecting an appropriate quality of service and maintaining this quality of service even when a network connection spans subnetworks of dissimilar quality
- Handling network layer management activities, including activation and error control

which addresses a different layer. Level 1 addresses the physical layer, level 2 addresses the data link layer, and level 3, sometimes called the packet level, addresses the network layer. Recommendation X.25 defines how a packet terminal interfaces with a packet switched network.

TRANSPORT LAYER

The *transport layer* is responsible for transferring transport service data units, or complete *messages*, between two session entities at an agreed-on level of service quality. The transport layer is not concerned with the specific route that is used through the network; it is simply concerned with the reliable, cost-effective transfer of messages. The transport layer is responsible for establishing transport connections between entities, transferring data, and releasing connections.

A transport connection acts as a virtual circuit between two parties and appears to be a simple point-to-point connection. This layer performs a function that is sometimes called "end-to-end" control and is responsible for taking action if a message is lost and for ensuring that a message is not delivered twice.

The transport layer offers a defined set of service classes. The service classes provide various combinations of factors, such as throughput, transit delay, connection setup delay, error rate, and availability. When a transport connection is established, a particular class of service is selected, based on the type of service requested by the session entity. The transport layer is then responsible for monitoring transmission to ensure that the appropriate service quality is maintained and, if not, for notifying the appropriate entity of the failure or degradation. The services provided by the transport layer to the session layer and many of the functions performed by the transport layer are summarized in Box 6.4.

SESSION LAYER

The *session layer* focuses on providing a set of services that are used to organize and synchronize the *dialog* that takes place between presentation entities and to manage the session service data units that are exchanged between them. The session layer maintains the dialog even if data are lost at the transport level. It is responsible for establishing, managing, and releasing session connections between presentation entities. There can be numerous concurrent session connections between a given pair of entities. A session connection can be mapped onto transport connections in a variety of ways. In the simplest case, a session connection uses a single transport connection. In more complex situations, one session might use a series of transport connections if, for example, a transport connection has to be terminated because of errors or failures. In other cases, a series of consecutive session connections might use the same transport connection.

A primary concern of the session layer is to manage dialog interaction. Three possible methods of interaction are defined:

- Two-way, simultaneous interaction, where both entities send and receive concurrently
- Two-way, alternate interaction, where the entities take turns sending and receiving
- One-way interaction, where one entity only sends and the other only receives

BOX 6.4   OSI transport layer

Services to the Session Layer

- **Transport Connection Establishment.** Establishment of a transport connection, of an agreed-on quality of service, between two entities defined by the session layer (At the time of connection establishment, a class of service can be selected from a defined set of available classes.)

- **Data Transfer.** Transfer of data in accordance with the quality of service negotiated when the connection was established

- **Transport Connection Release.** Release of a transport connection upon request by a session entity (The other session entity is also notified of the connection release.)

Transport Layer Functions

- Converting transport addresses for entities into network addresses. Several transport addresses can be associated with the same network entity, and thus several transport addresses might be mapped onto a single network address.

- Multiplexing multiple transport connections onto a single network connection or splitting a transport connection over several network connections as needed to optimize use of network connections

- Sequencing of data units transferred in order to ensure that they are delivered in the same sequence in which they were sent

- Detecting and recovering from errors

- Segmenting, blocking, and concatenation of data units

- Controlling data flow to prevent overloading of network resources

- Handling transport-layer supervisory activities

- Providing for expedited transfer of data units between session entities

Where the entities take turns sending and receiving, the changeover can be voluntary on the part of the entities, or it can be forced by the session layer upon request of the presentation entity. Box 6.5 lists the services that the session layer provides to the presentation layer and describes many of the functions that the session layer performs. Additional functions, currently not defined for the

BOX 6.5 OSI session layer

Services to the Presentation Layer

- **Session Connection Establishment.** Establishment of a session connection between two entities defined by the presentation layer

- **Session Connection Release.** Release of a session connection, in an orderly fashion and without loss of data, upon request of a presentation entity (This service permits either of the presentation entities to abort a session connection, in which case data might be lost. The release of session connection can also be initiated by one of the session entities supporting it.)

- **Normal Data Exchange.** Normal transfer of data between a sending presentation entity and a receiving presentation entity

- **Quarantine Service.** Request by a sending presentation entity that a specific number of session data units be held and not made available to the receiving presentation entity until specifically released by the sending entity (The sending entity can later specify that the data units be discarded instead of being sent to the receiving entity.)

- **Expedited Data Exchange.** Transfer of data on an expedited basis for high-priority traffic

- **Interaction Management.** Explicit control over whose turn it is to exercise certain control functions

- **Session Connection Synchronization.** Definition by presentation entities of synchronization points (The session layer provides services to reset a session connection to a resynchronization point and to restore entities to a defined state.)

- **Exception Reporting.** Notification to presentation entities by the session layer about exceptional conditions

Session Layer Functions

- Providing a one-to-one mapping between a session connection and a presentation connection at any given instant. Over time, however, a transport connection can use several consecutive session connections, and several consecutive transport connections might use a single session connection.

- Preventing a presentation entity from being overloaded with data by using transport flow control (There is no explicit flow control in the session layer.)

- Reestablishing a transport connection to support a session connection in the event of a reported failure of the underlying transport connection

- Handling session-layer management activities

session layer but considered candidates for future extensions, include the following:

- Sequence numbering of session service data units
- Brackets
- Stop-go transmission
- Security functions

PRESENTATION LAYER

The *presentation layer* is responsible for the presentation of information in a way that is meaningful to application entities. It is responsible for any data conversions that might be necessary before communication can take place. For example, in a computer network that supports advanced functions, incompatible devices should be able to communicate. The presentation layer handles any character code translation and data conversion that might be required. The presentation layer might also handle data compression and expansion functions that might be implemented to reduce the number of bits that are transmitted.

The presentation layer is concerned with the syntax used both for representing data and for the formatting of data. Representation of data deals with character sets and coding structures. Data formatting deals with the formats of data required by particular input and output devices. For either type, there can be up to three different types of syntax involved during a given session between two application entities:

- The syntax used by the sending entity
- The syntax used by the receiving entity
- The syntax used for the transfer of data

The three types of syntax can all be different, or any two, or even all three, can be the same. If they are different, the presentation layer is responsible for transforming from one syntax to another. Negotiations between the presentation entities that represent the application entities determine what transformations will be necessary and where they will be performed. These negotiations ordinarily take place when the session is initiated. Negotiations can also take place while the session is in progress. Box 6.6 lists the services that the presentation layer provides to the application layer and describes many of the functions that are performed in providing those services.

APPLICATION LAYER

The *application layer* provides application processes with a point of access to the system. The application layer provides a means for application processes to

BOX 6.6   OSI presentation layer

Services to the Application Layer

- **Session Services.** Provision to the application layer of all the services provided by the session layer
- **Syntax Selection.** Initial selection of a syntax and subsequent modification of the initial syntax selection
- **Syntax Transformation.** Code and character set conversion and modification of data layout

Presentation Layer Functions

- Issuing a request to the session layer for the establishment of a session
- Initiating a data transfer from one application entity or user to another
- Negotiating and renegotiating the choice of a syntax to be used in the data transfer
- Performing any required data transformation or conversion
- Issuing a request to the session layer for the termination of a session

access the system interconnection facilities in order to exchange information. It provides all functions related to communication between systems that are not provided by the lower layers. These functions include those performed by people as well as those performed by application programs. The OSI model does not currently define the specific functions that are performed by the application layer, but it does divide them into two categories. Box 6.7 lists the services that the application layer provides to the application process, or user, and describes the two broad categories of functions that are performed by the application layer.

Additional services, over and above those shown in Box 6.7, may also be provided. In addition, the application layer provides management services related to management both of the application processes and of the systems being interconnected. Management of application processes includes initializing, maintaining, and terminating the processes, allocating and deallocating resources, detecting and preventing deadlocks, and providing integrity, commitment control, security, checkpoint, and recovery control (this list is not exhaustive). Management of systems might include activating, maintaining, and deactivating various system resources, program loading, monitoring and reporting status and statistics, error detection, diagnosis and recovery, and reconfiguration and restart.

BOX 6.7   OSI application layer

Services to the Application Process

- **Identification.** Identification of the intended communication partners (for example, by name, address, description, etc.)
- **Availability.** Determination of the current availability of the intended communication partners
- **Authority.** Establishment of the authority of the partners to communicate
- **Privacy.** Agreement on the privacy mechanisms to be used in communication
- **Security.** Authentication of the identity of the intended communication partners
- **Cost Allocation.** Determination of cost allocation methodology to be used in communication
- **Resource Allocation.** Determination of the adequacy of available resources
- **Quality of Service.** Determination of the acceptable quality of service to be used with respect to such factors as response time, tolerable error rate, and cost
- **Synchronization.** Synchronization of cooperating applications
- **Dialog Discipline.** Selection of the dialog discipline to be used in communication, including the procedures to be used in initiation and release
- **Error Recovery.** Agreement on responsibility for error recovery
- **Data Integrity.** Agreement on the procedures for control of data integrity
- **Data Syntax.** Identification of constraints on data syntax (character sets, data structures, etc.)

Application Layer Functions

- Performing *common application functions*, functions that provide capabilities that are useful to many applications
- Performing *specific application functions*, functions that are required to service the needs of a particular application

OSI AND SNA COMPARED

Both SNA and the OSI model use a layered approach to their architectures, and in large part their definitions include similar services. However, there are some differences in the services that are specified and in how the services are distributed among the various layers. Figure 6.2 shows a deliberately oversimplified view of the correlations between the SNA and OSI layers. We will present a more detailed comparison of the major services provided by the two architectures.

SNA FUNCTION MANAGEMENT

SNA's function management layer corresponds to the combination of the application layer and the presentation layer in the OSI model (see Fig. 6.3). As part of the OSI application layer, a set of application management services is defined; these services relate to the management of OSI application processes. In general, SNA defines no counterpart to these management services. In SNA the management of applications is left to the applications that interface with SNA and is not defined as part of the SNA architecture. However, both SNA and OSI include definitions of services related to the overall management of network resources and to the monitoring of their status. In OSI these are the system management services that are defined in the application layer. In SNA these management services include configuration services, maintenance and management services, and network operator services.

In addition to management services, both OSI and SNA provide services that relate to the establishment and maintenance of sessions between network users for purposes of communication across the network. In OSI these are application services. In SNA these include session services and application-to-application services. As can be seen from Fig. 6.3, many of the functions performed at this level are common to both SNA and OSI.

Finally, both OSI and SNA define services that are related to the formatting and presentation of data. For SNA these are session presentation services; for OSI these services are performed in the presentation layer.

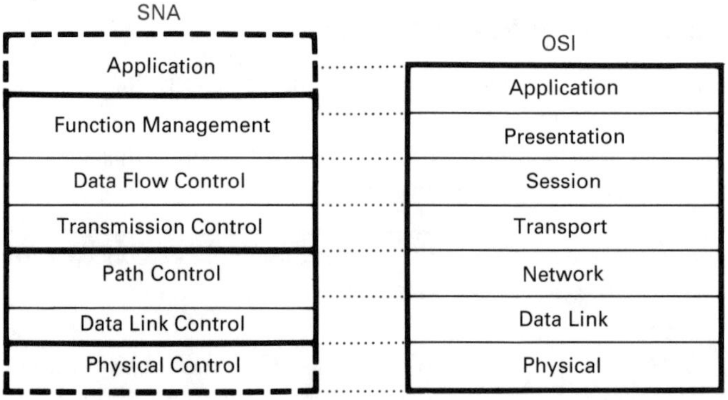

Figure 6.2   SNA and OSI layer correspondence.

SNA Function Management	OSI Application Layer
	Application Management • Initiation and termination of applications • Deadlock detection and prevention • Security • Checkpoint and recovery
Configuration Services • Activation and deactivation of nodes and links • Program loading and dumping • Reconfiguration and restarting of the network • Maintenance of network names and addresses • Maintenance of NAU and link status	**System Management** • Activation and deactivation of network resources • Loading of programs • Reconfiguration and restart of network • Monitoring and reporting of network status
Maintenance and Management Services • Identification and analysis of failures • Collection of test results and error statistics	• Detection, diagnosis, and recovery from errors • Monitoring and reporting of network statistics
Network Operator Services • Communication with network operator	
Session Services • Activation and deactivation of sessions • Verification of LU authority • Conversion of network names to network addresses • Determination of protocols and rules • Determination of virtual route • Initiation of request queuing	**Application Services** • Determination of availability of internal partners • Establishment of authority • Identification of intended partners • Agreement on dialogue discipline, responsibility for error recovery, and procedures for control of data integrity • Determination of quality of service • Determination of adequacy of resources
Application-to-Application Services • Program-to-program communication • Synchronization	• Information transfer • Synchronization • Agreement on privacy mechanisms • Authentication of intended partners • Determination of cost allocation methodology • Identification of constraints on data syntax
	OSI Presentation Layer
Session Presentation Services • Formatting of data streams • Compression and compaction of data • Formatting of data display	• Data representation syntax • Transformation between syntaxes • Data formatting syntax

Figure 6.3   Function Management vs. Application and Presentation layers.

SNA DATA FLOW CONTROL

The data flow control layer in SNA is analogous to the session layer in OSI. These layers are primarily concerned with the integrity of the overall data flow. Figure 6.4 shows the major services provided in each. Although the names used for a service in the two architectures may be different, their functions are often very similar. These services involve determining and managing the interactions involved in the transmission. These roughly comparable layers also demonstrate how SNA and OSI sometimes differ in the way in which services are assigned

SNA Data Flow Control	OSI Session Layer
• Determination of send/receive mode • Grouping of messages into chains • Identification of logical units of work with brackets • Control of request/response processing • Interruption of data flow, on request	• Management of transmission interaction • Providing quarantine services • Brackets (candidate for extension) • Synchronization • Stop-and-go transmission (candidate for extension) • Expedited data flow • Exception reporting • Security (candidate for extension)
SNA Transmission Control	**OSI Transport Layer**
• Session level pacing • Sequence numbering • Request/response headers • Multiple sessions sharing virtual route • Encryption	• Flow control • Sequencing of data units • Error detection and recovery • Multiplexing and splitting of transport connections into network connections • Monitoring quality of service • Conversion of transport addresses into network addresses • Segmenting, blocking, and concatenation of data units

Figure 6.4   Data Flow and Transmission Control vs. Session and Transport layers.

to layers. Two of the services included in the session layer—exception reporting and security—have their counterparts in the transmission control layer in SNA, not the data flow control layer.

SNA TRANSMISSION CONTROL   Figure 6.4 also shows the correspondence between the SNA transmission control layer and the OSI transport layer. Here again there are a number of parallel services and also a few differences. Monitoring of the quality of service, which is part of the transport layer in OSI, finds its counterpart in virtual route control, which is part of SNA's path control layer.

SNA PATH AND DATA LINK CONTROL   There is greater overlap between layers as we move down to the next two layers, as shown in Fig. 6.5. The services provided by the network layer of OSI find many matches in SNA's path control layer. These services provide transfer of data in a way that makes the physical network structure transparent to the higher layers. The path control layer in SNA also contains sequencing services that are involved in ensuring that data are properly reassembled. In OSI these services are part of the data link layer. The OSI data link layer also provides the services involved in controlling the transmission of data over a specific physical link. The corresponding SNA services are provided

SNA Path Control	OSI Network Layer
• Sequencing of message units • Sharing of explicit route by multiple virtual routes • Segmenting and blocking of message units • High-priority transfer	• Providing data units in sequence • Interruption of data flow, on request • Multiplexing • Segmenting and blocking of data units • Expedited data flow (optional) • Reset services (optional) • Release of network connection, on request
	OSI Data Link Layer
• Routing • Sequencing of message units across transmission group • Virtual route pacing	• Use of multiple physical connections for data link connection • Synchronization of receipt of data units • Flow control
SNA Data Link Control	
• Creation of link headers and trailers • Transmission of data over a physical circuit • Error detection and correction	• Delimiting data as frames • Transfer of data over a physical link • Error detection and correction

Figure 6.5 Path and Data Link Control vs. Network and Data Link layers.

by the data link control layer. A key standard that has been developed in support of the data link layer in the OSI model is high-level data link control (HDLC). The SNA counterpart to the HDLC protocol, as mentioned earlier, is synchronous data link control (SDLC), which is effectively a subset of HDLC.

PHYSICAL LAYER The *physical layer* in OSI, which is responsible for transmission of bits across a physical medium, does not have a counterpart in SNA. Rather than explicitly defining this layer, SNA assumes that this layer is defined outside the SNA architecture using various international standards.

SNA-OSI RELATIONSHIPS We have discussed both SNA and the OSI model as examples of different network architectures. However, SNA and the OSI model need not be viewed as competitive network architectures. SNA is an architecture designed to allow IBM to develop a wide range of hardware and software products that can be easily interconnected to form complex networks. The OSI model provides an architecture that is best suited for interconnecting what might otherwise be incompatible systems. The OSI model and its associated standards can be used as a basis for developing individual networks; however, the OSI model can also be used as a basis for interconnecting dissimilar networks. For example, OSI might be used to define architectural guidelines for interconnecting an SNA network with other proprietary or nonproprietary networks. Moreover, IBM offers support of the CCITT X.21 and X.25 recommendations within the SNA product line. In many ways, the two architectures can be viewed as complementary.

CORPORATION FOR OPEN SYSTEMS

IBM is actively involved in the development of standards that support OSI and, over the years, will provide SNA capabilities for coexisting with equipment and systems that conform to the OSI model. In 1985 an organization known as the Corporation for Open Systems (COS) was formed in the United States under the auspices of the Computer and Communications Industry Association. A number of large organizations, including IBM and many other computer manufacturers, have joined the COS, which has as its charter the monitoring of OSI standards development and also the monitoring of standards in the area of *integrated services digital network* (ISDN) development. ISDN standards have to do with the combining of all types of traffic, including voice, data, and images, over the same communication facilities.

SUMMARY

The OSI model provides a generalized model for system interconnection. It uses a layered architecture in which entities within a layer provide services to the next higher layer. The physical layer is responsible for the transmission of bit streams across a physical transmission medium. The data link layer is responsible for providing reliable data transmission from one node to another. The network layer is responsible for establishing, maintaining, and terminating network connections and transferring data across those connections. The transport layer is responsible for providing data transfer at an agreed-on level of service quality. The session layer provides services to organize and synchronize the dialog that takes place between presentation entities and to manage the data exchange. The presentation layer is responsible for syntax conversion related to the representation and formatting of data. The application layer provides a means for application processes to access the system interconnection facilities in order to exchange information.

Both SNA and OSI use a layered approach to their architectures. The two architectures have many similarities, although there are also many differences in the services that are provided and in the way those services are distributed among the layers. The SNA function management layer corresponds to the OSI application and presentation layers. SNA's data flow control layer corresponds to OSI's session layer. The transmission control layer of SNA corresponds to the transport layer of OSI. SNA's path control and data link control layers correspond to OSI's network and data link layers. The layer that corresponds to OSI's physical layer is defined outside the SNA architecture. The OSI model provides an architecture that can be used to interconnect dissimilar systems and, as such, can be viewed as complementary to SNA.

7 SNA PROGRAM PRODUCTS

Thus far we have examined SNA as an architecture, which defines formats and protocols that are independent of any particular product. In this chapter we will look at the key IBM software products used to implement SNA networks. The types of products we will look at fall into the following four categories:

- Telecommunications access methods
- Network control programs
- Application subsystems
- Network management programs

TELECOMMUNICATIONS ACCESS METHODS

Telecommunications access methods software resides in a host processor and provides an interface between the host processor and other resources in the network. Figure 7.1 shows the relationship between an SNA telecommunications access method and the SNA components described in earlier chapters. If the host processor is a node that contains an SSCP, the SSCP is contained within the access method. Likewise, the physical unit, path control network components, and boundary functions are all part of the access method. The logical units are implemented partially within the access method and partially within either an application subsystem (described later in this chapter) or an application program.

There are three primary SNA telecommunications access methods: Advanced Communications Function for the Telecommunications Access Method (ACF/TCAM), Advanced Communications Function for the Virtual Telecommunications Access Method (ACF/VTAM), and Advanced Communications Function for the Virtual Telecommunications Access Method—Entry (ACF/

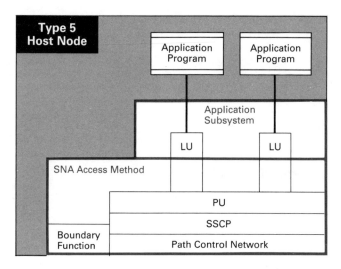

Figure 7.1   SNA Telecommunications Access Method.

VTAME). These three access methods all perform similar functions. ACF/
TCAM and ACF/VTAM are designed to be run on a host processor that runs a
version of the MVS operating system; ACF/VTAME runs under the control of
the VSE operating system and is the VSE counterpart of ACF/VTAM. ACF/
TCAM supports a number of data queuing functions that are not provided by
either ACF/VTAM or ACF/VTAME.

All three access methods control transmission of data to and from local
devices that are attached directly by channels. ACF/TCAM and ACF/VTAM
also permit communication between the host processor and remote devices via
a communications controller. ACF/VTAME provides such communication with
remote devices by using a communications adapter. The telecommunications
access methods do not require any knowledge of intermediate connections, such
as other communications controllers or communications links, in order to communicate with other parts of the network. The access methods also provide
communication with non-SNA devices, such as non-SNA 3270 terminals. Functions that are performed by all three telecommunications access methods include
these:

- Identifying network resources by name, without any knowledge of their loca-
  tions or addresses
- Controlling allocation and sharing of network resources, such as terminals,
  communications links, or communications controllers
- Initiating, maintaining, and terminating sessions for both logical units and non-
  SNA devices
- Transferring data as part of a session

- Queuing data and passing data directly to application subsystems (TCAM only)
- Allowing the network operator to monitor and modify network operations
- Allowing the network configuration to be modified while the network is in operation
- Detecting and correcting problems in the network

A useful feature, available with ACF/TCAM and ACF/VTAM, is the multisystem networking facility (MSNF). It supports communication across domains where several host processors are involved, which may be running different telecommunications access methods. The functions performed by MSNF include these:

- Initiating, maintaining, and terminating sessions between network resources that reside in different domains
- Allowing control of a communications controller to be shared by several host processors or to be transferred from one host processor to another

NETWORK CONTROL PROGRAMS

In a second major category of SNA software that is used to implement an SNA network are the network control programs that run in communication controllers.

ACF/NCP

The primary SNA network control program is called Advanced Communications Function for Network Control Program (ACF/NCP). ACF/NCP resides in the communications controller and interfaces with the SNA access method in the host processor to control communications across the network. It supports both single-domain and multiple-domain networks. Figure 7.2 shows how SNA components are incorporated in ACF/NCP. ACF/NCP contains path control network components, a PUCP, a physical unit, and boundary function elements.

ACF/NCP controls the physical operation of the links in a network and performs routine transmission functions. It also performs bit assembly and disassembly, code translation, polling, routing, error recovery, line tests, device tests, and other physical management functions.

A copy of ACF/NCP residing in a communications controller is commonly called a *network control program* (NCP). A system programmer defines an NCP by coding a set macros that describe the network or portion of the network that the NCP is to control. A separate macro defines each communication line and each device. The communication line macros specify characteristics such as speed, half-duplex or full-duplex operation, line protocol, and type of connection. The device macros specify the characteristics of each physical device. The

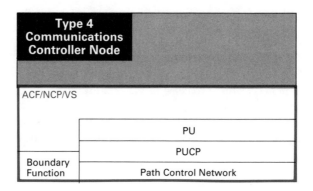

Figure 7.2   SNA Network Control Program.

complete set of macros is assembled and link-edited by a host processor and stored on the host processor in load module form. When the network is established, the telecommunications access method retrieves a copy of the NCP from the appropriate load module library on the host processor and transmits it to the communications controller. NCPs are downloaded to both local and remote communications controllers in the same manner. After a communications controller receives its NCP, the controller initializes itself and is then ready to operate as part of the SNA network.

NTO

The set of software called the Network Terminal Option (NTO) may also reside in the communications controller. The NTO allows ACF/NCP to support certain non-SNA terminals as part of an SNA network. If NTO is used, ACF/NCP appears as shown in Fig. 7.3. The logical units shown use the services of NTO to make it appear to the network as if the non-SNA terminals are actually SNA devices.

ACCESS METHOD– NCP INTER- RELATIONSHIP

A telecommunications access method and network control program, in cooperation, are the major software products used to implement and operate an SNA network. We will look now in more detail at how these programs interrelate, using ACF/VTAM and ACF/NCP as examples. Figure 7.4 illustrates the relationship between ACF/VTAM and NCP in a channel-attached communications controller. Information passes between ACF/VTAM and NCP over the channel. The basic unit of information that is transferred is the *path information unit* (PIU).

ACF/VTAM controls all communication that takes place between ACF/VTAM and NCP. NCP must always be prepared to receive a message from the access method. When NCP has a message to send to ACF/VTAM, it first sends

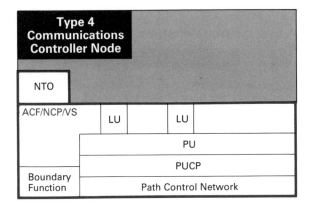

Figure 7.3   ACF/NCP/VS with NTO.

an attention interrupt to the host computer. It then waits for ACF/VTAM to issue a read channel program and then sends the message. NCP can indicate that it has additional data to send by setting a read attention as part of the message.

When NCP receives a PIU from ACF/VTAM, it first determines if it is destined for its subarea. If so, NCP determines the appropriate node to which to forward it and sends it on to that node. If the message is not intended for a node in its subarea, NCP uses its routing table to determine the next subarea in the message's route and sends the PIU to that node. When NCP receives a PIU from the network, it determines whether the message is destined for the host. If so, it issues an attention interrupt and sends the message to the access method as just described. If not, the NCP determines the next subarea in the message's route and passes the message on. For cross-domain sessions, messages may pass through the NCP in an intermediate node without being processed by ACF/VTAM in that node's host processor.

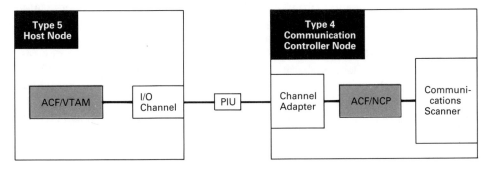

Figure 7.4   ACF/VTAM-NCP communication.

DEFINING NETWORK INFORMATION TO ACF/VTAM

ACF/VTAM and NCP both require access to information about the network in which they operate and the options that are to be used. For ACF/VTAM, some of this information is stored in tables that must be coded, assembled, and link-edited prior to activating ACF/VTAM. A *logon mode,* or *logmode,* table contains lists of protocols to be used for a particular session. These protocols address issues such as pacing, the use of brackets, and send/receive mode. When a session is initiated, a logmode table and a particular entry in that table are either specified or determined by default. The logmode table entry determines the protocols to be used during the session. A logmode table is provided with ACF/VTAM. Additional tables can be coded, if desired, by the installation.

Another table used by ACF/VTAM is the *class-of-service* (COS) table. Each entry in the COS table consists of a list of virtual route number–transmission priority pairs. When a session is initiated, an entry in the COS table may be specified or determined by default. The virtual route and transmission priority to be used for the session are then selected from the list that makes up that entry. A COS table is not provided with ACF/VTAM but can be coded by the installation if desired. If there is no COS table or no suitable entry, a set of default values is used to determine the virtual route and transmission priority.

In addition to the logmode and COS tables, ACF/VTAM uses *path definition sets* to route messages it sends. A path definition set contains information related to a destination subarea. For a given destination subarea it indicates, for each explicit route number, the adjacent subarea to which to send the message and the transmission group to use. The path definition set also indicates the mapping of virtual route numbers to explicit route numbers for that destination subarea. Path definition sets must be coded by the installation and stored in the appropriate ACF/VTAM library.

ACF/VTAM also requires information about the resources in its domain and their configuration. A system programmer provides this information by coding a set of macros that are also stored in an ACF/VTAM library. A macro is coded for each application program and device in the domain. For application programs, a unique program name must be supplied. Optionally, information can be included on the types of sessions to be established, the operating system, and the types of ACF/VTAM instructions and exits that are used. For devices, the macros specify device characteristics, device addresses, and ACF/VTAM options that apply to each device. Resource macros can also group individual resources, which are called *minor nodes,* into collections called *major nodes.* The resources that make up a major node can then be activated or deactivated as a group.

A *start option list* and *configuration list* must also be coded and stored in an ACF/VTAM library. When ACF/VTAM is activated, the start option list provides information about optional ACF/VTAM facilities to be used. The configuration list identifies the major nodes that are to be automatically activated as part of ACF/VTAM startup.

DEFINING NETWORK INFORMATION TO NCP

As described previously, a set of macros must be coded, assembled, and link-edited in order to generate the NCP used in a particular node. These macros describe all lines and devices that are controlled by the NCP node. A set of path definition statements must also be coded for the node. For each destination subarea reached via a node, the path definition statement indicates the adjacent subarea that is the next node on the route for each explicit route and the transmission group to be used. NCP macros can also contain information that is used by ACF/VTAM. One macro is used to describe the communications controller to ACF/VTAM and to specify ACF/VTAM options to use when this NCP is activated.

APPLICATION SUBSYSTEMS

Application subsystems form another category of programs that may be involved in an SNA network. Typical examples of application subsystems are transaction processing systems and interactive support systems. Typical transaction processing systems that implement SNA support include CICS/VS, IMS/VS, DPPX/DMS, and ACP/TPF. Typical SNA interactive support systems are TSO, VSPC, and VM/VCNA. These systems interface with other SNA products and contain part of the code that implements logical units. Application programs or end users are then able to use the services of the application subsystem; through those services they have access to the SNA network.

Figure 7.1 showed the relationships that exist between an application subsystem and an SNA access method in a host processor. Figure 7.5 shows the relationships that exist in a peripheral node. A peripheral node typically contains a control program that is implemented in hardware, software, or a combination of the two. The control program contains path control network components, a PUCP, a physical unit, and portions of the code that implements logical units. The application subsystem contains the remainder of the logical unit implementation code. The logical units are then accessed via the application subsystem by either application programs or end users.

NETWORK MANAGEMENT PROGRAMS

In addition to telecommunications access methods and network control programs, which support transmission of data throughout the network, there are also a number of application programs that provide network management functions.

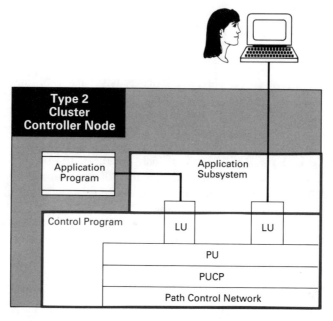

Figure 7.5   Peripheral node with application subsystem.

NCCF   The Network Communication Control Facility
                           (NCCF) provides enhanced operator control for mul-
tiple-domain networks. With NCCF a network operator can use a single terminal
to issue commands to any host processor on the network. There may also be
several distributed operator terminals. Functions provided by NCCF include
these:

- Recording and accessing data concerning problems in the network
- Employing user-written command processors and lists to perform special functions
- Communicating with network operators in other domains
- Dividing control of the network among different network operators, each operator being responsible for a specific portion of the network
- Providing access to both local and remote operator terminals

NCCF also provides database and communications facilities related to collecting, storing, and retrieving data about network errors. This provides a base for another network management program, the Network Problem Determination Application (NPDA), which provides problem determination services.

NPDA The Network Problem Determination Application (NPDA) is a program designed to help with on-line problem determination. It does this by collecting, monitoring, and storing data that relate to network problems and then allowing network operators to display these data. NPDA uses NCCF services, and any terminal used to display NPDA data must be designated as an NCCF terminal. NPDA provides data at several levels of detail, down to the level of a specific error or failure. At the lowest level, information is provided about the probable cause of the problem. NPDA can be used by an NCCF operator to request and display statistical maintenance data on nodes either in that operator's domain or in other domains throughout the network.

NLDM The Network Logical Data Manager (NLDM) collects information about sessions and routes and allows a central operator to examine that information to help in identifying network problems. NLDM collects information for both single-domain and cross-domain sessions about the logical routes currently being used by active sessions. NLDM also collects response time data. NLDM runs as an application under NCCF and uses system functions provided by NCCF.

NETVIEW Netview is a network management product that combines the capabilities of several of the individual products covered previously. It includes the functions that are part of NCCF, NLDM, and NPDA, as well as some of the functions that are part of VTAM Node Control Application and Network Management Productivity Facility.

Netview is designed to make it easier to use these functions in an integrated manner and to provide network operators with greater flexibility in configuring and managing networks. It provides a consistent use of color and function keys across the different functions and makes it easier for the network operator to move from one function to another. Through the use of the network status monitor facility the operator may access data on a particular network segment or see an overview of all network resources. Netview helps detect hardware and software errors and problems with accessing a particular application. It also provides links to other sources of network diagnostic information, including the Token Ring Network Manager, 3728 matrix switch, and 586X modems.

OTHER PROGRAM PRODUCTS The programs described in this chapter are those that play a key role in implementing SNA and are most directly involved with the transmission of data through the network. There are many other program products, however, that are used in SNA networks: general-purpose programs, such as operating systems, utilities, and language processors, that are part of the overall computing environment as well as programs that are specifically designed to provide network management or support functions.

SUMMARY   Telecommunications access methods reside in host processor and provide an interface between the host processor and the other resources in the network. They control transmission of data to and from directly attached devices and to and from other parts of the network via a communications controller or communications adapter. Key telecommunications access methods are ACF/TCAM, ACF/VTAM, and ACF/ VTAME. The primary network control program, which runs in a communications controller, is ACF/NCP. It manages the physical operations of the links in a network and performs routine transmission functions. NTO, another network control program, allows ACF/NCP to support certain non-SNA terminals as part of an SNA network.

ACF/VTAM controls all communication that takes place between ACF/ VTAM and NCP. Network information is defined to ACF/VTAM using the log-on mode table, class-of-service table, path definition sets, application program and device macros, start option list, and configuration list. Network information is defined to NCP using NCP macros. Some of the information in NCP macros may also be used by ACF/VTAM.

Application subsystems interface with SNA products and contain part of the code that implements logical units. Application programs or end users use the services of the application subsystem to access the SNA network. Network management programs include NCCF, NLDM, NPDA, and Netview. NCCF provides enhanced operator control for multiple-domain networks. NLDM collects information about sessions and routes and allows a central operator to examine that information to help in identifying network problems. NPDA collects, monitors, and stores data related to network problems and allows network operators to display the data. Netview combines the capabilities of NCCF, NLDM, and NPDA in a single integrated product.

PART II **ADVANCED FACILITIES**

8 ADVANCED PROGRAM-TO-PROGRAM COMMUNICATION

The facility called *Advanced Program-to-Program Communication* (APPC) provides one of the more advanced capabilities of SNA. APPC is designed to support network capabilities that go beyond the simple connection of a terminal user with an application program. We will begin our investigation of this powerful feature by examining in greater detail the characteristics of the LU-to-LU session. As discussed earlier, an LU-to-LU session is a formal connection between two network users that allows them to communicate.

LU-TO-LU SESSIONS

For two network users to communicate, a session must be established between the logical units that represent the two users. An LU-to-LU session is a temporary connection that exists only as long as is required for the users to exchange data. At the time the LU-to-LU session is established, agreement is reached on the protocols that will be used during the session. These protocols specify such things as data format, the amount of data to be sent before a reply is requested, and procedures to be performed if an error occurs.

LU AND NETWORK-USER RELATIONSHIP

The relationship between network users and logical units is not necessarily one to one. Figure 8.1 shows one possibility. Here a single logical unit represents two network users and can be involved in separate sessions on behalf of these users. Figure 8.2 shows another possibility. In this case, a single user is involved in two concurrent sessions. For example, an application program might be communicating with several terminals at the same time. Figure 8.3 shows how two logical units can have multiple concurrent sessions established between them. These are known as parallel sessions. Each

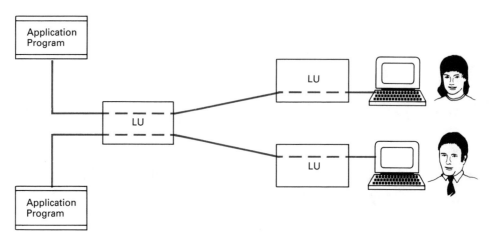

Figure 8.1   LU with more than one session.

LU-to-LU session in which a particular logical unit participates uses a set of resources in that logical unit. The component within the logical unit that provides that set of resources is called a *half-session*.

LOGICAL UNIT TYPES

A particular SNA product typically does not implement all possible SNA functions; instead, a number of subsets of SNA functions have been defined. Each different subset of SNA functions is assigned to a particular type of logical unit, or *LU type*. SNA products are classified according to the LU type, or types, they support. An SNA product can support more than one LU type. For example, application subsystems, such as CICS/VS and IMS/VS, typically support several LU types and thus are able to communicate with various types of devices or other subsystems.

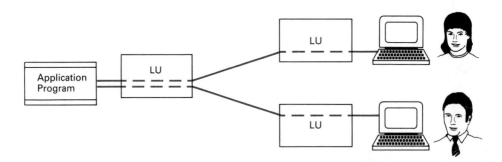

Figure 8.2   More than one session for one user.

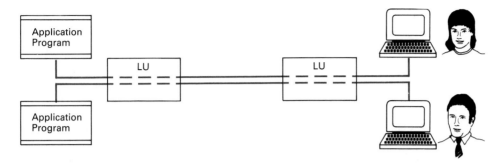

Figure 8.3   Parallel sessions.

For two logical units to establish a session, they must both support a common LU type. The LU type designation, then, helps to identify which SNA products will be able to communicate with which other products. In general, the LU type corresponds to a particular form of communication. For several LU types, the LU type corresponds either to a particular device type or to the type of *data stream* that is transmitted during the session. A data stream is defined as the allowable characters, including control codes, that flow between the two logical units. Box 8.1 describes the data streams that SNA supports. Box 8.2 gives brief descriptions of the various LU types that are currently defined by SNA.

For a given LU-to-LU session, both LU half-sessions that are participating in the session must be of the same LU type. However, as we have seen, a given logical unit can support more than one LU type. Where this is the case, the logical unit can participate in concurrent LU-to-LU sessions using different LU types. For example, a logical unit could participate in a type 4 session with one session partner and at the same time participate in a type 2 session with another session partner.

ADVANCED PROGRAM-TO-PROGRAM COMMUNICATION

The LU types initially defined as part of SNA were LU 0 through LU 4 and were oriented toward communication between an application program and a terminal. LU 6 defines a general-purpose interprogram protocol that avoids the limitations associated with the terminal-oriented LU types. LU 6 provides support within SNA for *distributed transaction processing*. Distributed transaction processing allows user application processing to be executed cooperatively on various interconnected computing systems. Distributed transaction processing can also involve the distribution of other resources, including databases, across the network. Advanced Program-to-Program Communication (APPC) is designed to provide enhanced SNA support for applications that require these types of facilities. APPC

BOX 8.1   Typical data streams

- **SNA Character String Data Stream.** An SNA character string (SCS) data stream consists of a string of EBCDIC bytes, in which data characters and SNA character string (SCS) controls are intermixed. The primary purpose of the SCS control codes is to provide a generalized, device-independent method for controlling the formatting of a visual presentation medium, such as a display screen or a printed page.

- **SNA 3270 Data Stream.** An SNA 3270 data stream consists of user data and commands employing control codes that govern the way data are handled and formatted for 3270-type terminal equipment.

- **SNA 5250 Data Stream.** An SNA 5250 data stream consists of user data and commands employing control codes that govern the way data are handled and formatted for 5250-type terminal equipment.

- **User-defined Data Streams.** A user-defined data stream is any data stream whose contents are defined outside the SNA architecture. Some higher-level architectures that are related to SNA define user-defined data streams. For example, the office information architectures that are used in implementing office systems implement a data stream called the *Revisable Form Text* data stream for representing documents in an internal, revisable form and a data stream called the *Final Form Text* data stream for representing documents in final, page-image form.

BOX 8.2   Logical unit types

- **LU Type 0.** LU 0 allows the SNA formats and protocols to be augmented by formats and protocols defined by the network user. This LU type is most often used in cases where the device or data stream being supported does not fit the definitions used for other LU types. In early SNA networks LU 0 was used for situations not covered by the other LU types that were initially defined. However, now that LU 6 has been defined, there is less need for LU 0. User-defined data streams are typically used with LU 0 sessions. Examples of SNA products that support LU 0 are JES2 Network Job Entry (NJE) and the IBM 3600 Finance Communication System.

- **LU Type 1.** LU 1 is designed to support sessions in which an application program communicates with a terminal that can implement several input/output devices, such as printers, card readers, and some types of storage

BOX 8.2 *(Çontinued)*

devices, using an SNA character string data stream. The terminal might be operating in an interactive, batch data transfer mode or in a distributed processing environment. Products that support LU 1 include the IBM 3767 communication terminal and IBM 3270 printers.

- **LU Type 2.** LU 2 is designed to support sessions in which an application program communicates with a single 3270-type display terminal using the SNA 3270 data stream. An IBM 3277 display station is an example of a product that supports LU 2.

- **LU Type 3.** LU 3 is designed to support sessions in which an application program communicates with a single printer using an SNA 3270 data stream. The IBM 3284 printer attached to a 3791 controller uses this LU type.

- **LU Type 4.** LU 4 is designed to support several types of sessions. One type is a session between an application program and either a single-device or multiple-device terminal operating in an interactive, batch data transfer or distributed processing mode. This type of session is similar to an LU 1 session. LU 4 also supports word processing applications and some types of peer-to-peer communication between two terminals. LU 4 uses the SNA character string data stream. A product that supports LU 4 is the IBM 6670 information distributor.

- **LU Type 6.** LU 6 is designed to provide peer-to-peer communication between application subsystems or application programs. The application subsystems can be of the same type, as when one CICS subsystem communicates with another CICS subsystem, or they can be of different types, as when a CICS subsystem communicates with an IMS/VS subsystem. The *remote resource access capability* provided by LU 6 allows application subsystems to distribute resources, such as files and queues, throughout the network and still have transparent access to them. The *Transaction Processing Program* (TPP) *conversational capability* of LU 6 allows application subsystems to distribute application programs throughout the network and allows these programs to cooperate in processing transactions. LU 6 sessions can use any desired data stream, including SNA character string data streams, SNA 3270 data streams, and various user-defined data streams. LU 6 is detailed in the discussion of Advanced Program-to-Program Communication later in this chapter.

- **LU Type 7.** LU 7 is designed to support sessions in which an application program communicates with a 5250-type display terminal using an SNA 5250 data stream. An example of a product that supports LU 7 is an IBM 5251 information display.

has been designed to meet three broad requirements that make it possible to implement distributed transaction processing systems:

- Providing a common program-to-program communication protocol that can be used by a wide variety of products
- Encouraging the development of compatible distributed applications to be run on these products
- Providing a common method for intelligent communication among distributed processes

Advanced Program-to-Program Communication implements a single logical unit type, known as LU 6.2, that supports all types of program-to-program communication, including peer-to-peer communication between peripheral nodes. Part of the LU 6.2 architectural definition is a set of uniform architected services that can be used in a standard manner by cooperating processes. Supporting LU 6.2 is a physical unit type, called PU 2.1, that supports peer-to-peer communication among peripheral nodes. With earlier LU types, communication typically operated in a master-slave fashion, where one of the communicating partners had greater responsibility for error recovery. With APPC there is symmetry of operation; the communicating applications are given equal control, and both may be responsible for error recovery.

LU 6.2

As we have already discussed, the architectural base for APPC is a specific version of LU type 6 known as LU 6.2. A key concept in LU 6.2 is that of a *conversation*. A conversation is a connection between two programs over which the two programs communicate. A conversation employs a session between two LUs that represent the two communicating programs. This session is used as the mechanism for exchanging data across the network. Typically, a conversation lasts only a short time, often the time it takes to process a single transaction, and a series of conversations can use the same session, one after the other. Each conversation is handled within SNA in the form of a bracket. Conversations provide an efficient way of using the network, since they avoid the overhead of initiating a new session for each conversation.

PARALLEL SESSIONS

LU 6.2 defines an option that allows parallel sessions between logical units. Parallel sessions can be used for a number of purposes, including increasing the bandwidth of the connection between two logical units, balancing transmission loads, providing for duplex communication, and providing different priorities for transmission. Using parallel sessions avoids the overhead associated with having to use separate LUs for each session. The overhead associated with multiple LUs includes multiple LU names for the same application subsystem and multiple control blocks within the application subsystems.

PRIMARY VERSUS   With the older LU types the assumption is typically
SECONDARY LU   made that one of the LUs represents an application
                      program and the other represents a terminal. In ses-
sions between these older LU types the application program is always the primary LU and has responsibility for error recovery. With LU 6.2 either of the
two LUs has the capability of acting as the primary LU. As part of session
initiation when LU 6.2 is used, agreement is reached as to which LU will act
as the primary LU and which will act as the secondary LU in that session.

SYNCHRONIZATION   In distributed transaction processing systems, re-
                      sources that are required to process a particular trans-
action can be distributed throughout the network, and application processes may
work cooperatively in performing the required processing. Synchronization capabilities are particularly important in such systems. LU 6.2 offers three levels
of capability for synchronization processing:

- **No Synchronization.** When this level of support is chosen, the LU provides
  no synchronization services.

- **Confirm Synchronization.** With this level of support, a definite response is
  required by each cooperating program after that program has completed the
  processing of a transaction. This allows all application programs to agree that
  processing has been completed without error. At this level any error recovery
  is the responsibility of the programs that are involved in processing a transaction.

- **Syncpoint Synchronization.** With this level of support certain resources are
  defined to the LU as protected. The LU is then responsible for the commitment
  of changes to these protected resources. If an error occurs at any time during
  the processing of a transaction, it is the responsibility of the LU automatically
  to back out any changes that were made to protected resources during the processing of the transaction. A resynchronization capability is also provided to
  handle failures that occur during synchronization processing. The two LUs exchange information on the status of protected resources at the time of the failure
  and then perform the processing necessary to restore the resources to a synchronized state.

LU 6.2 PROTOCOL   LU 6.2 uses a *protocol boundary* to define services
BOUNDARY   provided. The protocol boundary consists of set of
                      verbs and parameters whose functions and formats
are defined as part of SNA. Application subsystems, such as CICS/VS and

IMS/VS, and other programs that implement LU 6.2 must provide the services defined by these verbs.

A particular product that has its own application programming interface, such as CICS/VS, might elect to use its own programming language or syntax to represent the LU 6.2 verbs to its application programs. In other words, application programs might issue CICS commands in requesting SNA functions; however, CICS would translate these requests into the required SNA services, as defined in the LU 6.2 protocol boundary. Thus application developers who are designing and coding distributed transaction processing systems can design these systems based on the common functions that LU 6.2 makes available without being concerned about differences between particular products or with their ability to communicate with each other across a network. The protocol boundary provides a common language and conceptual basis upon which to design the system. For those who are responsible for implementing products that provide an application programming interface, the LU 6.2 boundary function verbs specify the facilities that the product must offer if it is to be considered an implementation of LU 6.2.

In summary, the architectural definition of LU 6.2 specifies a consistent set of functions, formats, and protocols that can be used in implementing conversations between programs that run in separate, interconnected computing systems.

ARCHITECTED MODELS

The services provided by the verbs that make up the LU 6.2 protocol boundary can be used to implement a wide range of functions. They support the capability of having "any-to-any" connections throughout the network. LU 6.2 also offers built-in support for certain predefined sets of functions that take the form of *architected models*. These architected models are also known as *SNA service transaction programs*.

Some of the architected models provide support functions, such as synchronization or the regulation of the number of parallel sessions that are supported by an LU. Another LU 6.2 architected model is the Document Interchange Architecture (DIA), which defines a set of protocols that can be used in exchanging documents among various processors and devices that are part of an office system environment. We will examine this aspect of LU 6.2 in Chapter 9.

REVISED VIEW OF THE LOGICAL UNIT

When we first introduced the concept of the logical unit in this book, we described it as a port or entry point through which a network user accesses an SNA network for purposes of communication with another network user. LU 6.2 still provides this function; however, its greater range of functions allows us to take a broader view of the role of the logical unit. LU

6.2 can be viewed as providing a complete run-time environment for application programs that implement transaction processing systems. To the application program, the LU-to-LU session is another resource it shares, in much the same way that other types of system resources are shared under the control of the operating system. In effect, SNA can then be viewed as a distributed operating system, in which logical units perform the roles of loosely coupled processors.

SUMMARY

An LU type defines a set of functions that a logical unit provides. LU type 0 allows SNA formats and protocols to be augmented by formats and protocols defined by the network user. A typical LU type 1 session might provide communication between an application program and a terminal that implements several input/output devices. A typical LU type 2 session might handle communication between an application program and a 3270-type display device. A typical LU type 3 session might support an application program that communicates with a 3270 printer device. An LU type 4 session is designed to provide peer-to-peer communication for certain types of systems. An LU type 6 session provides general program-to-program communication capabilities. A typical LU type 7 session might support an application program that communicates with a 5250 display station.

Advanced Program-to-Program Communication provides a common program-to-program communication protocol, implemented via LU 6.2. LU 6.2 implements the concept of a conversation, which is a connection between two programs over which they communicate. A series of conversations can use the same LU-to-LU session. An option of LU 6.2 allows parallel concurrent sessions between two logical units. Both logical units must be capable of acting as the primary LU. LU 6.2 offers three levels of synchronization processing, including full syncpoint synchronization, in which the LU is responsible for backing out changes to protected resources when errors occur during transaction processing. LU 6.2 defines a broader role for the logical unit in the transaction processing environment. In addition to providing a port into the network, LU 6.2 provides a complete run-time environment for distributed application programs.

9 LOGICAL UNIT 6.2 IMPLEMENTATION

To achieve compatibility among the various devices and application subsystems that implement LU 6.2, SNA uses an approach that is based on the rigorous definition of *subsets of facilities*. LU 6.2 defines a base set of capabilities that is mandatory and must be included in all products that implement APPC. Additional optional sets of facilities are also defined. If a product implements an optional set, it must support all the facilities that are part of that set. Also, there are different levels of option sets. If a higher-level option set is implemented, all prerequisite lower-level sets must also be implemented. In this way, two different products are guaranteed of being able to communicate at the highest level that they have in common. LU 6.2 maintains the layered approach that is the basis of SNA. Individual layers communicate with their counterparts in the opposite node. The flow of data from one layer to another operates in the same manner as for any other LU type.

LU 6.2 FUNCTIONAL CAPABILITY

In discussing LU 6.2 capabilities we will often use the term *transaction program*. Transaction programs are also called *transaction processing programs* (TPPs). Although LU 6.2 is most often used to implement transaction processing systems, its services are not limited to transaction processing. So this book uses the term *transaction program* to refer to any type of application program that makes use of LU 6.2 facilities, either directly or through an intermediary, such as an application subsystem. To support transaction programs, LU 6.2 provides capabilities in three major functional areas:

- **Communications.** The primary goal of LU 6.2 and APPC is to provide the ability for transaction programs to communicate via conversations across the SNA network.

- **Distributed Error Recovery.** Distributed transaction processing typically involves the control and coordination of resources that are distributed across the network. When failures occur, it is important to be able to restore these distributed resources to their original states and to resume communications. LU 6.2 provides protocols that address this type of error recovery.

- **Resource Management.** LU 6.2 provides services necessary for the management of the distributed resources that are used as in implementing distributed transaction processing systems.

CONVERSATION TYPES

From the viewpoint of the transaction program, the basic mechanism for accessing LU 6.2 functions is the *conversation,* defined in Chapter 8 as a connection between two transaction programs, which allows them to communicate via the underlying LU 6.2–to–LU 6.2 session.

There are two types of conversations defined as part of LU 6.2: *basic* conversations and *mapped* conversations. With mapped conversations, application programs do not have to be concerned with any specialized data streams that are used by a specific product. In a mapped conversation, all data being sent as part of a conversation are converted into a standard format, called the *generalized data stream,* and are automatically converted back into their original form at the receiving end. With a basic conversation, no automatic conversion is performed, and a program on one side of the conversation must be able to handle the data stream that is used by the program on the other side. Programs that use basic conversations also have greater responsibility for error recovery.

Basic conversations are part of the base set of LU 6.2 facilities and thus are part of any LU 6.2 product implementation. Mapped conversations form one of the option sets and may or may not be included in a particular product. Any product that provides an application programming interface for writing transaction programs, however, must provide the mapped conversation capability.

BASE-LEVEL FACILITIES

The set of base-level facilities defined for LU 6.2 includes the following functions:

- Allocating a conversation, sending and receiving data, and deallocating a conversation
- Invoking a remote program as part of allocation
- Requesting and yielding control of the data flow between two programs
- Sending error information to a program
- Synchronizing the processing of two programs involved in a conversation

The two lower levels of synchronization (no synchronization and confirm synchronization) are provided in the base-level facilities set. Syncpoint synchronization is one of the option sets.

MAPPED CONVERSATION OPTION SET

The mapped conversation option provides application programs with an interface that is easier to use than that provided by basic conversations. Functions provided by an LU that implements the mapped conversation option set include these:

- **Function Management Header Compatibility.** Earlier versions of LU 6 (LU 6.0 and LU 6.1) used certain types of function management headers for application-specific purposes. LU 6.2 continues to support these headers to allow continued use of applications and products that were developed prior to the definition of LU 6.2.

- **Data Mapping.** A transaction program that sends data has the option of specifying that the data are to be mapped, which involves transforming or translating the data from one format to another. This may be a simple byte-to-byte transformation or the conversion of a complex data structure into a stream of data suitable for transmission. Mapping can be performed by the sending LU, by the receiving LU, or by both.

- **Data Stream Handling.** Mapped conversation services in the LUs handle all formatting requirements for the data stream that is sent from one transaction program to another. When the mapped conversation option is used, transaction programs have no need to be concerned with the data stream that flows through the network.

- **Error Detection.** Mapped conversation services in the LUs provide for the detection of remote program errors and for performing the processing required to handle local program errors.

SYNCPOINT OPTION SET

Syncpoint synchronization processing forms a second major option set. With syncpoint processing, the resources that are used to implement a distributed transaction processing system can be specified as protected. When an LU implements the syncpoint option set, it provides the following functions for protected resources:

- **Commitment Control.** All of the transaction programs that are involved in the processing of a transaction indicate when the end of a unit of work has been reached. When the LU receives notification from all the transaction programs, the LU considers all changes that were made to protected resources to be permanent and releases any locks that may have been placed on these resources.

- **Backout.** If a transaction does not reach an appropriate conclusion—for example, if an error occurs—the LU backs out any changes that were made to protected resources and restores them to their original states. Changes are backed out either to a previous syncpoint or to the beginning of the transaction.

- **Resynchronization.** If a session fails, the LU handles the processing required to restore protected resources to a synchronized condition. This is done without any involvement of the transaction programs.

OTHER OPTION SETS

A number of additional option sets are defined as part of LU 6.2, including these:

- **Program Initialization Parameter (PIP) Data.** At the time a transaction program is allocated, it may send certain initialization parameters to its partner transaction program in the form of PIP subfields. The System/38 system software uses this facility.

- **Performance Options.** Certain verbs and verb parameters can provide better application program performance. For example, a program may wish to initiate a transmission even though a send buffer has not been filled.

- **Parallel Sessions.** The ability to have parallel sessions between two logical units is a key option in LU 6.2. Parallel sessions offer improved performance over a single session, since new units of work can be queued against several sessions rather than waiting for one. Parallel sessions also avoid the overhead that would be required if multiple LUs in a single node were used to handle the parallel sessions.

LU 6.2 PROTOCOL BOUNDARY VERBS

As discussed in Chapter 8, the LU 6.2 protocol boundary is defined in terms of a set of verbs and their associated parameters. The verb names and their syntax are defined by the SNA architecture, and we will use the SNA names and syntax in describing boundary function verbs in this book. However, a product that implements LU 6.2 and provides an application programming interface may choose to use different names and different syntax to represent these verbs in its protocol boundary with the application programs. The application program boundary, however, must map this syntax back to the functions defined as part of LU 6.2. This is shown conceptually in Fig. 9.1 As part of the application program interface, an application program may specify a function such as WRITE or READ. These statements must be mapped by the application subsystem to the corresponding LU 6.2 functions, which are defined by the SEND and RECEIVE verbs. LU 6.2 verbs are divided into three categories: basic conversation verbs, mapped conversation verbs, and control operator verbs.

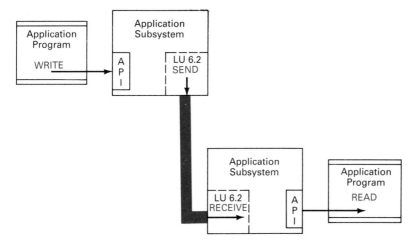

Figure 9.1   Application program interface (API) and LU 6.2 protocol boundary.

Basic Conversation Verbs

The basic conversation verbs can be divided into those that are part of the base set and those that are options. Box 9.1 describes the verbs that are part of the base set. The base set verbs permit the following operations:

- allocation and deallocation of a conversation
- obtaining information about a conversation
- sending and receiving data
- obtaining confirmation that data have been successfully received
- transmission of a request for permission to send data
- sending notification of a program error to the partner program.

Box 9.2 lists the basic conversation verbs that are implemented when various option sets are included. The option set verbs provide the following operations:

- syncpoint processing
- performance options
- the use of PIP data during conversation initialization.

Mapped Conversation Verbs

Certain mapped conversation verbs make up the minimum support set, and additional verbs constitute option sets beyond the mapped conversation option. The minimum support set is very similar to the base set of the basic conversa-

BOX 9.1   Base set verbs

- **ALLOCATE.** This verb is used to allocate a conversation with a remote transaction program. Parameters for this verb include LU—NAME, which gives the name of the LU that represents the remote program; TPN, which gives the name of the remote program; MODE—NAME, which specifies session properties for the conversation; and SYNC— LEVEL, which specifies a synchronization level of either NONE or CONFIRM.
- **GET—ATTRIBUTES.** This verb returns information about a conversation, including mode name, partner LU name, and synchronization level.
- **DEALLOCATE.** This verb deallocates a conversation.
- **CONFIRM.** This verb sends a confirmation request to a remote transaction program, to determine if the program has successfully received data.
- **CONFIRMED.** This verb sends a confirmation reply in response to a CONFIRM.
- **SEND—DATA.** This verb causes data to be sent.
- **RECEIVE—AND—WAIT.** This verb is sent by a transaction program that is ready to receive data and causes the program to wait until the data are received.
- **REQUEST—TO—SEND.** This verb notifies a transaction program that its partner program requests permission to send data.
- **SEND—ERROR.** This verb informs the remote transaction program that a program error has occurred. The program issuing the SEND—ERROR is placed in the send state and the remote program is placed in the receive state.

tion verbs. The differences are that a mapped conversation rather than a basic conversation is started by the allocation process, and any data stream formatting is done outside the transaction programs. The mapped conversation verbs are listed in Box 9.3.

Control Operator Verbs

Box 9.4 lists the control operator verbs that are used in controlling certain aspects of the sessions established between two logical units. These include verbs that control the number of sessions supported for a particular logical unit, verbs used to activate and deactivate LU-to-LU sessions, and verbs that allow access to system definition parameters for the local logical unit.

BOX 9.2 Option set verbs

- **FLUSH.** This verb causes data in a send buffer to be transmitted.
- **PREPARE__TO__RECEIVE.** This verb causes a program to change from the send state to the receive state.
- **SYNCPT and BACKOUT.** These verbs, plus various parameters on other verbs, are used to specify syncpoint processing.
- **SECURITY parameter of ALLOCATE.** This parameter provides access to security information requested by the remote LU.
- **PIP parameter of ALLOCATE.** This parameter is used to provide initialization data during conversation allocation.

BOX 9.3 Mapped conversation verbs

Minimum Set Verbs

- MC__ALLOCATE
- MC__RECEIVE__AND__WAIT
- MC__SEND__DATA
- MC__CONFIRM
- MC__CONFIRMED
- MC__DEALLOCATE
- MC__REQUEST__TO__SEND
- MC__SEND__ERROR

Option Set Verbs

- MC__FLUSH
- MC__PREPARE__TO__RECEIVE
- SYNCPT and BACKOUT
- SECURITY parameter on MC__ALLOCATE
- PIP parameter on MC__ALLOCATE

BOX 9.4   Control operator verbs

Session Number Verbs

- **INITIALIZE—SESSION—LIMIT.** This verb establishes the maximum number of sessions that can be active for a particular logical unit.

- **RESET—SESSION—LIMIT.** This verb resets to zero the session limit for a particular logical unit.

- **CHANGE—SESSION—LIMIT.** This is an optional verb that allows a program to request a change in the session limit.

- **PROCESS—SESSION—LIMIT.** This is a verb used in processing the other three verbs related to the number of sessions.

Session Activation and Deactivation Verbs

- **ACTIVATE—SESSION.** This verb activates a session.

- **DEACTIVATE—SESSION.** This verb deactivates a session.

System Definition Parameter Verbs

- **DISPLAY.** This verb returns the values of the system definition parameters, including the total LU-to-LU session limit, the remote LU name, the set of properties associated with a particular mode name, and session limits for local LU and mode combinations.

- **DEFINE.** This verb causes system definition parameters to be set or modified.

SAMPLE CONVERSATIONS   The verbs defined as part of the LU 6.2 protocol boundary support a number of types of conversation flows. Figure 9.2 shows an example of conversation flow that implements a simple one-way conversation with no confirmation. The ALLOCATE and SEND—DATA commands place data in a buffer. The DEAL-LOCATE command forces it to be sent, even if the buffer is not full. When the allocation information is received by the logical unit on the receiving end of the conversation, program Y is started and receives the data being sent. This is an example of an *asynchronous* conversation. Notice that program X has finished its processing and has terminated its side of the conversation before program Y even begins processing.

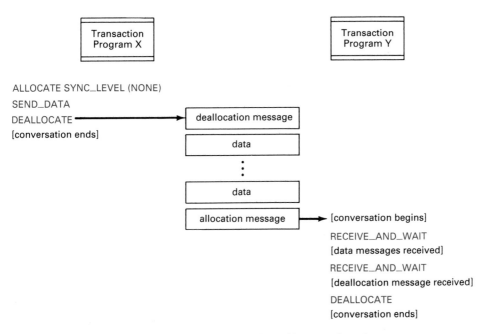

Figure 9.2 One-way conversation with no confirmation.

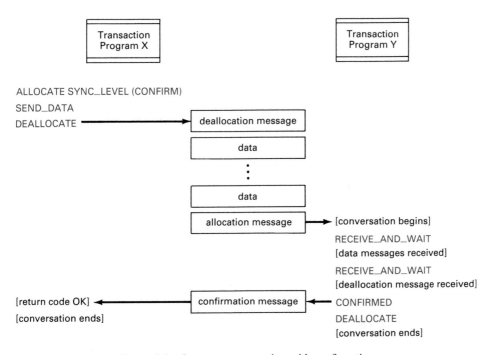

Figure 9.3 One-way conversation with confirmation.

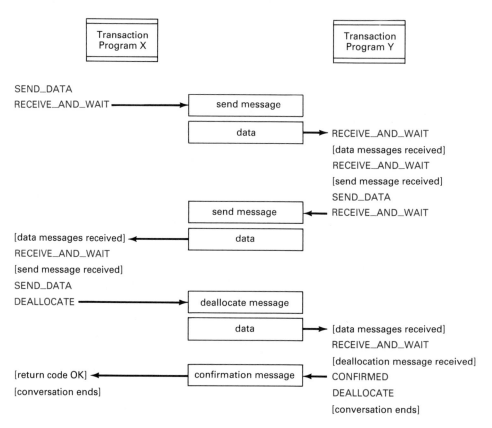

Figure 9.4 Two-way conversation.

Figure 9.3 shows an example of a one-way conversation with confirmation. Processing is the same as for a one-way conversation with no confirmation, except that the conversation is not ended for program X until a response is received from program Y.

Figure 9.4 shows an example of a two-way conversation. Here the programs alternately send and receive data until one of the programs issues a DEALLOCATE command. When a final confirmation is received from the other program, the conversation is ended.

PERIPHERAL NODE SUPPORT

To support the any-to-any connectivity that is the goal of LU 6.2 and APPC, it is necessary that peripheral nodes as well as host nodes be able to support LU 6.2 functions. This has had two key implications for peripheral nodes.

Prior to LU 6.2, peripheral nodes were unable to support parallel sessions and were not capable of assuming the role of the primary LU in a session. In order to provide these capabilities, an enhanced version of the type 2 node was developed. This enhanced version is known as a *type 2.1* or *T2.1 node.*

TYPE 2.1 NODE

The type 2.1 node offers several capabilities not provided in the original type 2.0 node. One area that has been enhanced is that of connectivity. The T2.1 node supports peer-to-peer connections where the T2.0 node did not. The T2.1 node also supports multiple links and multiple sessions.

Peer-to-Peer Connection

Peer-to-peer communication means that logical units in one T2.1 node can participate in sessions with another T2.1 node without the need for host node involvement. Prior to LU 6.2, there were certain specific systems, such as the System/34, 5520, and 6670, that were able to communicate in a peer-to-peer fashion. With LU 6.2 and the T2.1 node, this type of communication now has general architectural definition and support.

Multiple Links and Sessions

Another enhancement is the T2.1 node's ability to have multiple links and to support multiple sessions. A T2.1 node may have multiple links to other nodes. Each of these links may be to a subarea node or to another T2.1 node. A T2.1 node also has the capability of supporting multiple sessions, including parallel sessions with another T2.1 node. A T2.1 node can participate in simultaneous sessions with other T2.1 nodes and with a subarea node. For a session with a subarea node, the T2.1 node functions in the same way as the original type 2 node, using boundary function support in the subarea node. For sessions between T2.1 nodes, one of the T2.1 nodes will act as the primary LU and the other as the secondary LU. The ability to act as a primary LU is another enhancement provided by the T2.1 node in order for it to support LU 6.2.

TYPE 2.1 NODE
FUNCTIONS

When a T2.1 node is connected to a subarea node, boundary function in the subarea node provides routing services. The establishment and termination of sessions is controlled by the SSCPs that control the domains that contain the nodes involved in the session. For a T2.1-to-T2.1, or peer-coupled, connection there is no subarea node or SSCP involved. The two T2.1 nodes communicate directly, and there is no routing of data through intermediate nodes. Rather than a PUCP, a T2.1 node contains a *single-node control point,* or *SNCP.* The SNCP provides a subset of SSCP functions. It has the capabilities for initiating and

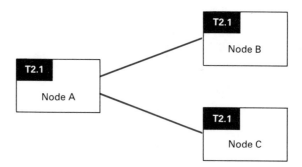

Figure 9.5   Multiple PU Type 2.1 links.

terminating sessions between T2.1 nodes and provides the necessary control functions for those sessions.

TYPE 2.1 NODE   A T2.1 node can support a number of network con-
CONFIGURATIONS   figurations. One of these configurations consists of
                         multiple point-to-point links to other T2.1 nodes, as
shown in Fig. 9.5. In this case, it is possible for a node to act as the primary
LU on one link and as the secondary LU on another. A T2.1 node can also
support a multipoint configuration, where it is directly coupled with a series of
T2.1 nodes through a single link. This is shown in Fig. 9.6. Here one node
(node A in the figure) is the primary LU and the other nodes on the link are all
secondary. A T2.1 node can also participate in a hybrid configuration, where it
attaches both to a subarea node and directly to other T2.1 nodes. This is illustrated in Fig. 9.7. As shown in the figure, there can be parallel links between
two T2.1 nodes. These are treated as distinct links and not as transmission group
facilities.

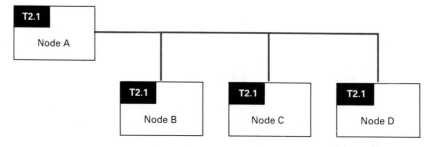

Figure 9.6   Multipoint configuration.

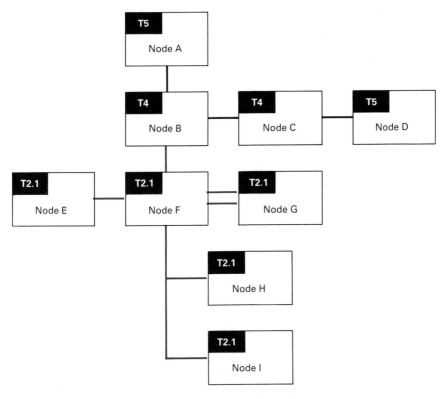

Figure 9.7 Hybrid configuration.

Direct Communication

Direct LU-to-LU communication can be implemented in either of two ways. If a T2.1 node is connected to a subarea node, it may participate in sessions with other LUs, anywhere in the network, using normal subarea routing facilities. Boundary function in the attached subarea node performs the necessary address translation and routes messages across intermediate nodes as necessary. In Fig. 9.7, for example, node F can participate in a session with a logical unit in node D using nodes B and C as intermediate nodes and using boundary function facilities in node B. Direct communication can also take place over directly coupled T2.1 nodes. In Fig. 9.7, node F can communicate directly, for example, with node B or node G.

Indirect Communication

For peer-coupled T2.1 nodes, direct LU-to-LU sessions can be established only between directly coupled, or adjacent, nodes. In Fig. 9.7, for example, an LU-to-LU session cannot be established directly between node E and node G. These nodes can communicate indirectly by each establishing a session with node F. However, it would be the responsibility of the transaction program to provide the routing and queuing functions needed to pass data between node E and node G.

SUMMARY   LU 6.2 supports basic and mapped conversations. With mapped conversations, application programs are not concerned about specialized data streams. LU 6.2 provides its services through a defined set of verbs and parameters known as the protocol boundary. The protocol boundary comprises three categories of verbs: basic conversation verbs, mapped conversation verbs, and control operator verbs. The PU type 2.1 node supports peer-to-peer connections between peripheral nodes and allows a peripheral node to have multiple links to other nodes. A T2.1 node can communicate directly with a subarea node and with adjacent T2.1 peripheral nodes. A T2.1 node can support parallel sessions with another T2.1 node.

10 OFFICE AUTOMATION ARCHITECTURES

The Advanced Program-to-Program Communication facility has provided the basis for many extensions to the basic SNA architecture. The extension called *SNA Distribution Services* (SNADS) is particularly important in the area of office automation systems. SNADS provides a generalized architecture for asynchronous distribution services that are used to implement office information architectures and a comprehensive *document interchange architecture*.

OFFICE INFORMATION ARCHITECTURES

IBM has defined architectures that deal with the interchange of the type of information required in implementing an office system network. The architectures are known collectively as the *office information architectures*. Office information systems are concerned with the exchange of information, where that information takes the form, primarily, of text documents. The text information can be formatted in a variety of ways, including messages, notes, memos, letters, and formal reports having a complex format. For simplicity, we will refer to text information in all forms simply as *documents*.

A typical office system provides services related to the processing of documents, including these:

- Creating documents
- Revising documents
- Distributing documents
- Storing and retrieving documents

A key requirement for an office information system is not only to provide document processing services but also to provide for the interchange of documents both within an individual office system and between dissimilar office systems. Document interchange capabilities should include the ability to handle documents without regard to their specific content or formatting requirements. An office information system should also be able to deliver documents to users throughout the network, without regard to whether a user is currently using the network. To meet these requirements, IBM has developed two office system architectures:

- **Document Content Architecture.** The document content architecture (DCA) deals with the form and meaning of the content of a document that is being interchanged within an office system. It defines the data streams that are used to store and interchange documents within the system.

- **Document Interchange Architecture.** The document interchange architecture (DIA) addresses how documents and requests for document distribution and processing services are communicated throughout an office system network. It defines the protocols and data structures that are used to interchange documents and other information.

DOCUMENT CONTENT ARCHITECTURE

A document can be represented in the system in one of two forms: *revisable text* or *final-form text*. Figure 10.1 shows the differences between revisable form and final-form documents. A document in revisable form might contain control information that describes how it is to be formatted, and it can be modified by anyone who receives the document or has access to it. A document in final form is already formatted and arranged in pages for presentation on a printer or display device. Heading and footing information is repeated as appropriate on each page. The document might also contain control codes for displaying the document on an output device.

DCA includes separate architectures for revisable-form text and final-form text. Each architecture defines the structure of the data stream used to represent the document within the office system network. The revisable-form-text document content architecture defines how the text of a document is to be represented. It also defines the structure to be used for formatting control information and prescribes how office systems are to interpret the control information. The final-form-text document content architecture defines a simpler data stream that can be processed by a workstation and can more easily be presented on a printer or display screen.

DOCUMENT INTERCHANGE ARCHITECTURE

It is important to note that the document interchange architecture does not deal with the content of documents. It defines only the protocols and data formats needed for the transparent interchange of documents

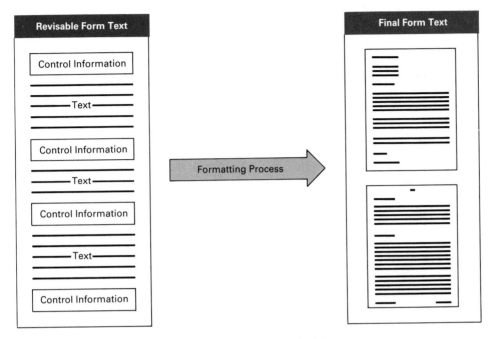

Figure 10.1   Revisable form and final-form text.

in an office system network. The definition of an office system network within the document interchange architecture is based on components that can be divided into three categories:

- **Source Nodes.** A source node acts on behalf of an end user to initiate and control the interchange of information, including documents, with recipient nodes.

- **Recipient Nodes.** A recipient node acts on behalf of an end user to control and receive information, including documents, sent by source nodes.

- **Office System Nodes.** Office system nodes provide services to source and recipient nodes, including routing, receiving, delivering, and storing information. Office system nodes provide document library storage capabilities and exchange information with other office system nodes as necessary to distribute information through the network.

DIA SERVICES

There are four categories of service that are defined as part of the document interchange architecture: document distribution services, document library services, application processing services, and DIA session services.

DOCUMENT DISTRIBUTION SERVICES   Document distribution services are used to deliver documents from a source node to one or more recipient nodes. Delivery can take place directly from a source node to a recipient node, or a document can be routed through an office system node for later delivery to the recipient node. The basic functions provided by document distribution services are listed in Box 10.1.

DIA Sessions

Since there can be no guarantee that a particular user of an office system network is currently logged on, document distribution services must operate on an asynchronous basis. It is not necessary for a source node to establish a session directly with each recipient node, nor is it necessary that both nodes be active at the same time in order to request the delivery of a document from one node to another. Instead, a user establishes a session between a source node and an office system node, and the document to be distributed is passed from the source

BOX 10.1   Document distribution functions

- Distributing documents and other information to one or more recipient nodes. Users can specify a distribution list to be used for distributing a document. A copy of the document is then sent to each recipient on the list.

- Allowing prioritization of a distribution request, so that higher-priority documents or information can be delivered faster than documents or information with lower priority

- Classifying documents as *personal* so that only authorized recipients have access to them

- Providing feedback on problems or errors encountered during document distribution

- Providing confirmation-of-delivery facilities. A sender can request a confirmation notice indicating receipt of a document from each recipient. DIA assigns a unique distribution document name to each distribution request. Confirmation notices specify this unique name, which allows DIA to correlate confirmation or error messages with the original distribution request. A sender can also cancel an outstanding confirmation-of-delivery request.

- Providing, on the recipient end, information on documents available for delivery, delivering documents, and canceling the delivery of documents node to the office system node. If necessary, the document is passed from one office system node to another until the document reaches the office system node that is associated with the recipient node. When the recipient node eventually establishes a DIA session with its associated office system node, that office system node can handle the final delivery of the document.

Node Addresses

Each source node is identified by a *source address,* and each recipient node has a *recipient address.* Each source and recipient node is associated with a single office system node. An office system node is identified by either an *originating node address* or a *destination node address.* When an office system node is supporting a source node, it is considered to be an originating node; when that same office system node is supporting a recipient node, it is considered to be a destination node. Originating node addresses and destination node addresses are unique throughout an office system network. Source and recipient addresses, however, need be unique only within the group of source and recipient nodes that are associated with a particular office system node.

An office system node can be both the originating node and the destination

BOX 10.2 Office system node functions

Originating OSN Functions

- Assigning a unique document distribution name to each distribution request and returning that name to the source node
- Storing requests, documents, and other information to be distributed
- Routing documents and other information to other office system nodes that are serving as the recipient nodes for the distribution
- Correlating confirmation-of-delivery messages with the original distribution request and providing status information to the source node

Destination OSN Functions

- Queuing distribution requests and documents until they can be delivered to the recipient node
- Identifying documents queued for delivery for recipient nodes
- Delivering documents and canceling delivery upon request of a recipient node
- Sending confirmation-of-delivery messages to the originating OSN

node, in which case the originating node address and the destination node address are the same. Similarly, the same node can be both a source node and a recipient node, in which case the source address and the recipient address are also the same.

Office System Node Functions

The services provided by an office system node (OSN) can be divided into two categories, according to whether the node is functioning as an originating or destination node. *Originating node OSN functions* are used when a source node is in session with an office system node; *destination node OSN functions* are used when the office system node is in session with a recipient node. Box 10.2 lists typical originating and destination node OSN functions.

DOCUMENT LIBRARY SERVICES

Document library services form the second major category of DIA services. These services mainly handle the storing and retrieving of documents. When a document is stored in a library, a *document profile* is created for it. This profile contains a set of descriptors for the document, which might include the name of the document, its authors, subjects it covers, the date on which it was created, and so on. In a document retrieval request, a user can specify any of the information that is contained in a document's profile to provide a means for searching for and identifying the requested document. For example, a user can ask for a list of all documents created by a particular author on a certain subject. Based on the list returned, the user could then request by name the retrieval of one or more of the listed documents. Typical document library services are listed in Box 10.3.

BOX 10.3   Document library functions

- Filing, retrieving, and deleting documents from the library
- Assigning a unique library-assigned document name to each document filed and returning that name to the end user who requested that the document be filed
- Searching document profiles and returning to the end user who requested the search a list of documents that match the search criteria

BOX 10.4   Application processing functions

- Requesting the execution of application programs in an office system node
- Requesting the addition or deletion of descriptors in a document profile
- Invoking programs that format documents

APPLICATION PROCESSING SERVICES

A third category of DIA services is application processing services. These services define commands that cause an office system node to perform a variety of functions, including manipulating document profiles and transforming a document from revisable to final form. Some of the functions performed by application processing services are listed in Box 10.4.

DIA SESSION SERVICES

The final category of DIA services is DIA session services. DIA session services issue commands needed to establish a session between two DIA processes. As part of establishing a session, agreement is reached on the scope of the work to be performed. The various services that are part of DIA are grouped into *function sets;* each set includes all the commands needed to provide a specific, well-defined unit of work. DIA defines a wide range of functions, and not all will be included in a particular product implementation. Communication and interface capabilities between products are then based on the function sets they have in common. Some of the function sets defined are listed in Box 10.5. As

BOX 10.5   DIA session functions

- Transmitting a document from a source node to an office system node, from a source node to a recipient node, or from an office system node to a recipient node
- Storing, retrieving, and deleting documents from a library
- Modifying descriptors in a document profile

part of establishing a session, DIA session services determine that the two DIA processes have appropriate function sets in common to accomplish the exchange of information.

DOCUMENT INTERCHANGE UNIT

As discussed earlier, DIA defines two data streams, a revisable-form-text data stream and a final-form-text data stream, that are used for exchanging documents. These data streams are transmitted through the network in units called *document interchange units* (DIUs). The components that make up a DIU are described in Box 10.6.

The various components of the DIU can be broken down into subcomponents. A document profile in the document unit is an example of a subcomponent. All components and subcomponents have a format that begins with an *introducer*. An introducer is a structured field that uniquely identifies the component or subcomponent and specifies its length. Using an introducer for each component means that a DIU is completely self-defining and can vary in length. When a DIU is transported across an SNA network, the entire DIU is treated as

BOX 10.6   DIU components

Prefix	Command Sequence	Data Unit	Document Unit	Suffix

- **Prefix.** This identifies the unit of information as a DIU.

- **Command Sequence.** This indicates the specific DIA function to be performed, such as "distribute a document," "retrieve a document," or "search for a document."

- **Data Unit.** This is an optional component that contains data relating to a command sequence. An example of its use might be to contain the distribution list when a document is being distributed to a number of recipients.

- **Document Unit.** This contains the document profile and might also contain the text of the document. This field is optional and is used only when a document profile or the document itself is sent from one DIA process to another.

- **Suffix.** This indicates the end of the DIU. It might optionally contain information about any error conditions encountered during transmission.

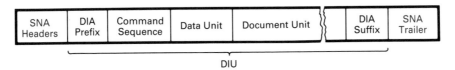

Figure 10.2   SNA headers and trailers.

a message unit. SNA adds the appropriate headers and trailer required for transmission across the network and then removes them when transmission is completed. This process is illustrated in Fig. 10.2.

SUMMARY

IBM's office information architectures handle the transparent interchange of information in an office system network. The document content architecture defines the structure of the data streams used to represent documents within the office system network. There are architectures for both revisable-form and final-form text. The document interchange architecture defines the protocols and data structures used to interchange documents.

In DIA, source nodes initiate and control the interchange of information, including documents, with recipient nodes. Office system nodes provide services to source and recipient nodes. There are four service categories defined as part of DIA. Document distribution services deliver documents from a source node to one or more recipient nodes. Document library services provide for the storing and retrieving of documents. Application processing services provide various application functions, including modifying document profiles, transforming text from revisable form to final form, and invoking user-requested application processes. DIA sessions services are used to establish a session between two DIA processes. DCA data streams are carried in document interchange units (DIUs). A DIU consists of a prefix, command sequence, data unit, document unit, and suffix.

11 SNA DISTRIBUTION SERVICES

It is desirable, from both the user's and IBM's viewpoint, for an office system network to be able to use SNA transport facilities. By using SNA facilities, an organization can avoid duplicating network and transmission facilities and can instead build on network facilities that are already in place. SNA was initially designed, however, to provide *synchronous* transmission facilities, whereby the two network users exchanging information are in session with each other and are concurrently active. Office system communication, in contrast, must allow for *asynchronous* transmission. An office system must be able to receive documents, distribute them throughout the network, queue them, and later deliver them upon request of the recipient. IBM's response to this requirement is *SNA Distribution Services* (SNADS). SNADS provides an asynchronous distribution capability that can be used by SNA applications. SNADS services have been used to implement the functions defined as part of DIA and thus allow an office system network to use SNA facilities.

SNADS consists of a set of architected transaction programs that make use of LU 6.2 and APPC services to distribute information. These programs, called *distribution transaction programs,* are interconnected and cooperate to perform asynchronous data distribution functions. Application transaction programs interface with SNADS and make requests to send or receive information using the distribution services. A program that requests distribution is known as an *origin* application transaction program; a program that receives the distribution is known as a *destination* application transaction program.

DISTRIBUTION SERVICE UNIT   The element in SNADS that an application transaction program communicates with is called a *distribution service unit* (DSU). A DSU consists of the distribution transaction programs that are located within a logical unit in an SNA node. The various DSUs in an SNA network are interconnected, and the connection between two DSUs is called a *distribution connection*. A distribution connection between two DSUs allows a synchronous SNA session to be established between the two DSUs. The distribution connection exists whether or not there is an active SNA session in progress. A DSU can assume different roles. A DSU that services an origin application transaction program is an *origin DSU*. A DSU that services a destination application transaction program is a *distribution DSU*. A DSU that is used to establish a distribution path from the origin DSU to a destination DSU is known as an *intermediate DSU*.

DSU INTERFACES   Figure 11.1 illustrates the relationships that exist when SNADS is used. Users are represented by application transaction programs that request distribution services from DSUs. The DSUs, in turn, use SNA services as defined by LU 6.2. The SNA services provide transmission of information across the path control network. The DSU interface to SNA uses the standard verbs defined as part of the LU 6.2 protocol boundary. The application transaction programs use the *distribution protocol*

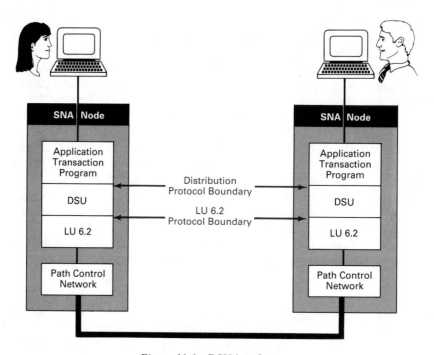

Figure 11.1 DSU interfaces.

boundary to request services of the DSU. The distribution protocol boundary consists of the following three verbs:

- DISTRIBUTE___DATA
- DISTRIBUTE___STATUS
- RECEIVE___DISTRIBUTION

**INTERCHANGE
UNITS**
The basic unit of data that is handled in SNADS is called an *interchange unit*. It uses the coding structure defined for the document interchange unit (DIU) defined in DIA (see Chapter 10). Each component within the unit has an introducer field that identifies the component and specifies its length. Thus the entire unit is self-defining. SNADS defines two types of interchange units: a *distribution interchange unit* is used for the actual distribution of information, and an *acknowledge interchange unit* is used either to confirm that distribution has been accomplished or to report that an error condition has been encountered.

Figure 11.2 shows the formats of the two interchange units. Both begin with a prefix field and end with a suffix field, which together serve to delimit the unit. The command field contains the control information required to perform whatever function is being requested. The control information includes any necessary command parameters. For example, if the function requested is to distribute a document, the command field will contain a DISTRIBUTE command code plus the names of the recipients and the name of any distribution transaction program needed for processing. The object field contains the actual information that is being distributed. It is possible to have more than one object in a distribution interchange unit and also to have no object, for example, when only a command field is required to implement a particular function.

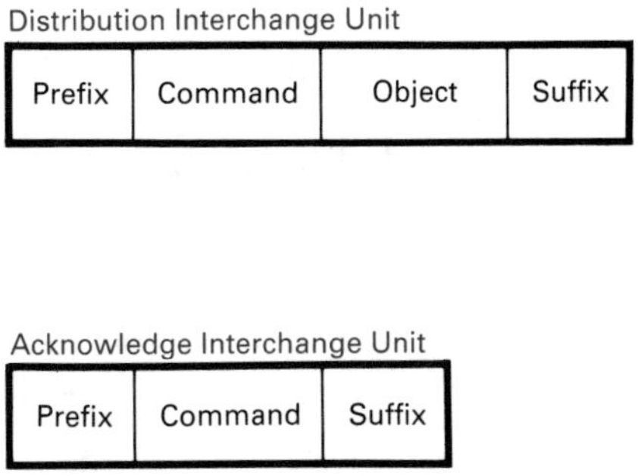

Distribution Interchange Unit

Prefix	Command	Object	Suffix

Acknowledge Interchange Unit

Prefix	Command	Suffix

Figure 11.2 Interchange Unit formats.

SNADS NAMES AND ADDRESSES   As with any network-related architecture, names and addresses are key architectural considerations. SNADS naming and addressing is based on the following:

- Each user is identified by a name, called a *distribution user name* (DUN).
- Each DSU is identified by a name, called a *distribution service unit name* (DSUN).
- Each user is associated with one, and only one, DSU at a given time. That DSU's name (DSUN) is the user's address.

The DSU name consists of two parts: the *routing group name* (RGN) and the *routing element name* (REN). The routing group name can be used to group DSUs. The routing element name is used to identify each DSU in the group. Figure 11.3 shows the RGN being used to group DSUs on a geographical basis. DSUs in Chicago are in one group, and those in Milwaukee are in another. DSUs in Chicago are given an RGN of "CHI" and those in Milwaukee "MIL". The REN (Z1, Z2, etc.) must be unique within an RGN but can be duplicated between groups, since the full compound name will be unique. It is important to note that the use of an RGN is not required by the architecture. A DSU name can consist only of an REN, in which case all RENs must be unique throughout the network.

The user name is also a two-part name, consisting of a *distribution group name* (DGN) and a *distribution element name* (DEN). Typically, the distribution group name is used to identify a group of related users, for example, all the users that belong to a particular department or division. The members of the

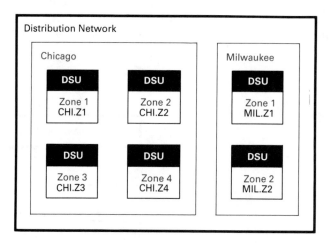

Figure 11.3   Routing group name and routing element name.

accounting department could be given names such as ACCT.ANDERSON, ACCT.BROWN, ACCT.CARTER, and so on, while those in personnel might be PERS.SMITH, PERS.THOMPSON, and the like. The distribution element name then identifies a particular user within the group.

RELATIONSHIP OF USERS AND DSUs

Figure 11.4 shows possible relationships that might exist between users and DSUs. An entire distribution group might be associated with a single DSU, as is the case for PERS and RD. Or a distribution group might be split over several DSUs, as with SALES and ACCT. Similarly, a single DSU might be associated with one or several distribution groups.

DISTRIBUTION DIRECTORIES

To service distribution requests, SNADS must be able to convert a distribution user name into the appropriate DSUN that forms that user's address. The approach taken in SNADS is to use *distribution directories* for this purpose. Figure 11.5 shows a complete distribution directory for the distribution network shown in Fig. 11.4. With this type of directory, a user's address is determined

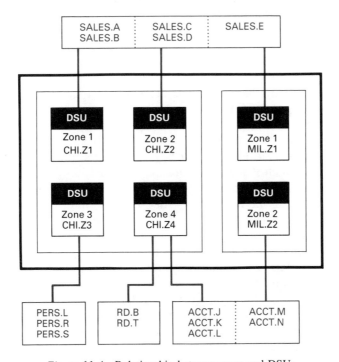

Figure 11.4   Relationship between users and DSUs.

Distribution Directory

DUN	DSUN
SALES.A	CHI.Z1
SALES.B	CHI.Z1
SALES.C	CHI.Z2
SALES.D	CHI.Z2
SALES.E	MIL.Z1
ACCT.J	CHI.Z4
ACCT.K	CHI.Z4
ACCT.L	CHI.Z4
ACCT.M	MIL.Z2
ACCT.N	MIL.Z2
PERS.L	CHI.Z3
PERS.R	CHI.Z3
PERS.S	CHI.Z3
RD.B	CHI.Z4
RD.T	CHI.Z4

Figure 11.5 Complete distribution directory.

simply by looking up the user's name in the directory. If a user's address changes, that entry in the table is changed to reflect the new address, and the change is transparent to other users.

Because of space conditions and directory maintenance requirements, however, it may not be desirable to store a complete directory at every DSU. A facility called a default entry is provided that allows for DSUs to use only a subset of the complete directory. A default entry uses an asterisk (*) to indicate all possible values for a particular portion of the name. For example, SALES.* refers to all distribution user names that have a DGN of SALES.

Figure 11.6 demonstrates the use of default entries. If a user at CHI.Z1 sends a distribution to ACCT.K, the distribution directory at CHI.Z1 routes it to CHI.Z4, where it is recognized as belonging to a user at that DSU. If the user at CHI.Z1 sends a distribution to ACCT.M, the distribution directory at CHI.Z1 again sends it to CHI.Z4. At CHI.Z4 the distribution directory routes it on to MIL.Z2, which is the actual destination DSU in this case.

Default entries can route a distribution through several different DSUs before it either arrives at the recipient's actual DSU or an error is identified. This chaining of directories can also be used to handle address changes. If, for example, the address for ACCT.K were changed to MIL.Z1, the directory at CHI.Z4 could simply be changed to reflect the new address and ACCT.K added to the directory at MIL.Z1. In this way, distributions routed to the old address (CHI.Z4) would be directed on to the new address (MIL.Z1). Choices about the use of defaults in distribution directories are left to the network administrator. The advantages of reduced storage space and directory maintenance must be balanced against the possible overhead that is incurred when distributions are routed through intermediate DSUs.

CHI.Z1

DUN	DSUN
SALES.A	CHI.Z1
SALES.B	CHI.Z1
SALES.C	CHI.Z2
SALES.D	CHI.Z2
SALES.E	MIL.Z1
PERS.*	CHI.Z3
RD.*	CHI.Z4
ACCT.*	CHI.Z4
.	Error

CHI.Z4

DUN	DSUN
ACCT.J	CHI.Z4
ACCT.K	CHI.Z4
ACCT.L	CHI.Z4
ACCT.*	MIL.Z2
RD.B	CHI.Z4
RD.T	CHI.Z4
RD.*	Error
.	CHI.Z1

Figure 11.6   Default entries.

DSU STRUCTURE

Figure 11.7 shows the various components that make up a DSU. The services and queues shown in the diagram provide the processing needed to use SNA synchronous transmission facilities to support asynchronous distribution requirements. Presentation services provide the interface to the application transaction programs involved in a distribution request. They process the distribution protocol boundary verbs used to issue a request to send or receive a distribution.

A distribution request causes an entry to be added to the input queue. When a recipient requests delivery of a distribution, an entry is removed from an output queue. Routing and directory services determine where each entry in the input queue should go. If the entry has reached its destination DSU, it is placed in an output queue. If it must be sent to another DSU, it is placed in a next DSU queue. Transport services process entries in the next DSU queues and are responsible for transporting them to the next DSU along their route. Transportation of the distribution is accomplished by means of SNA transmission facilities, which are invoked using the LU 6.2 protocol boundary verbs. When a distribution reaches the next DSU, it is entered into that DSU's input queue, where it is then processed by routing and directory services.

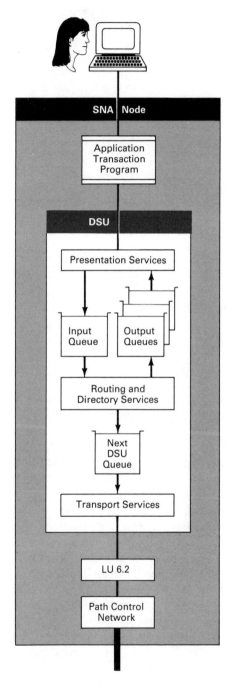

Figure 11.7 DSU components.

ROUTING   Sending a distribution through the distribution network might involve the use of intermediate DSUs. The series of DSUs a distribution must pass through to reach its destination is called its *route*. Figure 11.8 repeats the distribution network shown earlier, with the distribution connections between the various DSUs shown using red lines.

Suppose that SALES.A wishes to send a distribution to SALES.E. The distribution request is processed at CHI.Z1, and the distribution is placed in the input queue there. Routing and directory services use the distribution directory to determine that the distribution must be passed on to MIL.Z1. There are two

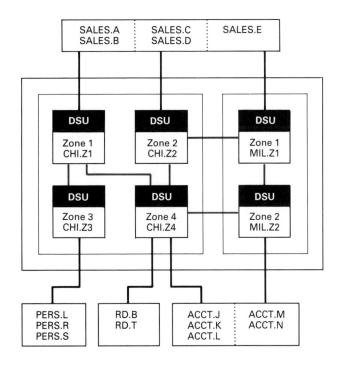

Distribution Directory

DUN	DSUN
SALES.A	CHI.Z1
SALES.B	CHI.Z1
SALES.C	CHI.Z2
SALES.D	CHI.Z2
SALES.E	MIL.Z1
ACCT.J	CHI.Z4
ACCT.K	CHI.Z4

Figure 11.8   Distribution network routes.

137

possible routes that could be used to reach MIL.Z1 from CHI.Z1. One route uses CHI.Z4 and CHI.Z2 as intermediate DSUs, and the other uses CHI.Z4 and MIL.Z2. Based on service-level considerations, which will be described in more detail shortly, routing and directory services determine which route to use and thus the next DSU along that route. The distribution is then placed in the appropriate DSU queue, and transport services transport it to the input queue of the next DSU, CHI.Z4. This continues until the distribution reaches the destination DSU, MIL.Z1. There the distribution is placed in an output queue, where the destination user, SALES.E, is able to access it.

DISTRIBUTION SERVICE LEVEL   *Distribution service level* (DSL) in a distribution network is similar to class of service in an SNA network. It allows users to specify their service requirements and then becomes the basis for choosing a particular route through the network. The distribution service level allows for the specification of requirements in three areas. The first area is *priority*. A data distribution can be given either a HIGH or a LOW priority. There is also a FAST priority that can be used for expedited delivery. A priority of FAST is usually reserved for small objects that do not require much capacity. There is also a priority called STATUS that can be used to expedite status distributions. Status distributions are used to send information about the status of distribution requests.

A second area where a service level can be specified is *capacity*. Capacity relates to the storage capacity that a DSU has and is used to ensure that a distribution is not sent to a DSU that has inadequate storage capacity to handle the distribution. Capacity can be specified using various size values or as INDEFINITE.

The third area specified by DSL is *protection*. Possible protection specifications are PROTECTED and NONE. If PROTECTED is specified, a DSU protects a distribution against communications or system failures. With this protection specification, the capability is provided for restoring a distribution if a failure occurs. With the NONE specification, a distribution might be lost if a failure occurs.

ROUTING TO THE NEXT DSU   The destination DSU name and distribution service level are used together to determine the next DSU to which a distribution is transported as it passes along its route to its final destination. The distribution service level also determines the class of service given to the transmission as it passes through the SNA network.

Figure 11.9 shows a sample routing table that might be used to determine the next DSU for a distribution. Using our previous example, the destination DSUN is MIL.Z1. If the DSL were specified as A, which might stand for LOW

Routing Table

DSUN	DSL	LU Name	Mode	Queue
⋮	⋮	⋮	⋮	•
MIL.Z1	A	LUX	BULK	Q2
MIL.Z1	B	LUY	FAST	Q1
MIL.Z1	C	LUY	FAST	Q2

Figure 11.9   Routing table.

priority and INDEFINITE capacity, the routing table specifies that a distribution with this combination should be sent next to the DSU at the logical unit named LUX, and a mode name of BULK should be used for the transmission. SNA converts the mode name into a class-of-service specification and, based on that specification, determines an appropriate virtual route and transmission priority to use. The routing table shows that if a different DSL is specified, a different route will be used. If the DSL were B, which might correspond to a smaller capacity and a HIGH priority, the distribution would be routed via logical unit LUY with a mode name of FAST. The routing table also specifies a queue name. There can be multiple queues for a given combination of LU and mode name. These queues are processed in a specified order. For example, Q1 might be processed before Q2. This allows the queues to be used to separate distributions having different priorities that are being sent via the same LU and mode name. In the table this is shown by assigning to Q1 distributions to MIL.Z1 with DSL B and assigning to Q2 those with DSL C. The order of the queue processing then ensures that higher-priority distributions are sent first.

DISTRIBUTION PROCESSING

The DSL plays a major role in determining the processing that is performed when a distribution reaches its destination DSU. When a distribution reaches its destination DSU, routing and directory services select the appropriate output queue in which to place it and start a distribution transaction program to process it. The queue that is used and the distribution transaction program that is started are determined on the basis of recipient name, DSL, and destination transaction program name (TPN), which is included as a parameter in the distribution. There can be one queue for a given destination transaction program, or several queues can be defined. How these queues are handled is largely product-specific and might be different at different DSUs in the network.

SNADS RELATIONSHIP TO LU 6.2

As part of next DSU queue processing, transport services cause distributions to be transmitted from one DSU to another. This is done through the use of LU 6.2 services. Transport services consist of two transaction programs, DISTRIBUTION__SEND and DISTRIBUTION__RECEIVE.

These programs interface with LU 6.2 using the standard LU 6.2 protocol boundary verbs and are viewed by LU 6.2 as any other transaction program. The communication between two DSUs takes place using a LU 6.2 conversation that is established between the logical units that contain the DSUs. This is illustrated in Fig. 11.10. DSU A in logical unit X uses the DISTRIBUTION__ SEND program to communicate with the DISTRIBUTION__RECEIVE program in DSU B, which is located in logical unit Y. This communication is done using a conversation that has been established between the two logical units. Figure 11.11 shows a sample conversation that is used to send a DIU from one DSU to the next. A separate SEND verb is used for each element of the DIU. When the entire DIU has been received, the conversation ends.

To increase throughput it is possible to start multiple instances of DISTRIBU-TION__SEND and DISTRIBUTION__RECEIVE, communicating between several logical units or between the same two logical units. This depends on the underlying LU 6.2 capability that the LU has to establish parallel sessions.

Beyond the standard communication facilities supported by LU 6.2, SNADS provides additional facilities to the application transaction programs it supports. These facilities include hold/release processing for recoverable errors and notification facilities. Both of these facilities are discussed next.

HOLD/RELEASE PROCESSING   At times during a distribution transmission, errors can occur, from which recovery can be effected by retransmitting the distribution. An example of this type of error might be when a DSU runs out of storage capacity. At a later time, when other queued distributions have been forwarded, the DSU might have the capacity to accept the transmission. When this type of error is detected, the receiving DSU sends a message telling the sending DSU to stop transmission temporarily. The sending DSU suspends transmission, places a hold on the queues involved, and deallocates the conversation then in progress. At a later time the receiving DSU sends another message, causing the transmission to be

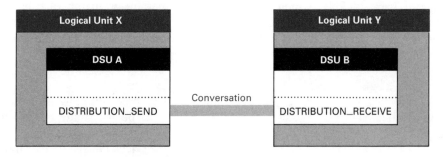

Figure 11.10   DSU use of LU 6.2 conversation.

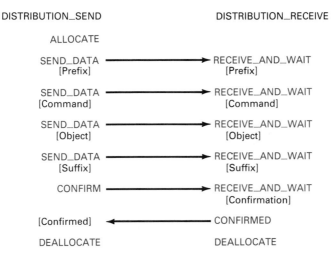

Figure 11.11 Distribution conversation.

resumed. The sending DSU then releases the hold on the queues, allocates a new conversation, and attempts again to transmit the distribution. If, after repeated attempts, the transmission still fails, it can be treated as an unrecoverable error, with an appropriate message being sent to the originating user.

NOTIFICATION FACILITIES   SNADS also provides a facility that lets a user be notified about the status of a distribution request. To do this, each distribution request is assigned a *unique distribution identifier* (UDI). All copies of the distribution being sent carry this UDI. A destination transaction program then returns status information indicating whether the distribution was received by the recipient or if an error occurred. The status information carries the UDI, which allows it to be correlated to the original distribution request. Typically, the status information is sent back to the originator of the request, although it is possible to specify that it be sent to some other user. The status information is sent using a DISTRIBUTE__ STATUS verb. It might contain information for a single recipient or for several recipients. If it is for several recipients, each can have a different status.

Notification facilities provide generalized services that can be employed by many architectures. To provide this generality, status is reported using two fields: *status type* and *status data*. The status type field indicates with which application architecture the status is associated. Each application architecture, such as DIA, is assigned certain status type values. Each application architecture can then define the format and meaning of the status data for its status types.

SERVERS SNADS has been designed to handle the transmission of objects of widely varying size. This is necessary if it is to support application architectures such as DIA, where the information being transferred can range from a brief message to a large report or other document. One consideration in providing this type of service is how to access the objects being distributed at both the originating and destination ends. The approach used by SNADS is to employ *servers* to retrieve and store distribution objects. Figure 11.12 shows the relationship between origination and destination DSUs and their servers. The servers are not part of the distribution network and are not directly defined by SNADS. They interface to the DSUs in much the same way as an application transaction program does, using a set of verbs that make up the server protocol boundary. Some of the functions provided by these servers are listed in Box 11.1.

As a result of server processing, the originating DSU receives an object in the form of a byte stream that is ready for transmission. The role of the distribution network is then to transmit that byte stream unchanged to the destination DSU. The object being transmitted consists of two parts: an object prefix and an object byte stream. The object prefix specifies the name of the server to be used by the destination DSU. This server is then responsible for any processing to be performed on the object at the receiving end and for writing the object directly into the recipient user's space.

SPECIFIC VERSUS GENERAL SERVERS The servers that are used by originating and destination DSUs are known as specific servers, since they deal with objects in their application-specific form. There are also general servers, which are used by intermediate DSUs. A general server is responsible for reading and writing an exact copy of an object being

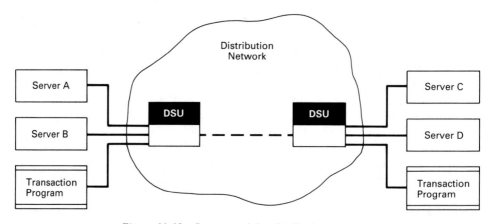

Figure 11.12   Servers and the distribution network.

BOX 11.1   Server functions

- Using the appropriate data management routines to read or write the objects being distributed
- Encoding and decoding the data, as required by the application
- Applying techniques such as compression or decompression to transform the data stream for transmission
- Processing profiles, such as the DIA document interchange profile, and processing catalog entries as necessary to use and maintain libraries
- Synchronizing access to objects and providing locking protocols to ensure that an object is not modified until all necessary copies have been transmitted

forwarded. A general server is not required to perform any application-specific processing and thus is considered to be part of the distribution network.

SNADS AND DIA   SNADS provides a generalized architecture for asynchronous data distribution using an SNA network. As such it is capable of supporting many types of applications. Office systems, by their very nature, have a requirement for asynchronous distribution. As discussed in Chapter 10, the document interchange architecture (DIA) has been developed to support the interchange of documents in an office system. SNADS has been designed to be compatible with DIA and provides the services needed for document interchange. SNADS has been implemented in an office system environment in products such as DISOSS and the IBM 5520. As such it represents a significant enhancement in SNA's ability to support a variety of networking needs.

SUMMARY   SNA distribution services (SNADS) provides an asynchronous distribution capability that can be used by SNA applications. It consists of a set of architected transaction programs, called distribution transaction programs, that use LU 6.2 to perform asynchronous data distribution. The element in SNADS that an application transaction program interfaces with is a distribution service unit (DSU). The DSUs use LU 6.2 services to transmit information across the SNA network. The basic unit of communication in SNADS is an interchange unit. It consists of a prefix, a command field, an object field, and a suffix.

Each SNADS user is identified by a distribution user name (DUN), which consists of a distribution group name (DGN) and a distribution element name (DEN). Each DSU is identified by a distribution service unit name (DSUN), which consists of a routing group name (RGN) and a routing element name (REN). Each user is associated with one DSU, and its DSUN serves as the user's address. Each DSU has a distribution directory that is used to convert user names into addresses. Distributions are routed from DSU to DSU until the destination DSU is reached. The distribution service level is used to specify service requirements and to determine the particular route used.

SNADS provides hold/release processing, which supports retransmission in the case of recoverable errors. It also provides notification facilities that allow the originating user to check the status of all recipients of a distribution. Servers are used to access objects at both the originating and destination ends of a distribution. They employ appropriate data management routines to retrieve and store distribution objects and handle any formatting required to prepare the object for transmission. SNADS provides a generalized architecture for asynchronous data distribution using an SNA network. It has been designed to be compatible with DIA and provides the services needed for document interchange in an office system.

12   SNA NETWORK INTERCONNECTION

SNA allows for complex networks to be built, with numerous host processors and communications controllers interconnected in a variety of ways. However, there are some restrictions that must be observed. For example, the network names given to the network resources—logical units, physical units, SSCPs, and links—must be unique. The addressing mode, whether 16- or 23-bit, and the split that is used for 16-bit addressing, must be uniform throughout the network. Similarly, mode names and class-of-service names must also be consistent. As the number of SNA networks has grown, there has also been a growing requirement for these networks to be able to communicate with one another or to be interconnected. From the user's perspective, it is desirable that the interconnection of networks be transparent and that it appear to the user as if all the separate interconnected networks actually form a single network. The user should not have to be concerned with what physical network a particular resource resides in.

Actually to combine individual networks into a single, larger network requires considerable work. Any duplicate network names need to be changed and network redefinition performed. Users would then have to change application programs and operating procedures in order to use the new network names. If the addressing modes were not the same in all the various individual networks, significant changes would be required to make addressing modes uniform throughout the combined network. Differences in class-of-service and mode names would also have to be resolved. SNA provides a more practical approach to interconnecting networks through the use of a facility called *SNA Network Interconnection* (SNI). With SNI, *gateways* can be constructed between networks that allow users to communicate across networks without being aware that more than one network is involved.

SNA GATEWAY　　A gateway that interconnects SNA networks consists of two components: a gateway SSCP and a gateway node. Figure 12.1 illustrates an SNA gateway. The gateway SSCP belongs to only one of the individual networks; the gateway node belongs to both networks. Each network recognizes the gateway node as a subarea node within that network. A gateway SSCP typically resides in a host processor, and a gateway node typically resides in a communications controller. It is possible to configure a gateway with several SSCPs or gateway nodes. For simplicity, though, we will assume a single SSCP and a single gateway node in our initial examples. The gateway provides two primary services:

- Translating network names and addresses as messages and requests cross from one network to another
- Providing a virtual route for transmission with a consistent class of service across networks

**NETWORK NAME
AND ADDRESS
TRANSLATION**　　One potential complication in interconnecting networks is that there may be duplicate network names or addresses between two different networks. If this is the case, a reference to a particular name or the use of a particular address could be ambiguous. SNI avoids this by using *alias names* and *alias addresses* when referring to resources in another network. When a message or request crosses the boundary between two networks, the gateway translates alias names and addresses to actual names and addresses within the new network.

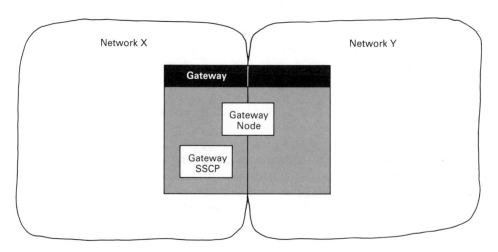

Figure 12.1　SNA gateway.

Name Translation

Figure 12.2 shows a simple example of network name translation. Suppose a logical unit in network X with the name LUA wishes to communicate with a logical unit in network Y with the name LUB. Since there is a logical unit in network X with the name LUB, an alias name must be given to LUB in network Y by which it is known in network X. In this example it has been given the name LUBY. Similarly, LUA has been given the name LUAX in network X. Alias names are defined at the time that the interconnection facilities between the two networks are set up.

The alias names do not have to indicate to what network a resource belongs, although a decision may be made to use a naming convention that incorporates some sort of network designation. This can help to decrease the likelihood of creating duplicate names as new resources are added to the network. In the example shown it is not necessary for LUA to know that LUB is part of network Y—all LUA needs to know is that there exists somewhere a logical unit with the name LUBY with which it wishes to communicate. To LUA, LUBY appears to be a resource belonging to the gateway node, and LUA directs its request for session establishment to that node. The gateway translates the name LUBY to the actual name used in network Y (LUB) before passing on the request. The gateway also translates the name LUA to its alias in network Y, LUAX. To LUB in network Y, it appears that a session is being established with logical unit LUAX, which is a resource belonging to the gateway node.

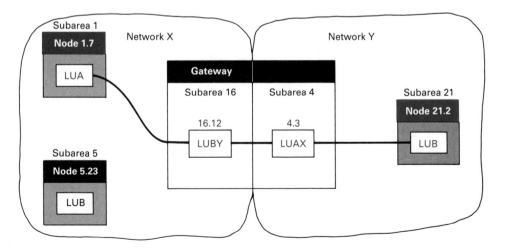

Figure 12.2   Gateway translation of network names and addresses.

Address Translation

Once a session has been established, all messages pass through the gateway, where network addresses in the transmission header undergo translation. A message unit sent by LUA will specify as the destination address a network address based on the gateway's address in network X. In the example in Fig. 12.2, the gateway is defined as subarea 16 in network X. As part of session initiation, LUB is assigned an alias address in network X (16.12 in the example). This is the address specified in messages sent by LUA. When a message from LUA reaches the gateway, the gateway translates this address to the actual address of LUB in network Y, which is 21.2. The address of LUA, which is contained in the transmission header as the sending address, is also translated. This address is changed from its actual address in network X (1.7) to its alias address in network Y (4.3). The alias addresses in network Y reflect the fact that the gateway is part of subarea 4 within network Y.

A particular alias address is assigned to a logical unit only for the duration of a session. When a session ends, that alias address can be used to represent another logical unit. In this way, a gateway node can represent a large number of resources. The maximum number of element addresses that the gateway node can support limits only the number of resources actively involved in sessions at a given time, not the total number of resources in the network being represented.

As part of address translation, any differences in address splits between networks are also resolved. Alias addresses are in the appropriate format for the network in which they are used, which may differ from the format used for the actual address in its network. In this way, logical unit A in one network is able to communicate with logical unit B in another network in the same way that it would if logical unit B were part of logical unit A's network. In effect, the interconnection of the two networks is transparent to any two logical units that establish a session.

VIRTUAL ROUTES

When a session is established between logical units in different networks, the path between the logical units consists of multiple virtual routes. There will be a separate virtual route in each network, with the logical unit as one end point of the route and the gateway as the other end point. The gateway provides the interconnection between these virtual routes that is necessary for data transfer to take place. This is illustrated in Fig. 12.3, in which there is a virtual route between LUA in network X and the gateway and another virtual route between the gateway and LUB in network Y.

As part of session initiation, the original session request contains a class-of-service name that identifies a list of possible virtual routes that might be used for the session. When the session request passes to another network, the class-of-service name is translated. The translated name corresponds to a set of virtual

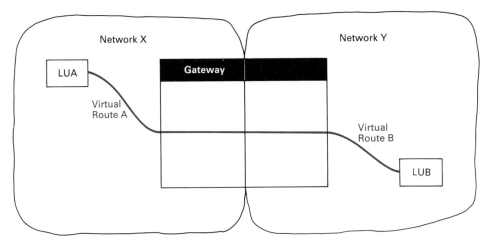

Figure 12.3   Virtual routes in a network interconnection.

routes in the other network that will provide the same level of service as in the original network. As part of the session initiation process, a virtual route is chosen within each network to be used as part of the path for this session. The class-of-service name translation, which is another service of the gateway, ensures that a consistent level of service is provided along the entire path.

GATEWAY   There are a number of possible configurations that
CONFIGURATIONS   can be used for gateways that interconnect networks.
                     Figure 12.4 shows the simplest—a single gateway
SSCP and a single gateway node. The gateway SSCP handles name and address

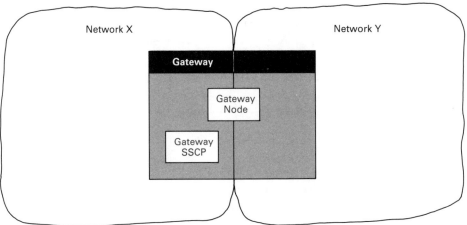

Figure 12.4   Single gateway.

translation for all session service requests and routes the service requests to the appropriate SSCP in either network. The gateway node handles network address translation for all messages that pass between the networks via this gateway. Overhead is reduced by avoiding the use of the gateway SSCP for processing messages. A simple gateway can also be used to interconnect more than two networks, as shown in Fig. 12.5. A session can be established between network Y and network Z even though the gateway SSCP is in network X.

SHARED CONTROL   It is also possible to have more than one gateway SSCP share control of a gateway node. This is shown in Fig. 12.6. Here each network contains a gateway SSCP. When several SSCPs are used in this way, it is possible to divide responsibility among them such that each SSCP needs to know the locations only of logical units that are part of the network in which it is located. This makes it possible to change a network's configuration without affecting the other networks.

PARALLEL PATHS   A single gateway SSCP can be used to control more than one gateway node, as shown in Fig. 12.7. This provides parallel gateways between two networks and allows for alternative paths to be used for sessions. If one gateway node is out of service or lacks

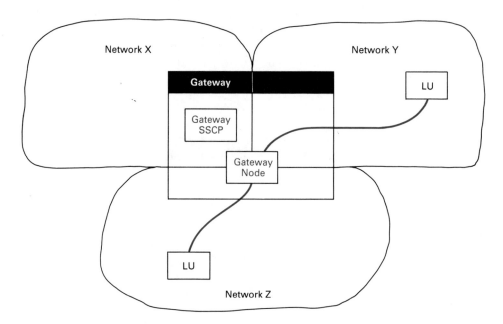

Figure 12.5   Single gateway interconnecting more than one network.

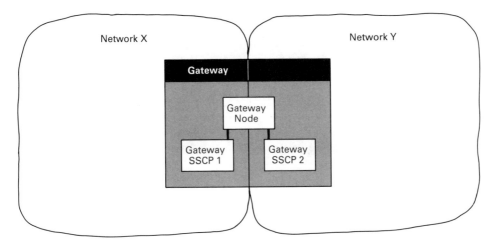

Figure 12.6 Shared-control gateway.

capacity to handle a session, another gateway node can be used. Figure 12.8 shows some alternative configuration possibilities for parallel gateways. The configuration shown in the upper part of the figure uses multiple gateway SSCPs and gateway nodes with no overlap or sharing between the gateways. The lower part of the figure shows a configuration with both shared control of a single

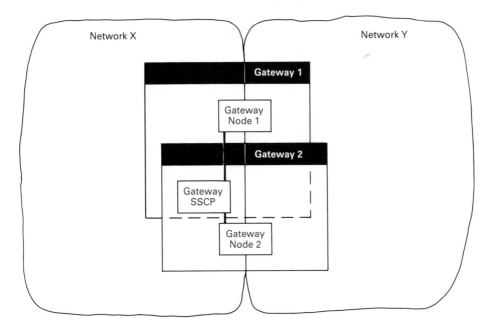

Figure 12.7 Parallel gateways.

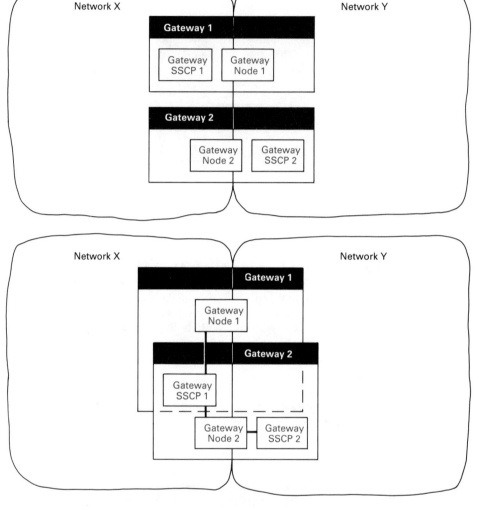

Figure 12.8 Parallel gateways–alternative configurations.

gateway node and a gateway SSCP with control of multiple gateway nodes. Other configurations are possible, since a gateway can be configured in any desired way.

CASCADED GATEWAYS

A series of gateways, known as *cascaded gateways,* can be used to interconnect networks. Figure 12.9 illustrates cascaded gateways. Given this configuration, a logical unit in network X can establish a session with a logical unit in

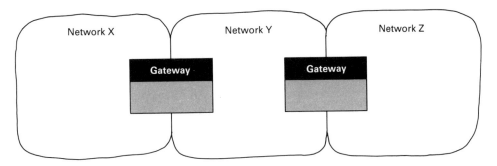

Figure 12.9   Cascaded gateways.

network Z, using network Y as an intermediary in the path. Any number of
networks can be successively linked in this manner. Figure 12.10 shows a special case of cascaded networks. Here the intermediary network (network Y)
consists of nothing more than an SDLC link between the two gateway nodes.
This type of configuration can be used to interconnect two networks with a
minimum of network redefinition. Existing nodes in each network are used as
gateway nodes, and only the link between them needs to be added to the network definitions. This avoids having to add a new subarea to either network
and making the changes to the routing tables that would be associated with the
addition of a subarea to each network.

**NETWORK
MANAGEMENT**

SNI, through the use of gateways, supports the transmission of data across interconnected networks. Issues of network control and management are also ad-
dressed. Existing commands that support cross-domain network operator control
can also be used to perform such functions as initiating or terminating sessions
with a logical unit in another network. Where necessary to avoid con-

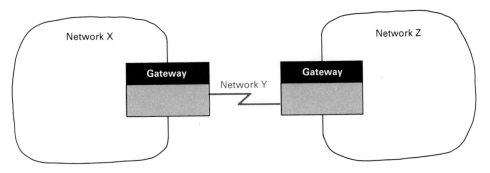

Figure 12.10   Cascaded gateways with minimal intermediary network.

fusion, messages and commands include network identifiers. These network identifiers can be used to limit the scope of a command to a particular network.

With standard operator control, operator commands issued in one network do not control resources in another network. However, with NCCF, it is possible to centralize control of interconnected networks and to give one network operator control of several networks. Problem determination is more complex in an interconnected network environment. Changes to the transmission header caused by address translation make it necessary to collect additional information for diagnosing session-related problems. NLDM, a key problem determination tool, has been enhanced to provide support for interconnected networks.

SUMMARY

SNA Network Interconnection (SNI) provides a way of interconnecting networks. A gateway, consisting of a gateway SSCP and a gateway node, provides translation of network names and addresses and implements a virtual route with a consistent class of service across networks. When a session is established, alias addresses are assigned to the communicating logical units to represent them uniquely in the other network. As a transmission passes from one network to another, the gateway node translates addresses in the transmission header into the form appropriate to the network the transmission is entering. When the session is initiated, the class-of-service name is also translated so that a virtual route is chosen in each network such that the transmission will have an equivalent level of service along its entire path.

Gateways have several possible configurations. A gateway may consist of a single gateway SSCP and gateway node. Several SSCPs can share control of a single gateway node. A single gateway SSCP can control several gateway nodes, providing parallel gateways. Parallel gateways may also use several gateway SSCPs and gateway nodes with no overlap. These configurations can be combined to form more complex configurations. A series of cascaded gateways can be used to interconnect networks in series. SNI extends SNA's capabilities, allowing separate networks to be interconnected in a way that is transparent to the users of the networks while maintaining the independence and autonomy of the networks involved.

13 DATA LINK CONTROL

The arrival of communications network architectures has brought about a steadily increasing complexity in network structures. Higher and higher levels of services are consistently being offered. But all these services must rely on precisely defined lower-level functions to ensure that data are efficiently and reliably passed between nodes.

The chapters in Parts I and II concentrated on SNA fundamentals and attempted to construct a conceptual framework to support a more detailed study of the various SNA layers. The chapters in Parts III, IV, and V present this detailed information. The chapters in this part examine in detail the functions that make up the two lowest SNA layers, those that implement the *path control network*. Part IV then discusses the next two SNA layers: transmission control and data flow control. Part V examines the two sublayers that make up the function management layer.

PATH CONTROL NETWORK

The path control network comprises the lowest two layers of SNA: *data link control* and *path control* (see Fig. 13.1). The data link control layer is responsible for controlling the transmission of data over links between network nodes. The path control layer is responsible for selecting the appropriate data link to use for transmitting a message unit, for determining the rate at which the nodes exchange data, and for controlling the sequencing of message units that are sent over parallel links. We will begin with the lowest layer, the data link control layer, and examine the *synchronous data link control* (SDLC) protocol. SDLC specifies the rules that govern the functions performed in the data link control layer of SNA. SDLC is the subject of Chapters 13 through 16. The path control layer is discussed in Chapters 17 and 18.

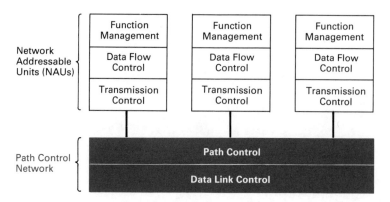

Figure 13.1 Path Control Network.

DATA LINK PROTOCOLS

Data are transmitted over a link using a *data link protocol*. As discussed in Chapter 3, the purpose of a data link protocol is "to transfer blocks of data without error between two devices connected to the same physical link." The protocol should have sophisticated error detection mechanisms and should be able

BOX 13.1 SDLC advantages

- The binary-synchronous protocol is character-oriented; SDLC is bit-oriented. A character-oriented protocol treats the data stream as a continuous stream of characters, some of which have a special significance to the protocol. A character-oriented data link protocol is sensitive to particular characters that appear in the data stream.

- A bit-oriented protocol does not perceive the data stream as a string of characters; instead it perceives it as a continuous bit stream. A bit-oriented protocol attaches no significance to the specific character set being used.

- The binary-synchronous protocol operates only in half-duplex mode; SDLC can accommodate half-duplex or full-duplex links.

- The binary-synchronous protocol requires messages to be acknowledged individually. SDLC allows several messages to be sent before expecting an acknowledgment. This advantage is particularly important on satellite links that have long propagation delays.

to handle any desired data format. It should also be able to perform these functions on a wide variety of full-duplex and half-duplex links. In some cases the protocol must also ensure that only one of several possible devices that are attached to the data link recognizes and accepts a message.

SNA supports two types of links: *data channels* and *SDLC links*. Data channels can be used where two devices can be connected directly by cable. SDLC links are used where a short, direct connection is impractical, and they can be implemented using various methods, such as telephone lines, fiber optics, satellite transmission, or microwave links.

SDLC is the primary SNA data link protocol and is designed to handle the wide variety of possible data links that SNA supports. Box 13.1 lists some of the advantages that SDLC has over the binary-synchronous protocol, a data link protocol that was commonly used prior to the widespread use of SNA. In general, transmission over an SDLC link is considerably faster than transmission over a binary-synchronous link.

SDLC LINK COMPONENTS

An SDLC link consists of the components shown in Fig. 13.2. The connection between two nodes is known as the *link connection*. For SDLC, the link connection ordinarily consists of two modems plus the physical circuit that connects the modems. The physical circuit might take the form of a twisted wire cable, a fiber-optic cable, or a satellite or microwave link. The modems convert binary signals to a form compatible with the physical connection being used. In some cases digital circuits might be used to implement a link connection. In this case the modems might be replaced with simpler devices, sometimes called *digital line drivers*. The *link stations* shown in Fig. 13.2 consist of the hardware and software within an SNA node that control the link connection and prepare data for transmission over it. Link stations are part of SNA's data link control layer.

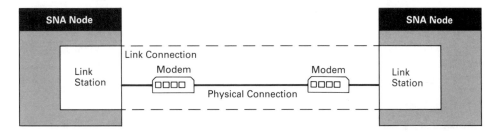

Figure 13.2   SNA data link.

PRIMARY AND SECONDARY LINK STATIONS

There are two types of link stations that are supported by the SDLC protocol:

- **Primary Station.** This station initiates a data transfer and is in control during the exchange of messages. It notifies each secondary link station when it can transmit data and when it should expect to receive data.
- **Secondary Station.** This station is contacted by the primary station and is controlled by the primary station during the exchange of a message.

There can be only one primary link station on a link at a given time. However, there can be several secondary stations on a link. All communication on a link takes place between the primary station and a secondary station; secondary link stations cannot directly communicate with one another. Link stations that are able to communicate with one another are known as *adjacent link stations*. Thus a primary link station and each of its secondary link stations are adjacent link stations. For a secondary link station, only the primary link station is adjacent. Since secondary link stations cannot directly communicate with any other secondary link stations, they are not considered adjacent.

POLLING

A secondary link station is able to send data to the primary link station only after it receives notification from the primary station that it is allowed to send. The primary station uses a process called *polling* to notify each secondary link station that it can send data.

SDLC DATA LINK CONFIGURATIONS

The SDLC protocol allows a primary station and one or more secondary stations to be connected in four different configurations:

- **Point to Point.** In the *point-to-point* configuration shown in Fig. 13.3, a single primary station is connected by a point-to-point link to a single secondary station. Each station in this configuration can send data to the other.
- **Multipoint.** In the *multipoint* configuration shown in Fig. 13.4, a single primary station is connected to two or more secondary stations. The primary station can send data that are addressed to one or more of the secondary stations.

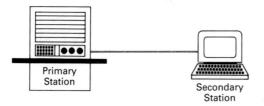

Primary Station

Secondary Station

Figure 13.3 Point-to-point configuration.

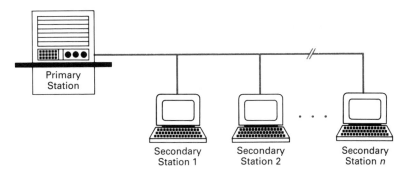

Figure 13.4   Multipoint configuration.

A secondary station can send data only to the primary station; one secondary station cannot send data to one of the other secondary stations.

• **Loop.** In the *loop* configuration shown in Fig. 13.5, the primary station is directly connected only to the first and last secondary stations on the loop. The primary station passes data to the first secondary station, which in turn passes them to the next secondary station, and so on until the data arrive back at the primary station. As in the multipoint configuration, the primary station can send data to one or more of the secondary stations; a secondary station can send data only to the primary station.

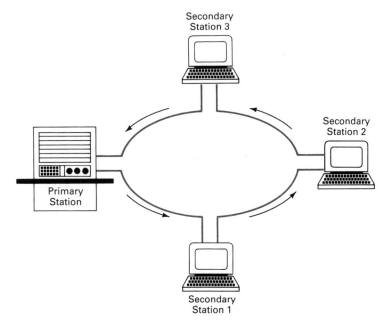

Figure 13.5   Loop configuration.

- **Hub Go-Ahead.** The *hub go-ahead* configuration, shown in Fig. 13.6, is a rare configuration used by some specialized equipment. Two channels are used: an inbound channel and an outbound channel. The primary station communicates with any and all of the secondary stations via the outbound channel. A secondary station can communicate only with the primary station via the inbound channel, which is daisy-chained from one secondary station to the next.

LINK STATION ADDRESSES

Each secondary link station has associated with it a set of *receive addresses* and a single *send address*. When the primary link station sends a message unit, an address is included as part of the message unit. If that address is included in the receive address set of a particular secondary link station, that station recognizes and accepts the message unit. Allowing each secondary link station to have a set of receive addresses allows a primary station to send message units to a group of secondary stations on the data link.

Figure 13.7 illustrates a situation in which each secondary has several receive addresses. In this example the primary station has seven different addresses that it can use for transmission. If the primary station needs to send a message unit to only one of the four secondary stations, the primary station will include in the message unit a *station address*. Valid station addresses in this example are A, B, C, and D. If, however, the primary station wishes to send a message unit to all of the stations, it might use address X. Address X is called a *broadcast address*. Since all of the stations have X in their receive address sets, they will all recognize and accept the message unit.

Suppose that secondary stations 1 and 2 perform one type of function and stations 3 and 4 perform a different type of function. In this case it is possible that the primary station may need to send data or control information to both stations 1 and 2 and to both stations 3 and 4. To send the same message unit to both stations 1 and 2, the primary station need only send a single message using address M. Both stations 1 and 2 will accept the message, whereas stations 3

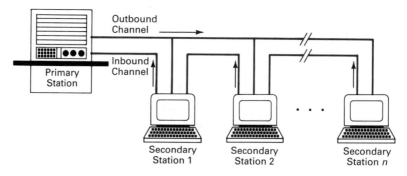

Figure 13.6 Hub go-ahead configuration.

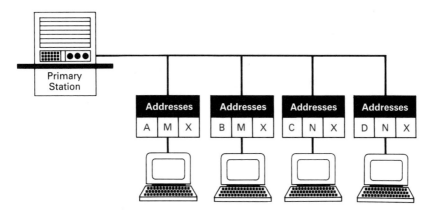

Figure 13.7   Secondary stations with more than one address.

and 4 will reject it. Similarly, if the primary station needs to send the same data to stations 3 and 4, it can send a single message using address N. Addresses M and N are called *group addresses.*

Any address value can be defined as a broadcast address or as a group address as long as all stations on the link interpret address values in the same way. Two address values are defined by the architecture. An address value of all zeros is interpreted as referring to no station; thus an address value of zero cannot be assigned as a station address. An address value that consists of all one bits is reserved for use as a broadcast address; however, a specific implementation may use other address values as broadcast addresses as well.

It is important to distinguish between the addresses used by SDLC and the network addresses and network names that are used by the higher-level layers of SNA. The higher-level layers work with network addresses and network names that uniquely identify network-addressable units within the total SNA network. The addresses used by SDLC are used to identify uniquely the stations that are attached to a single data link. In many cases an individual data link attaches only two stations. In some cases, as with multipoint data links and loops, several stations may share the same data link. However, it is rare for a single data link to be shared by more than a few stations, so the limit imposed by the 256 different bit configurations in a single-byte data link address is seldom reached in actual practice.

TRANSMISSION STATES

An SDLC link connection can be in one of four *transmission states* at any given time:

- **Active.** In the *active* state, control bits or bits representing message text are actively flowing between the primary and a secondary station on the link connection.

- **Idle.** In the *idle* state, no information is being transmitted. A continuous sequence of one bits is transmitted when the line is idling.

- **Transient.** The *transient* state represents the transition that takes place between the time that the primary station transmits a message unit to a secondary station and the time that the secondary station transmits a message unit back to the primary station.

- **Disconnected.** The line is in the *disconnected* state when the secondary station is physically disconnected from the primary station, as when a secondary station connected to a switched line is *on-hook*.

SDLC FRAMES

The message unit that is transmitted over an SDLC link is normally called a *frame,* although some SNA literature refers to the message unit that is transmitted over a data link as a *basic link unit* (BLU). We will use the more common term, *frame.* Some frames are originated by SDLC itself and are used to control the operation of the data link. Other frames consist of data or control information passed down from a higher SNA layer. As shown in Fig. 13.8, each frame is divided into three major parts: a header, a variable-length information field, and a trailer. Control information is carried in the header and the trailer. Frames originated by SDLC sometimes use the variable-length information field in the frame to contain control information. Other frames use the information field to carry basic transmission units (BTUs) that are passed down from the path control layer. Box 13.2 provides brief descriptions of the fields that make up an SDLC frame.

Notice that a single byte is normally used to contain the address in an SDLC frame. This address field always contains the address of a secondary station. Since all communication on the link takes place between a primary and a secondary station, the address of the secondary station is all that is needed to identify the source and destination of a frame; the address of the primary station is always implied. When the primary station is transmitting, the address field defines the address of the secondary station that is to receive the message. When a secondary station is transmitting, the address field contains the address of the secondary station that originates the message.

In many cases the address specified by the primary station is a station address that identifies a single secondary station. As described earlier in this chapter, however, the address might alternatively be a broadcast address that

Figure 13.8 SDLC transmission frame.

BOX 13.2 SDLC frame fields

- **Beginning Flag Field.** A frame begins with a flag field, consisting of a single byte that contains the unique bit configuration 0111 1110. A *bit-stuffing* technique, described in Chapter 14, guarantees that the only place where six consecutive one bits will occur is in a flag field.

- **Address Field.** The field that follows the flag field, normally a single byte in length, is interpreted as the data link address. The position of this field within the frame (the byte immediately following the beginning flag) defines this field as the address field. The address field contains the link address of the secondary station that is sending or receiving the frame. An extension to the architecture allows multiple-byte data link addresses, but this extension is seldom implemented.

- **Control Field.** The control field, normally a single byte in length, defines the type of information carried by the frame. This byte determines the type of frame being transmitted, conveys information necessary for the proper sequencing of frames, and carries control and polling information. The position of the control field within the frame (the next eight bits after the address field) defines this byte as the control byte. An extension to the SDLC architecture that is implemented by some device types allows for frames that carry two-byte control fields.

- **Information Field.** A variable-length information field in the SDLC frame is used to carry the data portion of the frame. It consists either of SDLC control information or of a BTU that has been passed to the data link control layer from the path control layer. Some frames that are originated by SDLC do not use an information field. SDLC does not place any minimum or maximum length restrictions on information fields, but it does require that the length be some multiple of eight bits. The receiving station knows where the first byte of the information field begins because it always immediately follows the control field. The information field can contain any desired bit configurations other than the flag configuration (0111 1110). Chapter 14 describes the bit-stuffing technique that is used to allow data to be transmitted that might contain the flag configuration.

- **Frame Check Sequence (FCS) Field.** The frame check sequence field contains a 16-bit cyclic redundancy check (CRC) value that is used for error detection. Error checking is performed on all bits in the transmission frame, including the bits in the address field, the control field, and the information field.

- **Ending Flag Field.** Another flag field (0111 1110) terminates each SDLC transmission frame.

allows a single frame to be recognized by all secondary stations on the link, or it might be a group address that is recognized by a specific group of secondary stations.

SUMMARY

The purpose of a data link control protocol is to control the transfer of blocks of data without error between two devices that are connected to the same physical link. SDLC is the primary data link protocol used with SNA. An SDLC link consists of at least two link stations, one in each node, and the link connection between them. A link connection often consists of two modems and the physical connection between them. Link stations that are able to communicate with each other are known as adjacent link stations. There are two types of link stations: primary link stations, which initiate and control the exchange of message units, and secondary link stations. The primary station uses a process called polling to notify a secondary link station that it can send data. There are four possible link configurations: point to point, multipoint, loop, and hub go-ahead. Each secondary link station has a set of receive addresses that determine which messages it recognizes and accepts. Having a set of receive addresses allows a message to be sent to a group of secondary link stations.

An SDLC link connection can be in one of four states: active, idle, transient, or disconnected. The message unit that is transmitted over an SDLC link is called a frame. A frame consists of a three-byte header, a variable-length data field, and a three-byte trailer. The header contains a beginning flag field, an address field, and a control field. The data field can contain either control information or a basic transmission unit (BTU) that is passed down from the path control layer. The trailer contains a frame check sequence field and an ending flag field.

14 SDLC FRAMES

A considerable amount of control information must be carried in each frame in order to meet the objectives of SDLC. Not only must the frames be received by the proper devices, but they must also be sequence-numbered so that multiframe transmissions can take place without the danger that lost frames will be undetected. Frames must carry information to control polling and error detection. Communication must be able to take place on links that have many users as well as those that have just a few. All this must be accomplished with the lowest possible ratio of control information to user data. In this chapter we examine the frame formats and components prescribed by SDLC and see how these frames meet the objectives the SNA system architects have set for SDLC.

SDLC TRANSMISSION FRAMES
Chapter 13 introduced the format of the SDLC transmission frame. This is repeated in Fig. 14.1. SDLC frames can be divided into the two major categories of *commands* and *responses*. A command is a frame that flows from the primary station to one or more secondary stations. A response is a frame that flows from a secondary station to the primary station. Normally, when the primary station sends a command, it expects a response or string of responses in reply. Some commands and responses are used to carry data; others are used to perform control functions. All commands and responses have the same basic format. The following are more detailed descriptions of each field in an SDLC transmission frame.

Beginning Flag Field

A *flag field,* shown in Fig. 14.2, begins each transmission frame. A flag consists of a single byte that has the following bit configuration: 0111 1110. A *bit-*

Figure 14.1   SDLC transmission frame.

stuffing technique, described in detail later in this chapter, guarantees that the only place where six consecutive one bits occurs is in a flag field.

Address Field

The *address field,* shown in Fig. 14.3, is present in all SDLC frames. However, on point-to-point links, the address field is not used and contains binary zeros. When the primary station is transmitting on a multipoint link or a loop, the address field of the frame contains the address of the secondary station that is to receive the message. As discussed in Chapter 13, the address field can address a single secondary station, a group of secondary stations (group function), or all secondary stations (broadcast function). When the secondary station is transmitting, the address field contains the address of the station that is originating the frame. In this case the destination is implied, since the destination of a message originated by a secondary station is always the primary station.

The address field normally consists of a single byte. However, an extension to the SDLC architecture, seldom implemented, allows for a multiple-byte address field. When the architectural extension is used, a one in bit position 7 of an address byte indicates that another address byte follows. Bit position 7 of the final address byte contains a zero. This allows for an address field of any desired size, as shown in Fig. 14.4.

Control Field

The control field, normally a single byte in length, defines what type of information is carried by the frame. An extension to the architecture (which is implemented more frequently than multiple-byte addresses) allows for frames that carry two-byte control fields. There are three basic types of SDLC frames; each has a different control field layout (see Fig. 14.5). The specific interpretation of

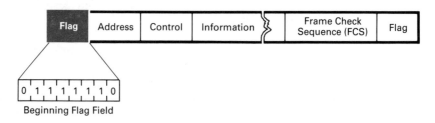

Figure 14.2   Beginning flag field.

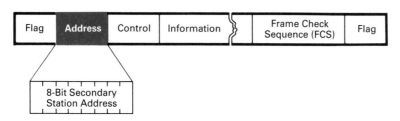

Figure 14.3   Address field.

the control field bits is discussed later in this chapter. The following are brief descriptions of each frame type.

- **Information Frames.** The primary function of an information frame (I-frame) is to carry user data. However, I-frames also carry some control information.

- **Supervisory Frames.** Supervisory frames (S-frames) are used to carry information necessary for supervisory control functions rather than user information. These functions include requesting transmission, requesting a temporary suspension of transmission, and performing control functions such as requesting polls, acknowledging the receipt of I-frames, and reporting on status. Normal, routine transmission over an SDLC link involves only I-frames and S-frames.

- **Unnumbered Frames.** Unnumbered frames (U-frames) are sometimes used to carry data but are most often used for special functions such as performing initialization procedures, controlling the data link, and invoking diagnostic sequences.

Information Field

The information field in an SDLC transmission frame is used to carry the data portion of the message. As shown in Fig. 14.6, the information field can be of any desired length, as long as the size is a multiple of eight bits, and the size can be zero bytes for some commands and responses. Although the architecture itself defines no maximum length, a particular device may set limits on the size

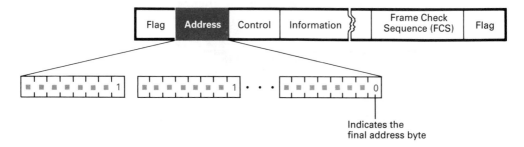

Figure 14.4   Multiple-byte address field.

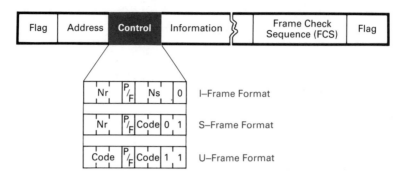

Figure 14.5 Control field.

of the information field based on the size of the buffer that is available. The content of the information field is of no significance to SDLC and is interpreted by higher SNA layers. It can consist of any sequence of bytes, using any desired character set.

Frame Check Sequence Field

The frame check sequence field contains a 16-bit cyclic redundancy check (CRC) value that is used for error detection. This two-byte sequence, shown in Fig. 14.7, is generated by the sending station. The address, control, and information fields are all included in the CRC computation.

Ending Flag Field

The end of the SDLC frame is marked by another flag field that contains the same bit configuration as the beginning flag field (0111 1110). The ending flag field is shown in Fig. 14.8.

TRANSPARENT OPERATION

SDLC always operates in *transparent mode,* meaning that any desired bit configurations can be used in the data carried in the frame's information field. Transparency is easier to achieve in SDLC than in character-oriented protocols, such

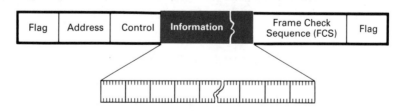

Figure 14.6 Information field.

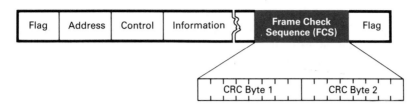

Figure 14.7   Frame Check Sequence field.

as the binary-synchronous protocol. This is primarily because the bit configurations for control functions, such as the functions performed by the address byte and the control byte, always appear in a fixed place in the frame. Therefore, any desired bit configuration can appear in any of the fields of the frame without confusion. The only requirement for achieving full transparency is to ensure that flag bytes (bytes that contain six consecutive one bits) are not transmitted in any part of the frame other than in the beginning and ending flag field positions. If a flag field appeared anywhere else in the frame, stations would have no way of knowing where a frame begins and ends. If the protocol is to be fully transparent, however, frames must be capable of containing bit sequences of any desired bit configuration, including bytes that contain the flag configuration (0111 1110). To handle data streams that contain any desired bit configuration, SDLC uses a technique called *zero-bit insertion* (sometimes called *bit stuffing*).

Zero-Bit Insertion

In transmitting the data between a beginning and ending flag, the transmitter inserts an extra zero bit into the data stream each time it detects a sequence of five one bits. The transmitter turns off the zero-bit insertion mechanism when it transmits an actual beginning or ending flag. In this way no consecutive sequence of six one bits is ever transmitted except when an actual flag is sent over the link.

Zero-Bit Deletion

A complementary technique called *zero-bit deletion* is used by the receiver in removing the extra zero bits. Whenever the receiver detects five one bits fol-

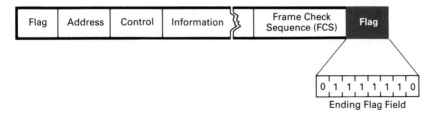

Figure 14.8   Ending flag field.

lowed by a zero bit, it discards the zero bit, thus restoring the bit stream to its original value. The bit-stuffing technique ensures that six one bits in a row will never occur except in a flag field. When the receiver detects six consecutive one bits, it knows that it has received an actual flag field.

SYNCHRONIZATION   In addition to making transparency possible, bit stuffing also helps SDLC stations maintain synchronization. Most SDLC stations use a technique called *non-return-to-zero encoding* (NRZI) in transmitting data. This technique is also sometimes called *zero-complemented differential encoding*. With this technique, a transition on the line occurs only when a zero bit is transmitted. Each time a one bit is transmitted, the line remains in the same state. The NRZI transmission technique is shown in Fig. 14.9. Since the receiving station is in synchronization with the sending station, it knows where each bit is in relation to time. Transitions are interpreted as zero bits; the lack of a transition is interpreted as a one bit.

Since transitions occur only for zero bits, very long sequences of one bits can cause long periods of time during which no transitions occur on the line. Zero-bit insertion ensures that no more than five consecutive one bits will ever be transmitted (except when transmitting a flag). This ensures that a transition will occur at least every five or six bit times, making it easy for the stations to stay in synchronization.

FRAME AND CONTROL FIELD FORMATS   The three types of SDLC frames, while all conforming to the same general format, have format variations that allow them to be used for different purposes.

I-Frame Format

Figure 14.10 illustrates the format of I-frames and shows how the control field bits are interpreted. Bit positions 6 and 7 in the control field identify the type of frame. An I-frame always has a zero in bit position 7. The remainder of the bits in the I-frame control field are used to contain a receive count, a send count, and a poll/final bit. With one-byte control fields, the two three-bit count fields allow up to seven frames to be sent between acknowledgments. Chapter 15 discusses how the two count fields are used. The poll/final bit is used for two different purposes depending on whether the transmitting station is the primary station or a secondary station. A primary station turns on the poll/final bit to

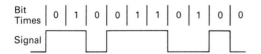

Figure 14.9 NRZI encoding. 0 bit = transition. 1 bit = lack of transition.

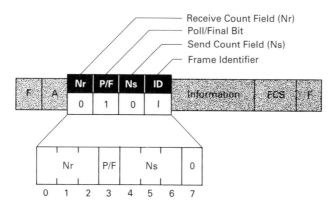

Figure 14.10   I-Frame control field format.

indicate that the primary station is *polling* the addressed secondary station. A secondary station turns on the poll/final bit to indicate that the frame is the *last frame* it intends to transmit back to the primary station.

S-Frame Format

Figure 14.11 illustrates the format of S-frames showing the control field layout. Notice that S-frames do not carry information fields. (No information field is a valid format variation since the information field is defined as consisting of any number of bytes, including no bytes.) When bit position 7 of the control field is one, bit position 6 further identifies the frame as being either an S-frame or a U-frame. 01 in bit positions 6 and 7 identifies the frame as an S-frame. The remainder of the bits in the S-frame control byte are interpreted as containing a receive count, a poll/final bit, and a two-bit function code. The function code bits identify the type of command or response the frame represents.

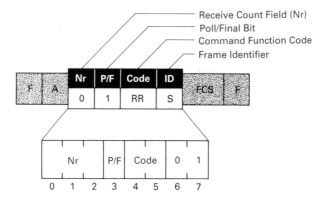

Figure 14.11   S-Frame control field format.

U-Frame Format

Figure 14.12 shows the format of U-frames, showing details for the control field. Some U-frame commands and responses have information fields; others do not. A 11-bit configuration in bit positions 6 and 7 identifies the frame as a U-frame. Bit position 3 is the poll/final bit. The remainder of the bits are interpreted as function code bits. The function code bits in a U-frame identify the type of command the frame represents. The five function code bits allow for up to 32 different bit configurations. A particular function code bit configuration can have a different interpretation depending on whether the frame contains a *command* that is being sent from the primary station to a secondary station or a *response* that is being sent from a secondary station back to the primary station. Thus the five bits can be used to represent up to 64 different functions, only some of which are actually used in SDLC.

TWO-BYTE CONTROL FIELDS   The SDLC architecture defines an additional mode that supports two-byte control fields. This mode is hardware-defined, and both the transmitting station and the receiving station must be operating in this mode in order for frame control fields to be properly formatted and interpreted. Figure 14.13 shows the formats of I-frame, S-frame, and U-frame control fields when the stations are operating in two-byte control field mode. Notice that in this mode, seven bits are used for count fields rather than three. This mode allows up to 127 frames to be sent before the transmitting station must wait for an acknowledgment. Two-byte control fields are often used over channels with long propagation delays, such as satellite links. The differences between one-byte and two-byte control field mode are discussed in detail in Chapter 15.

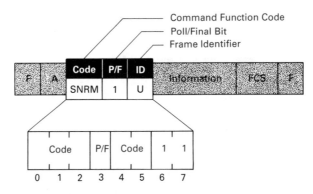

Figure 14.12   U-Frame control field format.

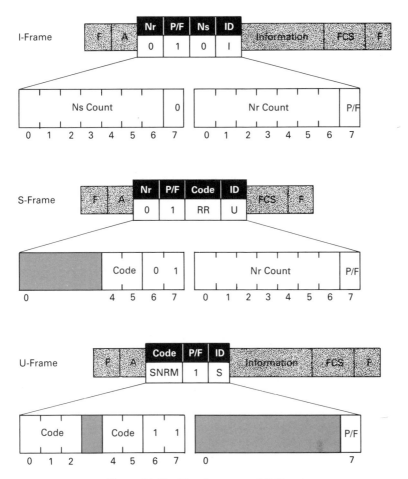

Figure 14.13 Two-byte control fields.

SUMMARY

The beginning flag field consists of a single byte with the configuration 0111 1110. The address field contains binary zeros on a point-to-point link and contains the link address of the secondary station for multipoint links or loops. The control field defines the frame type: I-frame, S-frame, or U-frame. If bit 7 is a zero, it is an I-frame. If bits 6 and 7 are 01, it is an S-frame. If bits 6 and 7 are 11, it is a U-frame. The information field can be any length that is a multiple of eight bits and can contain any sequence of bytes. The frame check sequence field contains a 16-bit CRC value that is used for error detection. The ending flag field consists of another byte with the configuration 0111 1110.

With zero-bit insertion, an extra zero bit is inserted into the data stream whenever a sequence of five one bits is detected. On the receiving side, whenever five one bits are followed by a zero bit, the zero bit is removed. In this way no consecutive sequence of six one bits is transmitted except as part of the beginning and ending flag fields.

The primary function of an I-frame is to carry user data. Its control field contains a receive count, a send count, and a poll/final bit, in addition to the zero bit that identifies it as an I-frame. S-frames are used to carry information necessary for supervisory control functions, such as requesting polls, acknowledging receipt of I-frames, reporting on status, or requesting temporary suspension of transmission. The S-frame control field contains a receive count, a poll/final bit, and a two-bit function code, as well as the 01 bits that identify it. U-frames are used for initialization procedures, to control the data link, and to invoke diagnostic sequences. The U-frame control field contains a poll/final bit and five function code bits, as well as the 11 bits that identify it.

15 SDLC DATA FLOW

This chapter examines the flow of frames that takes place between primary and secondary stations over an SDLC data link. It begins by examining the simplest case involving an acknowledgment after the receipt of each frame. After that, more complex data flows involving multiple frames between acknowledgments and various types of error situations are presented. Finally, the various types of commands and responses that are carried in S-frames and U-frames are examined.

ACKNOWLEDGMENTS One of the primary responsibilities of any data link protocol is to detect errors and, when an error is detected, to cause retransmission of the affected frames. To achieve this, frames that are transmitted require acknowledgments from the receiving station indicating whether or not frames were received correctly. In earlier data link protocols a sending machine needed to receive an acknowledgment for each frame it transmitted before it could send the next one. This procedure slowed the traffic somewhat, especially on half-duplex links, or when there was a lengthy propagation delay or long line turnaround time. In today's data communication environment, with more extensive use of high-performance links, it is particularly desirable to avoid frame-by-frame acknowledgment. SDLC's capability for transmitting multiple frames before requiring an acknowledgment is one of the primary reasons that SDLC can achieve higher throughput than earlier protocols, such as binary-synchronous. With one-byte control fields, SDLC allows a transmitting station to send up to seven frames to any given station before an acknowledgment is required. With two-byte control fields, up to 127 frames can be transmitted between acknowledgments.

SEND AND RECEIVE COUNTS

To ensure that no frames are lost and that all frames are properly acknowledged during a transmission, SDLC employs a system of *sequence numbering* to control frame transmission. All SDLC stations maintain counters that keep track of two counts: a *send count* (Ns) and a *receive count* (Nr) (see Fig. 15.1). These two internal counters are used to update the count fields in the control byte of the I-frames and S-frames that the station transmits. Figure 15.2 shows the format of an SDLC I-frame and an SDLC S-frame with some sample control field contents. I-frames carry both an Ns and an Nr field; S-frames carry only an Nr field. The transmitter always keeps track of how many frames it has sent, and the receiver keeps track of how many frames it has received. We will look now at how the send count and receive count fields are used to monitor and control data transmission.

DATA FLOW FOR INDIVIDUAL ACKNOWLEDGMENTS

The first data flow we will examine is a simple one in which individual I-frames are sent by the primary station, each of which is acknowledged by an S-frame from the secondary station. This data flow is illustrated in Box 15.1. The numbers in the illustration in Box 15.1 correspond to the step numbers in the description of the data flow. For simplicity, the steps in the data flow omit the FCS field verification step for each frame. Assume that this step is performed after each frame is received and that no transmission errors occur in this data flow. Each I-frame that the primary station sends has the poll/final bit set. This indicates that the secondary station must send a response back to the primary station after each I-frame is received. The process described in Box 15.1 can continue as long as the primary station desires to send frames to the secondary station using this procedure. A similar procedure can be used in sending I-frames in the opposite direction.

Nr AND Ns COUNT FIELD VALUES

Notice in Box 15.1 that the Nr counter in the primary station and the Ns counter in the secondary station remain set to zero throughout the entire process. This is because frames are being transmitted only in one direction. The information flowing back from the secondary station to the primary station consists only of S-frame acknowledgments. Only I-frames cause the Ns and Nr counts to be

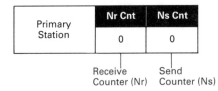

Figure 15.1   Send and receive counters.

I–Frame Format

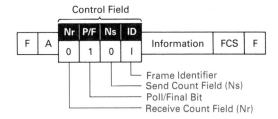

S–Frame Format

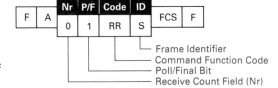

Figure 15.2   SDLC I-frame and S-frame formats.

updated. Since only S-frames are flowing from the secondary station to the primary station, the Ns count in the secondary station and the Nr count in the primary station remain the same. In more complex data flows, in which the receipt of I-frames by one station are acknowledged by I-frames flowing in the opposite direction, both sets of counters are updated and cause message sequencing to be checked in both directions.

MULTIPLE FRAMES BETWEEN ACKNOWLEDGMENTS   When individual acknowledgments are required, the sending station turns on the poll/final bit in each I-frame, indicating that the secondary station should send an acknowledgment after the receipt of each frame. However, individual acknowledgments are not required. If the poll/final bit is off in a received I-frame, the receiving station does not reply with an acknowledgment; instead it simply waits for the next frame. The next data flow, shown in Box 15.2, demonstrates how a sequence of I-frames can be sent with an acknowledgment requested only after the entire sequence of frames is sent. In this data flow the primary station sends a sequence of three I-frames, only the last of which has the poll/final bit set. The secondary station replies with an S-frame only after the third I-frame is received. This data flow again assumes that the FCS field value is correct after each frame is received. Notice

BOX 15.1   Individual acknowledgments

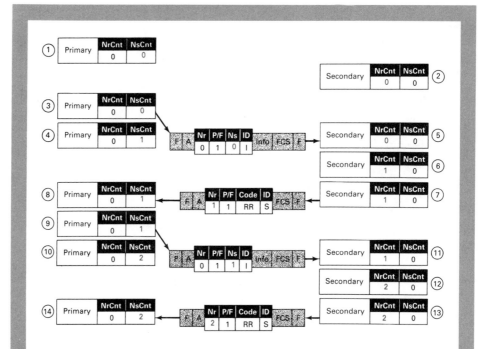

1. The primary station begins with its Ns counter set to zero indicating that the next frame it will *send* is frame 0. The value in the sender's Nr counter is not significant in this example, and its value is shown as 0.

2. The secondary station begins with its Nr counter set to zero, indicating that the next frame it expects to *receive* is frame 0. The value in the receiver's Ns counter is not significant in this example, and its value is also shown as 0.

3. The primary station formats an I-frame by setting the Ns and Nr count fields in the I-frame to the values in its internal counters (both currently 0) and turning on the poll/final bit. It then transmits frame 0. A 1 in the poll/final bit in a *command* (a frame sent from the primary station to a secondary station) indicates that the primary station is requesting a response to this frame.

4. The primary station adds 1 to its internal Ns counter, indicating that the next frame it will send is frame 1.

5. The secondary station receives frame 0. It compares the Ns count field in frame 0 with the value in its internal Nr counter. These two values are the same, which indicates that frame sequencing is correct.

BOX 15.1 *(Continued)*

6. The secondary station adds 1 to its internal Nr counter, indicating that the next frame it expects to receive is frame 1.

7. Since the poll/final bit in the received I-frame was on, the secondary station formats an S-frame as a positive acknowledgment for frame 0 and transmits the S-frame back to the sender. The secondary station turns on the poll/final bit in the S-frame response. A value of 1 in the poll/final bit in a *response* (a frame sent from a secondary station back to the primary station) indicates that this is the last frame the secondary station intends to send. The Nr field in the S-frame indicates to the primary station that the next frame the secondary station expects to receive is frame 1. It is important to note here that only the transmission of I-frames causes the Nr and Ns internal counter values to be updated; counter values are not updated when transmitting S-frames.

8. The primary station receives the S-frame acknowledgment and compares the received S-frame Nr field value with the value contained in its own internal Ns count value. Since they both contain the value 1, the primary station assumes that frame sequencing is correct and that frame 0 was successfully received by the secondary station.

9. The primary station formats a second I-frame by setting the Ns and Nr count fields to the value in its internal counters and again turning on the poll/final bit. It then transmits frame 1.

10. The primary station adds 1 to its internal Ns counter, indicating that the next frame it will send is frame 2.

11. The secondary station receives frame 1. It compares the Ns count field in the received frame with the value in its internal Nr counter. These two values are now both 1, indicating that it has received the proper frame.

12. The secondary station adds 1 to its internal Nr counter, indicating that the next frame it expects to receive is frame 2.

13. Since the poll/final bit in the received frame was again on, the secondary station formats another S-frame as a positive acknowledgment for frame 1 and transmits it back to the primary station. The Nr field in the S-frame indicates to the primary station that the next frame the secondary station expects to receive is frame 2.

14. The primary station receives the S-frame acknowledgment and compares the received S-frame Nr field value with the value contained in its own internal Ns counter. Since they both contain 2, the primary station assumes that frame sequencing is correct and that frame 1 was successfully received by the secondary station.

BOX 15.2   Multiple frames with no acknowledgment

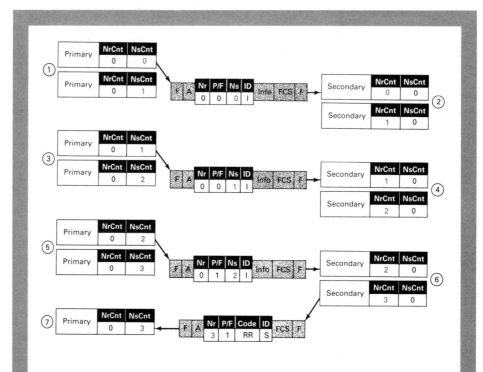

1. The primary station formats an I-frame by setting the Ns field to the current value of its Ns counter and turning off the poll/final bit. It then transmits frame 0 to the secondary station and updates its Ns count.

2. The secondary station receives the I-frame and compares the Ns field value to its Nr count. Since they are both 0, frame sequencing is correct. Since the poll/final bit was off, the secondary station simply updates its internal Nr counter and waits for the next frame.

3. The primary station formats frame 1 and sends it, again with the poll/final bit off, and updates its Ns count.

4. The secondary station receives frame 1 and compares the Ns field value with its internal Nr counter value. Since they are now both 1, frame sequencing is again correct. The poll/final bit was off, so the secondary station updates its Nr counter and waits for the next frame.

5. The primary station formats frame 2, sends it, and updates its Ns count. This time it turns on the poll/final bit, requesting a response from the secondary station.

BOX 15.2 *(Continued)*

6. The secondary station receives frame 2, verifies the Ns field value, updates its Nr counter, and examines the poll/final bit. Since the poll/final bit is on, the secondary station sends an S-frame acknowledgment back to the secondary station.

7. The primary station receives the S-frame acknowledgment and compares the received S-frame Nr field value with the value contained in its internal Ns counter. Since they both contain the value 3, the primary station assumes that frame sequencing is correct and that the three frames it sent were all successfully received by the secondary station.

again that the Nr count in the primary station and the Ns count in the secondary station remain unchanged, since no I-frames are flowing from the secondary station back to the primary.

ONE-BYTE AND TWO-BYTE CONTROL FIELDS   Chapter 14 introduced the fact that an SDLC station can operate with either one-byte or two-byte control fields. When a data link uses one-byte control fields, it is in *modulo-8* operation; when a data link uses two-byte control fields, it is in *modulo-128* operation. Figure 15.3 shows the I-frame control field formats for both one-byte and two-byte control fields. The following sections describe the differences between modulo-8 and modulo-128 operation.

Modulo-8 Operation

When stations operate in single-byte control field mode, Nr and Ns field values consist of three-bit values. Three-bit count values allow Nr and Ns values to range from 0 through 7. Modulo-8 operation allows a sending station to transmit up to seven frames in sequence before it must turn on the poll/final bit and request an acknowledgment.

Modulo-128 Operation

When stations operate in two-byte control field mode, Nr and Ns field values consist of seven-bit values, allowing values from 0 through 127. Modulo-128

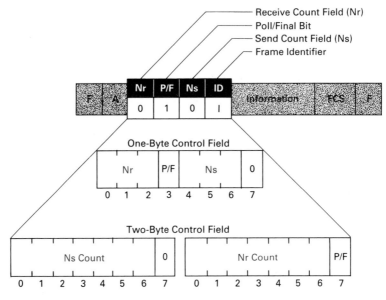

Figure 15.3   I-Frame format.

operation allows a sending station to transmit up to 127 frames in sequence before the poll/final bit must be turned on to request an acknowledgment. Stations use modulo-128 operation when channels with long propagation delays, such as satellite channels, are employed. It is important to note that an SDLC station must be specifically designed to operate with two-byte control fields, and modulo-128 operation is not supported by all SDLC stations. Also, if a primary station is operating with two-byte control fields, all secondary stations on that data link must also be capable of modulo-128 operation and must also use two-byte control fields.

Trade-offs

In deciding how many frames should be transmitted between acknowledgments, the hardware or software designer must evaluate several trade-offs. When channels with high error rates are used, relatively few frames should be sent between acknowledgments. This is because the frame-sequencing scheme only enables the receiver to inform the sender of the last frame that was received correctly. If an error occurs early in the transmission of a long sequence of frames, all the frames that are sent after the error is detected will have to be retransmitted. If a channel with a low error rate but with long propagation delay is used, a relatively large number of frames should be sent between acknowledgments, because the turnaround time required to send a high percentage of acknowledgments can cause line utilization to be unacceptably low.

SUPERVISORY FRAMES

In earlier data flows, S-frames were used as positive acknowledgments. In actual operation, S-frames can be used in a variety of additional ways to control the operation of the data link. Figure 15.4 shows the frame format for S-frames showing the control field layout for both modulo-8 and modulo-128 operation. Notice that the two bits provided for the function code allow up to four different S-frame commands and four different S-frame responses. Box 15.3 describes the three S-frame commands and responses that SDLC supports.

The next sections examine typical data flows that involve the transmission of S-frames in both directions along the data link. These flows illustrate the use of S-frames that carry the Receiver Ready (RR) and Receiver Not Ready (RNR) command/response codes.

RR POLLING, NORMAL FLOW

The RR-polling data flow is used to exchange messages between the primary and the secondary station.

With RR polling, the primary station begins by sending to the secondary station a frame that has the poll/final bit set. A frame sent

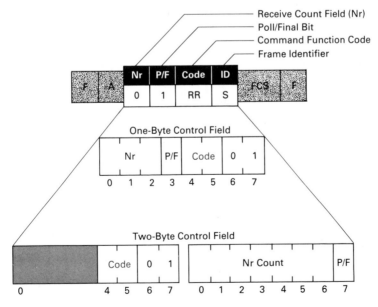

Figure 15.4 S-Frame format.

BOX 15.3 S-frame commands and responses

- **Receiver Ready (RR).** Used as a command by the primary station for polling and as a response by the secondary station to indicate that the receiver is ready to accept additional I-frames

- **Receiver Not Ready (RNR).** Used to indicate that the secondary station is not able to accept additional frames from the primary station

- **Reject (REJ).** Used to indicate certain types of errors in the Ns count field

BOX 15.4 RR polling, normal flow

BOX 15.4 *(Continued)*

1. The primary station sends an S-frame RR command to the secondary station asking if it has data to send. Notice that the poll/final bit is on, indicating that this is a poll.

2. The secondary station has a single I-frame of data to send, so it transmits it back to the primary station. Notice that the poll/final bit is on, indicating that this is the last I-frame the secondary station wishes to send.

3. The primary station acknowledges the receipt of the single I-frame and sends another S-frame RR command. Again the poll/final bit is on, asking the secondary station if it has any more data to send.

4. The secondary station this time responds by transmitting a sequence of three I-frames. Notice that the poll/final bit is on only in the last of the three I-frames. Also notice how the Ns count is updated after each frame is transmitted to control frame sequencing.

5. The primary station this time has data of its own to send, and it responds by transmitting four I-frames. Again the poll/final bit is on only in the last frame sent, which serves the same purpose as the S-frame RR-command poll and asks the secondary station if it has any data to send.

by the primary station that has the poll/final bit set performs the function of a poll, which asks the secondary station if it has data to send. If the secondary does not have data to send, it replies with a negative acknowledgment; if it has data to send, it sends the data in the form of I-frames. Box 15.4 shows a typical RR-polling data exchange. The receiving station is shaded in each step of the flow. Each poll that the primary station initiates is followed by a response from the secondary station. The data flow shown in Box 15.4 illustrates how RR polling can be used to control the transfer of data in both directions on a point-to-point data link.

The next three data flows show the data exchanges that take place when various types of errors occur. Each type of error causes a slightly different exchange of I-frames and S-frames.

RR POLLING, RECEIVER NOT READY

In the data flow illustrated in Box 15.5, an error occurs that causes a receiver-not-ready condition in the receiving station. A receiver-not-ready condition may be caused by some event such as a station's internal buffer filling up. This may cause one or more received frames to be discarded by the receiver, creating a mismatch between the receiver's Nr counter and the sender's Ns counter. In this data flow the secondary station signals that it is not ready by transmitting an RNR S-frame to the primary station. This indicates that the receiver-not-ready condition has occurred, and the Nr count value in

BOX 15.5   RR polling, receiver not ready

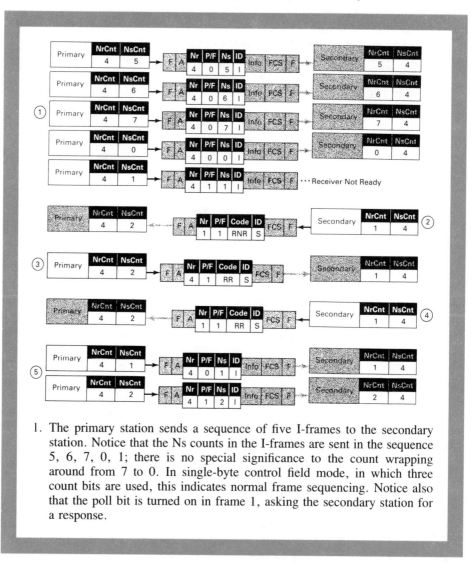

1. The primary station sends a sequence of five I-frames to the secondary station. Notice that the Ns counts in the I-frames are sent in the sequence 5, 6, 7, 0, 1; there is no special significance to the count wrapping around from 7 to 0. In single-byte control field mode, in which three count bits are used, this indicates normal frame sequencing. Notice also that the poll bit is turned on in frame 1, asking the secondary station for a response.

BOX 15.5 *(Continued)*

2. The secondary station receives the frames correctly but was not able to accept the final frame, possibly due to a buffer overflow. It responds by sending a *receiver not ready* (RNR) S-frame, indicating in the Nr count field that the next frame it expects to receive is frame 1. Since the primary station has already transmitted frame 1, this indicates that the secondary station was able to handle frames 5, 6, 7, and 0 but that it would like frame 1 sent again.

3. The primary station responds by issuing another poll request that, in effect, asks the secondary station if it is now ready.

4. The secondary station is now ready, and it responds to the poll with a *receiver ready* (RR) S-frame, again indicating that the next frame it expects to receive is frame 1.

5. The primary station resets its internal Ns count field back to 1 and then retransmits frame 1, followed by any additional I-frames it may have to send.

that frame indicates with which frame retransmission should begin. The primary station replies with another RR S-frame poll, which asks the secondary station if it is now ready to transmit. If the secondary station replies positively, the primary station retransmits the frames that the secondary station missed.

FRAME SEQUENCING ERROR

The S-Frame Reject (REJ) command or response is issued by a station that detects an error in frame sequencing. A frame sequencing error can occur when a transmission error causes one or more frames to be completely missed by the receiving station. A typical data flow associated with a frame sequence error is illustrated in Box 15.6. Here the secondary station has missed a frame, and it sends to the primary station a REJ command that tells the primary station with which frame retransmission should begin. The primary station then immediately responds by retransmitting the requested frames.

FCS ERROR

In all the foregoing data flows, we have assumed that the CRC value contained in the FCS field of each received frame matches the calculated CRC value that the receiving station gen-

BOX 15.6   RR polling, frame reject

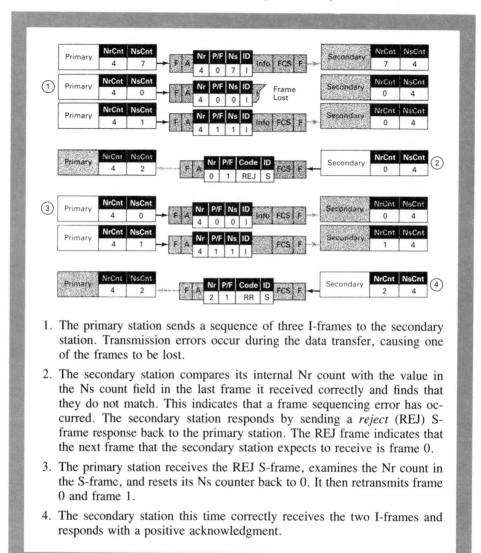

1. The primary station sends a sequence of three I-frames to the secondary station. Transmission errors occur during the data transfer, causing one of the frames to be lost.

2. The secondary station compares its internal Nr count with the value in the Ns count field in the last frame it received correctly and finds that they do not match. This indicates that a frame sequencing error has occurred. The secondary station responds by sending a *reject* (REJ) S-frame response back to the primary station. The REJ frame indicates that the next frame that the secondary station expects to receive is frame 0.

3. The primary station receives the REJ S-frame, examines the Nr count in the S-frame, and resets its Ns counter back to 0. It then retransmits frame 0 and frame 1.

4. The secondary station this time correctly receives the two I-frames and responds with a positive acknowledgment.

erates. When transmission errors occur while a frame is being sent, these values will not match. The receiving station must ask for that frame, and any sent after it, to be retransmitted. A typical data flow associated with this type of error situation is illustrated in Box 15.7. This time the error occurs while the secondary station is transmitting I-frames to the primary station. After the complete sequence of frames has been received, the primary station sends an RR S-frame poll that indicates the number of the frame with which the secondary station should begin retransmission.

FULL-DUPLEX
OPERATION

Prior to the use of distributed processing and computer networks, half-duplex operation of physical links was common and full-duplex operation was exceptional. However, with complex networks, such as those that are often implemented with SNA, it is desirable to have data flowing in both directions at once on many of the physical links. Figure 15.5 shows how an SDLC data link operates in full-duplex mode. This rather complex example shows the middle of a transmission sequence in which data messages are traveling in both directions. The user information flowing in one direction is independent of the data flow in the other. The vertical dimension represents time, and the arrows represent the frames that are flowing between the two stations.

We can assume that the transmission sequence shown in Fig. 15.5 has been going on for some time, since the sequence numbers at the beginning (top) of the sequence are not set at zero. The I-frame that is being transmitted from the secondary station at the top of the illustration has a send sequence number (Ns) of 2 and a receive sequence number (Nr) of 7, so it must have already transmitted at least two frames (Ns = 0 and Ns = 1). Since the receive sequence number of this frame is 7, we can infer that when the secondary station began transmitting this frame, the last *complete* frame that it had received from the primary station had a sequence number of 6. During the course of the transmission of frame Ns = 2, the secondary station received a frame from the primary station with a send sequence number of 7, so the receive sequence number is updated to 0.

There is only one S-frame shown in this example because most of the signals controlling the exchange of information are piggybacked on the information frames. Each I-frame carries both its own send sequence number (Ns) and the receive sequence number (Nr) of the frame to be received next. When an error occurs in frame Ns = 6, transmitted by the secondary station, the primary station detects the error and so does not update its Nr count. It keeps its Nr count at 6 in all the frames that it transmits from that point, indicating that the next frame it expects to receive should have a send sequence number (Ns) of 6. When the secondary station finally receives a frame from the primary station that has the poll/final bit set, it resets its Ns count field to the value contained in that frame (Ns = 6) and begins retransmitting frames from that point.

BOX 15.7   RR polling, FCS error

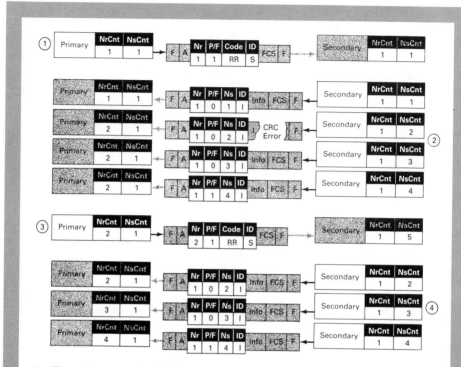

1. The primary station initiates a poll by transmitting an RR S-frame to the secondary station.

2. The secondary station transmits a sequence of four I-frames back to the primary station. In this particular case a transmission error occurs during the transmission of the second frame (frame 2).

3. The primary station detects a CRC error in frame 2 when it compares the value it generates by putting the frame through the CRC algorithm against the value contained in the FCS bytes received with the frame. It then stops updating its Nr count value for that and all subsequent I-frames. After it receives the final frame from the secondary station (frame 4, which has the poll/final bit on), it sends a *receiver ready* (RR) S-frame to the secondary station, indicating that the next frame it expects to receive is frame 2.

4. The secondary station compares the value in the Nr count in the received frame with the value in its own internal Ns counter. Since these do not match, the secondary station resets its Ns counter back to 2 and retransmits frames 2, 3, and 4.

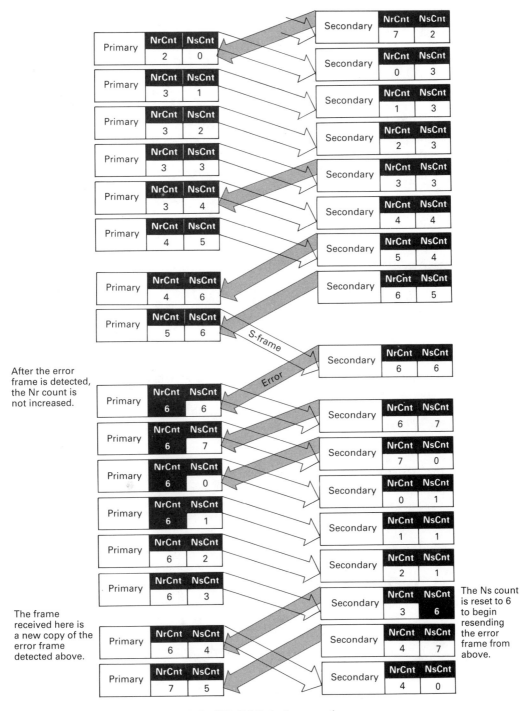

After the error
frame is detected,
the Nr count is
not increased.

The frame
received here is
a new copy of the
error frame
detected above.

The Ns count
is reset to 6
to begin
resending
the error
frame from
above.

Figure 15.5 SDLC full-duplex operation.

MULTIPOINT OPERATION

On multipoint lines such as that illustrated in Fig. 15.6 it is sometimes advantageous to interleave transmissions to several different secondary stations. When this occurs, a primary station does not send a whole group of frames to one secondary station before sending another group to a different secondary. Rather, the primary station may send the first frame in a group to one secondary station, then the first frame in another group to a second secondary, and so on until parts of several frame groups are sent to several different secondary stations. The primary might then proceed to send subsequent frames to each of the secondary stations in turn. This practice is particularly helpful when the speed of the secondary machines is considerably slower than that of either the primary station or the physical link. On a multipoint link that uses full-duplex lines, interleaved transmissions in both directions can occur simultaneously.

U-FRAME COMMANDS

The data flows that we have examined so far are typical of the flows that occur during normal operation of an SDLC data link. In addition to the supervisory functions that are performed by using S-frames, stations also transmit U-frame commands and responses to perform additional functions in initializing and controlling the data link.

Figure 15.7 shows the general format of a U-frame. Some U-frames have information fields and others do not. Notice that the control field in a U-frame has no count fields, thus freeing up five bits for the function code field. A five-bit function code allows for up to 32 commands and 32 responses; however, not all 32-bit configurations are currently used for SDLC functions. Box 15.8 provides brief descriptions of the U-frames currently defined by SDLC.

SDLC OPERATING MODES

A typical use for U-frames is initially to set the operating mode of a secondary station. The following are brief descriptions of secondary station operating modes.

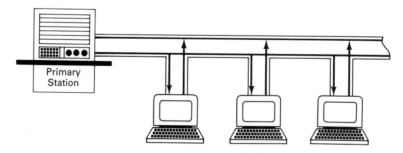

Figure 15.6 Full-duplex multipoint line.

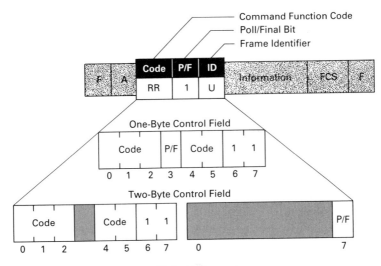

Figure 15.7 U-Frame format.

Initialization Mode

A station is in initialization mode before it actually becomes operational. Special U-frame commands are used to change the station from this mode to normal response mode. The primary station places a secondary station into initialization mode when it is necessary to perform some hardware-specific initialization procedure, such as downloading program code to the secondary station after powering up.

Normal Disconnected Mode

Disconnected modes are needed when a secondary station is to be prevented from appearing on the link unexpectedly while another interchange is taking place. In normal disconnected mode the station is logically and/or physically disconnected from the data link. No frames that carry user data can be transmitted or accepted, although the station may transmit or accept certain types of control frames in order to change the mode, cause the secondary station to identify itself, or poll the secondary station. A secondary station assumes normal disconnected mode at these times:

- When the station is first powered on or is enabled for data link operation
- Following certain types of failures, such as when a power failure occurs
- When a secondary station is first connected to the primary station on a switched line
- After a secondary station receives a Disconnect (DISC) command from the primary station

BOX 15.8 U-frame commands and responses

- **Unnumbered Information (UI).** A UI U-frame is used, as a command or a response, as a vehicle for transmitting information between stations under certain circumstances.

- **Set Normal Response Mode (SNRM).** A SNRM U-frame is sent from the primary station to a secondary station to place the secondary station into the normal SDLC operating mode.

- **Request Disconnect (RD).** An RD U-frame is sent from a secondary station to the primary station to request that the secondary station be disconnected and placed off-line.

- **Disconnect (DISC).** A DISC U-frame is sent from the primary station to a secondary station to place the secondary station off-line.

- **Disconnect Mode (DM).** A DM U-frame is sent from the secondary station to the primary station as a positive acknowledgment to a DISC command to indicate that the secondary station is now in disconnect mode.

- **Request Initialization Mode (RIM).** A RIM U-frame is sent from the secondary station to the primary station to request initialization. A typical initialization procedure may consist of downloading code from the primary station to the secondary station.

- **Set Initialization Mode (SIM).** A SIM U-frame command is sent from the primary station to the secondary station to begin initialization procedures.

- **Unnumbered Acknowledgment (UA).** A UA U-frame is sent from a secondary station to the primary station as a positive acknowledgment to a SNRM, DISC, or SIM command.

- **Frame Reject (FRMR).** Normal flows use the REJ and RR S-frames to indicate problems with frame sequencing and CRC errors. The FRMR command and response are used to indicate abnormal conditions. The command contains bits that indicate the reason for the rejection, such as an invalid or unimplemented command function code, a frame with an information field that should not have one, or a frame with an information field that is too big for the station's buffer.

- **Test (TEST).** TEST U-frames are exchanged as commands and responses in performing diagnostic procedures.

- **Exchange Station Identification (XID).** XID U-frames are sent as commands and responses in exchanging identification sequences between a primary and a secondary station. XID U-frames are most often used on switched lines to identify secondary stations that are requesting connection to the data link.

On a dial-up line, the DISC command causes the secondary station to place itself "on-hook," thus freeing the line for use by some other secondary station. On a leased line the secondary station remains physically attached to the line but is logically disconnected until a Set Normal Response Mode (SNRM) U-frame is received.

Normal Response Mode

Normal response mode is the normal SDLC operating mode. Figure 15.8 shows how a primary station places a secondary station into normal response mode. This is typically done immediately after a secondary station has been powered up or attached to a switched data link. After the SNRM/UA exchange, the secondary station is able to receive S-frames, I-frames, and U-frames in normal operation. In normal response mode one of the stations is identified as the primary station (the one that sends the SNRM command), and the other is defined as the secondary station (the one that receives the SNRM command and responds with the UA response).

When a secondary station is operating in normal response mode, the secondary station transmits data only after receiving a poll from the primary station. As seen earlier, a poll consists of a frame from the primary station that has the poll/final bit on. The secondary station's response may consist of one or more frames, and the station must indicate the last frame of the response. It cannot transmit again until it receives another poll.

SUMMARY

All link stations maintain counters that keep track of a receive count and a send count. When a frame is received, the receiving station compares the send count in the frame with the receive count in its internal receive counter. If both are the same, the frame has been received in the proper sequence. When a receiving station sends an acknowledgment, the sending station compares the receive count in the frame to its internal send counter. If both are the same, the receiving station has received all frames up to that point properly.

With full-duplex operation, messages may be sent in both directions at the same time. With multipoint operation, frames being sent to different secondary

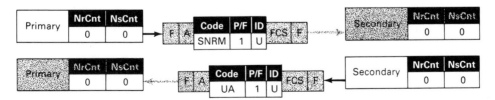

Figure 15.8 Setting normal response mode.

stations may be interleaved. If a one-byte control field is used, up to seven frames can be transmitted before an acknowledgment is requested. With a two-byte control field, up to 127 frames can be transmitted.

S-frames are used to determine if a station is ready to receive, is not ready to receive, or has received a frame with a frame sequencing error or a CRC error. U-frames are used, among other purposes, to change the operating mode of a station. A station is in initialization mode when it is being prepared to become operational. When it is in normal response mode, it is able to receive and transmit S-frames, I-frames, and U-frames as part of normal operation. When a station is in normal disconnected mode, it is logically and/or physically disconnected from the data link.

16 SDLC POLLING AND LOOP OPERATION

Throughout this book we have stated that the primary station initiates communications over a link either by sending an I-frame or by polling a secondary with a receive-ready S-frame. Most of the examples we have shown so far have been relatively simple and have used point-to-point links. The polling that takes place on a multipoint link is somewhat more complex than the data flows we looked at in Chapter 15. On a multipoint link, the polling technique that is most often used is called *roll-call polling*.

ROLL-CALL POLLING
With roll-call polling, the primary station sends a poll request to each secondary station in turn to ask whether that station has something to send. Figure 16.1 shows an example of roll-call polling over a multipoint line in which a primary station polls three secondary stations. The primary first polls secondary station 1 with an RR S-frame. In the example, station 1 has data to send, and it responds with an I-frame. If an acknowledgment is called for, the primary sends an acknowledgment in response to the I-frame. Next the primary polls station 2, which responds with an S-frame indicating that it has no data to send. Finally, the primary station sends a poll request to station 3, which responds with an I-frame.

This process is likely to be repeated over and over again. The primary will continue to poll the stations in sequence, and, when necessary, it will acknowledge frames and send frames to the other stations.

This simple sequence is appropriate when all of the secondary stations on a link transmit with approximately the same frequency. On many links, however, one secondary station transmits more often than another. For example, if

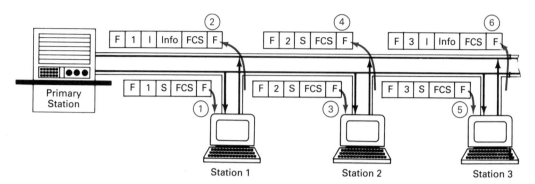

Figure 16.1 Roll-call polling.

station 1 sends more data than the other two stations, the primary station might use the following polling sequence:

1. Poll station 1
2. Poll station 2
3. Poll station 1
4. Poll station 3

The polling sequence is determined by the service order table defined in the NCP in the local communications controller.

LOOP OPERATION
The data flows examined so far have been associated with point-to-point and multipoint links. SDLC has additional U-frame commands that support operation over data links that are configured as loops. A typical SDLC loop is shown in Fig. 16.2. In a loop configuration only the primary station or one of the secondary stations transmits at any one time. The secondary stations transmit sequentially, as required, according to their physical sequence on the data link.

PRIMARY STATION SENDING
When the primary station transmits on the loop, it sends command frames that are directed at an individual secondary station or any group of secondary stations on the loop. Each frame transmitted by the primary station carries in its address field the address of the secondary station or stations to which the command is directed. When the primary station finishes transmitting, it begins transmitting a continuous sequence of one bits, which constitute a "go-ahead" signal.

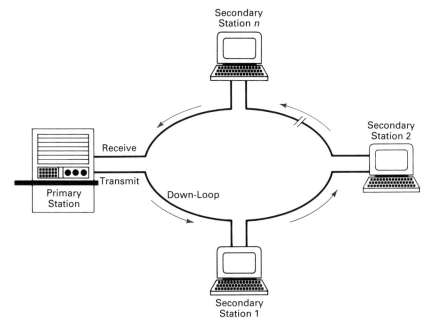

Figure 16.2   SDLC loop.

**SECONDARY
STATION
RECEIVING**

Each secondary station on the loop receives each frame transmitted by the primary station. Each station decodes the address field in the frame and accepts only commands intended for it. Each secondary station also serves as a repeater to relay each frame to the next station on the loop. All frames are relayed to the next station on the loop, including commands that are accepted by the station and those that are not.

**SECONDARY
STATION SENDING**

Before a secondary station can transmit on the loop, it must have received a frame intended for itself that constitutes a poll (poll/final bit on). It then formats its response and waits for the go-ahead signal from the primary station (continuous one bits). When the first secondary station on the loop that has a response detects the go-ahead signal, it converts the seventh of a sequence of seven one bits to a zero bit, thus creating a flag. It then sends its response down the loop to the next station, where it will eventually be relayed to the primary station.

The secondary station that sent the response then begins relaying the go-ahead signal down the loop to the next station. Other secondary stations down the loop each gets a similar opportunity to send a response to the primary sta-

BOX 16.1   Loop U-frame commands

- **Unnumbered Poll (UP).** A UP U-frame is used by the primary station to poll the secondary stations. The poll/final bit indicates whether or not the secondary station must respond.
- **Configure (CFGR).** The Configure U-frame is used as both command and response to perform loop configuration functions. A number of Configure subcommands are defined to control loop operation.
- **Beacon (BCN).** A secondary station begins transmitting a sequence of Beacon U-frame responses when it detects loss of signal at its input. This allows the primary station to locate the source of a problem on the loop.

tion. When the primary station receives frames from all the secondary stations on the loop that responded and again detects the go-ahead signal, it transmits its next frame to one or more secondary stations.

LOOP COMMANDS

Three additional U-frames are defined as commands and/or responses for SDLC loops. These are described in Box 16.1. The primary station on a loop can use the UP U-frame command to poll the secondary stations. Unlike a conventional poll, the UP U-frame can have the poll/final bit set either to zero or to one. When a secondary station receives a UP command addressed to it with the poll/final bit set to zero, that station can decide whether or not it should respond to the poll; if it has no response at that time, it normally does not respond to the poll. If a secondary station receives a UP U-frame with the poll/final bit set to one, that station must respond. The UP command is particularly useful on loops since it reduces the number of negative acknowledgments to polls that would result if normal RR-polling sequences were used on the loop.

SUMMARY

Roll-call polling involves the primary station contacting each secondary station in turn. The polling sequence can be set to any desired configuration. In a loop configuration only the primary station or one of the secondary stations can transmit at any one time. The secondary stations transmit sequentially, as required, according to their physical sequence on the data link. A go-ahead signal is passed around the loop, indicating when a station is allowed to send frames. With loop operations a secondary station is not always required to send an acknowledgment to a polling command, thus reducing transmissions on the loop.

17 PATH CONTROL

As discussed in Chapter 13, the path control network consists of two SNA layers: data link control and path control. In this chapter we will begin a more detailed look at the path control layer (see Fig. 17.1). We will examine the format of the transmission header that is appended by path control to the basic information unit. In Chapter 18 we examine the major services provided by path control. These services include routing data from node to node, segmenting and blocking messages, sequencing messages sent over multiple transmission links, controlling transmission priorities, and handling virtual route pacing. We begin by looking at the message units that pass to and from path control and discussing their relationship to the transmission header.

BASIC TRANSMISSION UNIT FORMAT

Figure 17.2 shows how the basic transmission unit (BTU) is built up as a message flows through the various SNA layers. The message unit that passes back and forth between transmission control and path

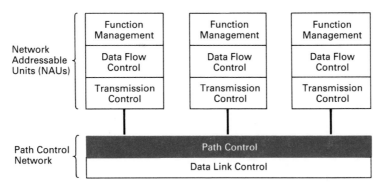

Figure 17.1 The Path Control layer.

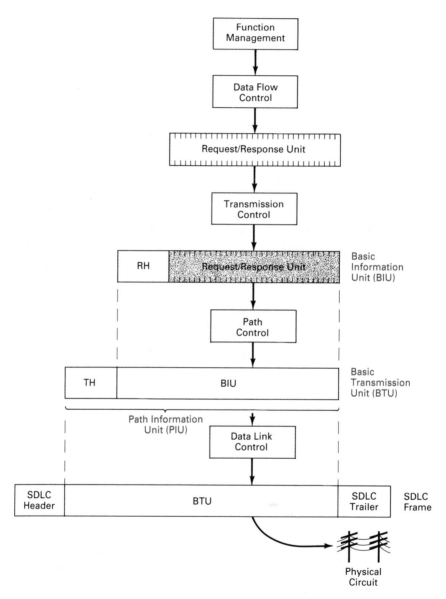

Figure 17.2 BTU format with a single PIU.

control is known as the basic information unit (BIU). Path control appends a
transmission header (TH) to the BIU to form a path information unit (PIU). The
message unit that passes back and forth between path control and data link
control is known as the basic transmission unit (BTU). Although Fig. 17.2
shows that the PIU and the BTU are the same, a BTU can comprise more than
one PIU. This is shown in Fig. 17.3. Data link control adds an SDLC header
and trailer to each BTU, whether it contains one or more PIUs, to form a frame,
which is the message unit transmitted over a data link.

TRANSMISSION   The transmission header in a BTU contains informa-
HEADER FORMATS   tion that allows the retrieval of individual PIUs from
                          the BTUs delivered to the destination path control
layer, as well as information related to routing, transmission priority, and sequencing of messages. The transmission header has several possible formats,
which are often referred to as *format identifier* (FID) types. Each FID type has
a different format. Box 17.1 describes the various transmission header formats
that SNA defines. The information carried in the transmission header depends
on the format of the header that is used. We will next examine the specific
elements that make up the transmission header for each format type.

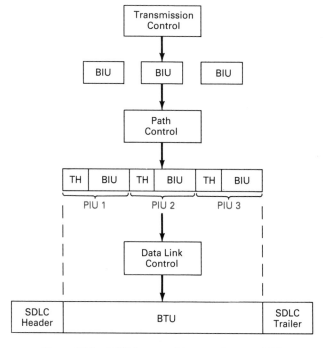

Figure 17.3 BTU format with more than one PIU.

BOX 17.1   Transmission header formats

- **FID0 (TH format 0).** When non-SNA machines are installed in an SNA system, the FID0 transmission header format is used for communication between a non-SNA device and an SNA node.

- **FID1 (TH format 1).** The FID1 TH format is used for communication between two subarea nodes where one or both does not support explicit route and virtual route processing.

- **FID2 (TH format 2).** The FID2 TH format is used for messages passed between a subarea node and a PU type 2 peripheral node. Peripheral nodes use a simplified addressing scheme, so the transmission header for this type of message uses local addresses rather than network addresses. The subarea node provides the boundary function address translation.

- **FID3 (TH format 3).** The FID3 TH format is used for messages passed between a subarea node and a PU type 1 peripheral node. As with FID2, local addresses rather than network addresses are used.

- **FID4 (TH format 4).** The FID4 TH format is used for messages passed between subarea nodes where both nodes are capable of supporting explicit route and virtual route processing.

- **FIDF (TH format F).** The FIDF TH format is used for special messages related to message sequencing that are passed between subarea nodes that support both explicit route and virtual route processing.

FID0 AND FID1 FORMAT

FID0 and FID1 headers use a similar format, which is shown in Fig. 17.4. The architecture of SNA is defined in the *SNA Format and Protocol Reference Manual* through the use of a high-level language called the *Format and Protocol Language* (FAPL), which has many similarities to PL/I. The abbreviations in parentheses that follow the names of the various transmission header fields are the FAPL data names used in the *SNA Format and Protocol Reference Manual* to define these fields. The following are brief descriptions of each of the FID0 and FID1 transmission header fields.

- **Format Identifier.** The first four bits of the first byte in the TH contain the *Format Identifier* (FID0 or FID1) field. This field identifies the header as FID0, FID1, FID2, etc.

- **Mapping Field (MPF).** The next field in a FID0 or FID1 header is a two-bit *Mapping Field,* which indicates whether the BIU has been broken into segments. The four possible bit configurations in this field are interpreted as follows:

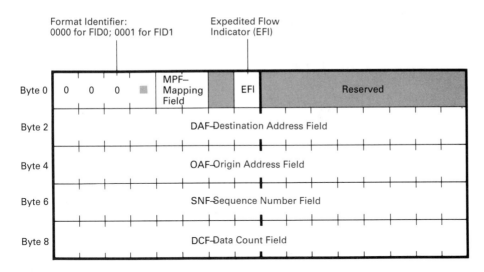

Figure 17.4   FID0 and FID1 TH header format.

00   The message unit is a middle segment of a BIU.
01   The message unit is the last segment of a BIU.
10   The message unit is the first segment of a BIU.
11   The message unit is a complete BIU.

- **Expedited Flow Indicator (EFI).** The next field, which follows a reserved bit, constitutes a one-bit *Expedited Flow Indicator* that specifies that the message is either a *normal flow* message (EFI = 0) or an *expedited flow* message (EFI = 1). Normal flow messages carry user information and some control information, and they are handled by the path control network in the order in which they are received. Expedited messages, in contrast, are used for certain critical control functions. These messages can jump the queues and are ordinarily handled before normal flow messages.

- **Destination Address Field (DAF).** Perhaps the most important field in the TH is the *Destination Address Field,* which carries the address of the message's destination node. For FID0 and FID1 the destination address is a full network address, including a subarea address and an element address.

- **Origination Address Field (OAF).** The transmission header also carries the address of the node at which the message originated. This information is carried in the *Origination Address Field*. The OAF is needed during the process of recovery after a network component has failed. The Origination Address Field is the same size as the Destination Address Field for FID0 and FID1 headers. Together, these two addresses completely identify a session.

- **Sequence Number Field (SNF).** A 16-bit sequence number is passed down to path control from transmission control and is eventually passed back from path control to transmission control in the destination node. This sequence number is carried in the *Sequence Number Field* and is used to ensure that messages are delivered to the receiving node in the same sequence as they were sent by the sending node. Expedited flow messages carry no sequence number, since these messages bypass normal flow queues and are not related to sequenced requests or responses. Instead, they carry a unique identification number that is unrelated to the sequence-numbering scheme of normal data flow.

- **Data Count Field (DCF).** The *Data Count Field* is employed in FID0 and FID1 headers to aid in separating PIUs that have been blocked together into a single BTU. This field indicates the length of each PIU, thus allowing path control to determine whether more than one PIU is contained in a BTU. If path control determines that PIUs have been blocked, the Data Count Field of each PIU is used to locate the transmission header of the next PIU in sequence.

FID2 FORMAT

Figure 17.5 shows the format of the FID2 header. The first byte has the same format as the FID0 and FID1 headers and contains the Format Identifier, Mapping Field, and Expedited Flow Indicator. The FID2 header contains a Destination Address Field and an Origination Address Field, but for the FID2 format the DAF and OAF contain local addresses instead of full network addresses. The FID2 header is used for communication between a subarea node and a PU type 2 peripheral node. The subarea node boundary function translates network addresses into local addresses and creates the FID2 header for messages passing to the PU 2 node. For messages sent by the PU 2 node, the boundary function translates local addresses into full network addresses. The Sequence Number Field serves the same function in the FID2 header as it does in the FID0 and FID1 headers.

FID3 FORMAT

The FID3 header, which is used for communication between subarea nodes and PU type 1 peripheral nodes, is shown in Fig. 17.6. The FID3 header is only two bytes in length. Its first byte contains the same information as the first byte in the previous headers. The second byte contains a *Local Session Identifier* (LSID), which in turn con-

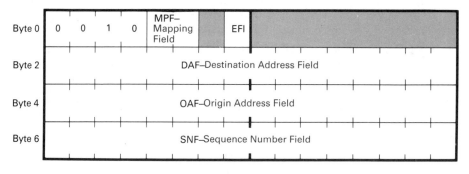

Figure 17.5 FID2 TH header format.

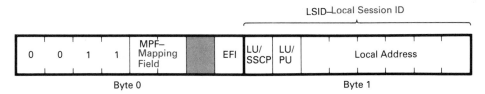

Figure 17.6   FID3 TH header format.

tains a local destination or origin address. A PU 1 node can support up to 64
LUs, so six bits are all that are required to represent the address of the PU or
LU in the PU 1 node involved in the session. The first two bits of the LSID
byte indicate the type of session to which the message relates. The four-bit
configurations are interpreted as follows:

	LU/SSCP	LU/PU
SSCP-to-PU session	0	0
SSCP-to-LU session	0	1
LU-to-LU session	1	1
Reserved	1	0

An LU in a PU 1 node can participate in only one session with another
LU at a time. So by knowing the type of session and the address of the local
LU or PU involved, the boundary function in the subarea node is able to identify
the session partner and to supply full network addresses for both the origin and
destination nodes.

FID4 FORMAT

The FID4 header format is the most complex of the
transmission headers. The header is complex because
of the broad range of functions that are supported by the header, including

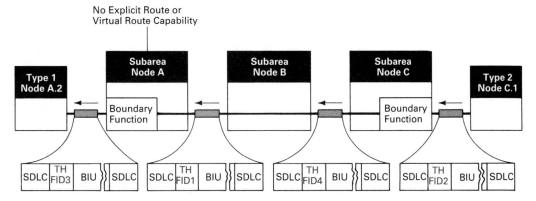

Figure 17.7   Header format conversion.

explicit and virtual routing, message sequencing, segmentation, and blocking. As a message passes from node to node along its route, different transmission headers may be required at different points along the route. Generally, a FID4 header is used when a message passes from one subarea node to another. If a peripheral node is involved at either end, either an FID2 or an FID3 header is used to pass messages to or from the peripheral node. If a subarea node along the route does not support the use of explicit and virtual routes, a FID0 or FID1 header is used for communication with that node as well. Figure 17.7 shows

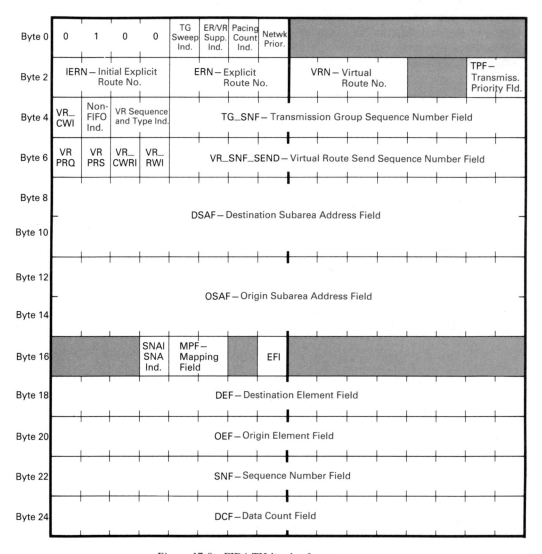

Figure 17.8   FID4 TH header format.

how different header types are used as a message unit passes over its route from an origin node to a destination node.

Figure 17.8 shows the format of the FID4 transmission header. Two of the fields in the FID4 header contain information related to header format conversion. The *ER and VR Support Indicator* (ER—VR—SUPP—IND) field indicates whether any node on the route does not support explicit and virtual routes. A value of 0 indicates that all nodes support them; a value of 1 indicates at least one node on the route does not. The *SNA Indicator* (SNAI) field indicates whether the message originated at or is destined for an SNA node or a non-SNA device. A value of 1 indicates SNA, 0 indicates non-SNA. This field, combined with the ER and VR Support Indicator, determines whether an FID0 or an FID1 header is used when a node not supporting explicit and virtual routes is reached.

ROUTING INFORMATION

Several of the fields in the FID4 contain information related to routing:

- **Explicit Route Number (ERN).** The *Explicit Route Number* field contains the explicit route number associated with the explicit route being used between the sending and receiving nodes in the direction the message is traveling.

- **Virtual Route Number (VRN).** The *Virtual Route Number* field contains the virtual route number used for this session.

- **Initial Explicit Route Number (IERN).** The *Initial Explicit Route Number* field currently contains the same value as the Virtual Route Number field.

- **Destination Subarea Address Field (DSAF) and Destination Element Field (DEF).** The *Destination Subarea Address Field* and the *Destination Element Field* contain the subarea and element addresses, which, when combined, make up the network address of the destination node.

- **Origin Subarea Address Field (OSAF) and Origin Element Field (OEF).** The *Origin Subarea Address Field* and the *Origin Element Field* contain the subarea and element addresses, which, when combined, make up the network address of the originating node.

SEGMENTING AND BLOCKING INFORMATION

The *Mapping Field* (MPF), as described earlier, contains information about the segmenting of a basic information unit. The *Data Count Field* (DCF), also described earlier, contains information used when several PIUs are blocked together into a single BTU.

PRIORITY INFORMATION

The *Transmission Priority Field* (TPF) indicates the transmission priority used for this session. Valid priority values are:

00   Low priority

01   Medium priority

10   High priority

The *Network Priority* (NTWK__PRTY) field indicates a special higher priority used for certain messages related to virtual route pacing. A value of 1 indicates the higher transmission priority. The *Expedited Flow Indicator* (EFI), as described earlier, indicates whether or not the message is to be expedited.

SEQUENCING
INFORMATION
There are several fields involved with sequencing of messages sent across parallel links in a transmission group. These fields are described in Chapter 18 when the topic of transmission group sequencing is discussed. Three fields are involved in the control of message unit sequencing:

- TG Sweep Indicator (TG__SWEEP)
- TG Non-FIFO Indicator (TG__NONFIFO__IND)
- TG Sequence Number Field (TG__SNF)

There are also fields concerned with the sequencing of messages across a virtual route. These fields are also discussed in Chapter 18 in the section on virtual route sequencing:

- Virtual Route Sequence and Type Indicator (VR__SQTI)
- Virtual Route Send Sequence Number (VR__SNF__SEND)

The FID4 header also contains a *Sequence Number Field* (SNF), which, as described earlier, is used either to identify messages or to provide sequence checking at higher SNA layers.

PACING
INFORMATION
Finally, there are several fields related to virtual route pacing. These fields are described in Chapter 18 in the section on virtual route pacing:

- Virtual Route Pacing Count Indicator (VR__PAC__CNT__IND)
- Virtual Route Change Window Indicator (VR__CWI)
- Virtual Route Pacing Request (VRPRQ)
- Virtual Route Pacing Response (VRPRS)
- Virtual Route Change Window Reply Indicator (VR__CWRI)
- Virtual Route Reset Window Indicator (VR__RWI)

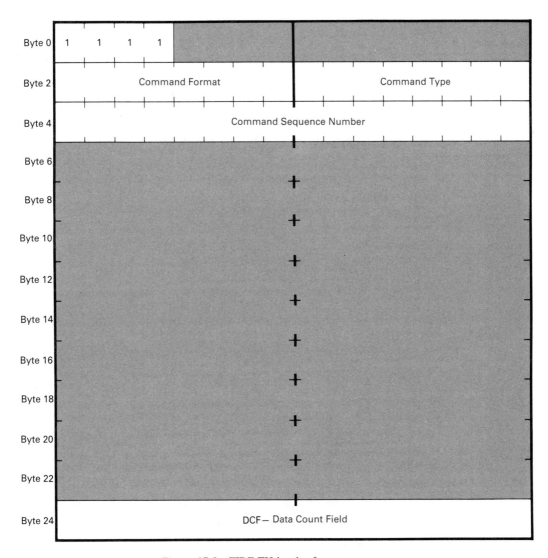

Figure 17.9   FIDF TH header format.

FIDF FORMAT

The FIDF header format is shown in Fig. 17.9. This header is used as part of the transmission group sequencing process and is discussed in the section on that topic in Chapter 18. In addition to the usual Format Identifier and Data Count Field, the FIDF transmission header contains the following fields:

- **Command Format.** Only one *command format* is currently defined, indicated by the value 01.

- **Command Type.** Only one *command type* is currently defined, indicated by the value 01.

- **Command Sequence Number.** The *Command Sequence Number* field identifies a particular message.

Box 17.2 provides a summary of all the various fields that can be found in a transmission header.

BOX 17.2   Transmission header fields

Function	Fields
Identification	Format Identifier
Routing	Destination Subarea Address Field Origin Subarea Address Field Destination Element Field Origin Element Field Explicit Route Number Virtual Route Number Initial Explicit Route Number
Segmenting BIUs	Mapping Field
Blocking PIUs	Data Count Field
Prioritization	Expedited Flow Indicator Transmission Priority Field Network Priority Field
Header Format Conversion	ER and VR Support Indicator SNA Indicator
Transmission Group Sequencing	TG Sweep Indicator TG Non-FIFO Indicator TG Sequence Number
Virtual Route Sequencing	VR Sequence and Type Indicator VR Send Sequence Number
Session Sequencing	Sequence Number Field
Virtual Route Pacing	VR Pacing Count Indicator VR Change Window Indicator VR Pacing Request/Response VR Change Window Reply Indicator VR Reset Window Indicator

SUMMARY Path control is the upper functional layer of the two layers that make up the path control network. It communicates with transmission control using message units called basic information units (BIUs). Path control is responsible for appending a transmission header (TH) to each BIU to form a path information unit (PIU). One or more PIUs are combined to form a basic transmission unit (BTU). The BTU is passed back and forth between path control and data link control.

There are various formats for the transmission header, which are designated as FID types. FID0 headers are used for messages passed between an SNA node and a non-SNA device. FID1 headers are used for messages passed between subarea nodes where one or both does not support explicit route and virtual route processing. FID2 headers are used for messages passed between a subarea node and a PU type 2 peripheral node. FID3 headers are used for messages passed between a subarea node and a PU type 1 peripheral node. FID4 headers are used for messages passed between subarea nodes where both nodes support explicit route and virtual route processing. FIDF headers are used for special messages related to message sequencing. The different header types differ in their formats and in the information they carry. The FID4 is the most complex header and supports all functions offered by path control.

18 PATH CONTROL SERVICES

This chapter examines the major services provided by the path control layer. These services include virtual route sequencing, basic information unit segmenting, subarea-to-subarea routing, blocking of path information units, transmission priority control, transmission group sequencing, transmission header conversion, and virtual route pacing. The primary services of path control are provided by three components: *virtual route control, explicit route control,* and *transmission group control.* If the subarea node is connected to one or more peripheral nodes, the path control layer must also include boundary function components. Box 18.1 summarizes the services that are provided by the various path control components.

VIRTUAL ROUTE SEQUENCING   One of the services provided by virtual route control is virtual route sequencing. Virtual route sequencing ensures end-to-end sequencing integrity for PIUs sent across the virtual route. When a virtual route is activated, a control block is created in the subarea node at each end of the route. Each control block contains two counters, one for messages it sends and one for messages it receives. When the virtual route is activated, these counters are initialized with consistent values at both ends. The values in these counters are maintained in a similar manner to the Ns and Nr counts used by SDLC stations in controlling SDLC frame sequencing (see Chapter 15).

When virtual route control at one end sends a PIU, it places its send counter value into the Virtual Route Send Sequence Number field of the FID4 header. It then increments its send counter by 1. When a PIU is received by virtual route control at the other end, it compares the sequence number in the TH header to its receive counter. If the values match, the receive counter is incremented by 1 and the PIU is processed. If they do not match, the PIU is

BOX 18.1   Path control component services

Virtual Route Control

- Virtual route pacing
- Virtual route sequencing
- BIU segmenting

Explicit Route Control

- Subarea-to-subarea routing

Transmission Group Control

- Transmission group sequencing
- PIU blocking
- Transmission prioritization
- TH header conversion

Boundary Function

- Message routing between subarea and peripheral nodes
- TH header conversion
- BIU segmenting

discarded. The sequence numbers for PIUs flowing in one direction are independent of the PIUs flowing in the opposite direction and are processed using separate counters.

Normal messages that travel over a virtual route are sequence-numbered and sequence-checked and are identified by the binary value 10 in the VR Sequence and Type Indicator field. Network control messages, identified by the value 00, and certain pacing messages, identified by the value 01, are not sequence-checked.

BIU SEGMENTING   As introduced in Chapter 17, virtual route control can segment BIUs into multiple PIUs when required. This process is illustrated in Fig. 18.1. On some transmission networks, long messages have to be segmented into smaller ones. One of the most common reasons for this segmenting is the limited buffer sizes of the nodes that the

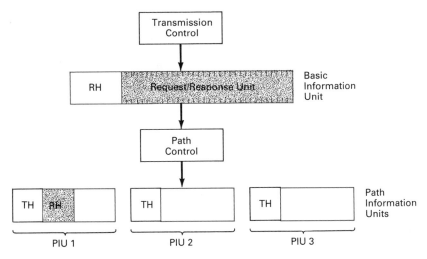

Figure 18.1 Segmenting a BIU.

message traverses on its passage through the network. The maximum message size that can be sent through the network is a function of the capabilities of the nodes in the path that the message takes. It is the responsibility of the path control layer to segment long messages into permissible lengths when this is required.

If a BIU is segmented, the Mapping Field in the TH header in each PIU is set to an appropriate value. The PIUs are then sent in the order that corresponds to the positions the segments occupied in the BIU. When the PIUs reach the destination subarea node, virtual route control reassembles the segments into the original BIU. Boundary function in a subarea node does not perform segment assembly. So BIUs destined for a peripheral node are never segmented when sent to the subarea node providing boundary function support. They may, however, be segmented by boundary function before being sent to the peripheral node.

SUBAREA-TO-SUBAREA ROUTING

Explicit route control is responsible for routing PIUs from one subarea node to the next along the explicit route. If the Destination Subarea Address Field in the TH header indicates that the local subarea is the PIU's destination subarea, the PIU is passed to virtual route control for processing. If the destination subarea is other than the local subarea, explicit route control determines the next subarea node to which the PIU should be sent and chooses the particular transmission group to use in sending it.

Each subarea node contains a routing table, an example of which is shown in Fig. 18.2. The destination subarea address and explicit route number, both

Routing Table

Destination Subarea	Explicit Route Number	Transmission Group Number	Next Subarea
3	5	1	7
3	8	2	7
3	12	1	2
4	6	4	5
4	7	1	7
6	15	3	2
.	.	.	.
.	.	.	.
.	.	.	.

Figure 18.2   Routing table.

of which are carried in the TH header, are used to determine the address of the next subarea node and the number of the transmission group to use. Using the routing table in Fig. 18.2, if a PIU were destined for subarea 3 and was using explicit route 8, it would be sent next to subarea node 7 using transmission group 2. (A specific transmission group is identified by its number and the addresses of the two subarea nodes it connects.) This information, along with the PIU itself, is passed to transmission group control. Transmission group control is then responsible for seeing that the PIU is transmitted properly to the next node.

BLOCKING PIUs   Transmission group control also has the ability to block several PIUs together for transmission across a link in the form of a single SDLC frame. This would be done primarily to reduce the overhead incurred by data link control. If several very short PIUs are traveling across the same link, it might be more efficient to send them in a single frame rather than to transmit each PIU in a separate frame, each with its own SDLC header and trailer.

Figure 18.3 illustrates the passage of a block of PIUs through an intermediate node. In this example, node A has blocked three PIUs into a single BTU because explicit route control has determined that they will all travel over the same link. These PIUs are not necessarily part of the same session.

When the BTU carrying the PIUs is sent to the proper SDLC component in node A, the BTU is enclosed in an SDLC frame and transmitted over the appropriate link to the SDLC component in node B. In node B the frame header and trailer are stripped off and the BTU is passed up to transmission group control in the path control layer. Transmission group control separates the BTU into its component PIUs and passes them on to explicit route control, which determines that each of them must travel over a different link to reach its ultimate destination. The PIUs are returned to transmission group control, which

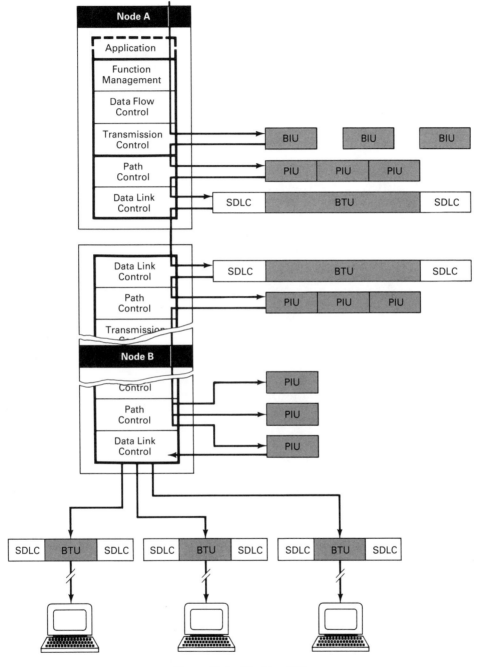

Figure 18.3 Blocking PIUs.

constructs three new BTUs, each of which contains a single PIU, and sends these BTUs to the appropriate SDLC components. There the BTUs are enclosed in frames and sent over the proper links on the way to their destination nodes.

Blocking is allowed only for transmission groups that consist of a single link. If blocking is performed, a BTU is constructed that contains the maximum number of currently available PIUs that are to be transmitted over that link, such that the BTU length does not exceed the maximum BTU length for that transmission group. Transmission group control uses the Data Count Field in the transmission header of each PIU to assemble and disassemble the PIUs.

TRANSMISSION PRIORITY

Transmission group control uses transmission priority to determine the sequence in which PIUs are transmitted. The Transmission Priority Field and Network Priority Field in the transmission header determine the priority of the PIU, as follows:

Network Priority	Transmission Priority	Priority Interpretation
1	—	Highest
0	10	.
0	01	.
0	00	Lowest

Based on the PIU's priority and the transmission group to be used for transmission, transmission group control inserts the PIU into a transmission group priority list. For PIUs with the same priority, the earliest to arrive is first on the list. PIUs are then removed from the list for transmission, PIUs with higher priorities first and, within priority, the oldest first. If higher-priority PIUs continue arriving at the node, or if transmission errors are frequent, lower-priority PIUs may end up remaining in the priority list for some time. An implementation-defined algorithm can be used to ensure the transmission of the lower-priority PIUs, based on the length of time they have been waiting.

TRANSMISSION GROUP SEQUENCING

When a transmission group consists of multiple links, different PIUs may be transmitted over the various links. When multiple links are used, it is possible for PIUs to be received at the destination node in a different sequence than that in which they were sent. This can be caused by transmission errors on one of the links, by having PIUs of different lengths, or by having different transmission rates associated with different links. Under some circumstances, duplicate PIUs can arrive at the destination node—for example, if a transmission error causes a PIU to be retransmitted over a different link.

Transmission group control provides a mechanism called transmission group sequencing that ensures that PIUs will be processed in the same sequence that they were sent. Transmission group sequencing applies only to PIUs sent over a transmission group with multiple links and with the TG Non-FIFO Indicator set to zero. If the TG Non-FIFO Indicator is set to one, sequencing is assumed to be an implementation-specific responsibility. When transmission group sequencing is performed, transmission group control in the sending node assigns a sequence number to each PIU, using the Transmission Group Sequence Number field of the FID4 header for this purpose. The sequence numbers run from 0 to 4095; when 4095 is reached, the value wraps around to 0. In the receiving node, transmission group control checks the TG sequence numbers of the PIUs being received. If PIUs are received out of sequence, they are held in a re-FIFO list until the PIU or PIUs are received that allow the PIUs to be passed to explicit route control in sequence. Also, any duplicate PIUs are discarded. Transmission group sequencing is handled independently for each direction of transmission over a multiple-link transmission group. PIUs flowing in one direction are sequenced separately from PIUs flowing in the other direction. Transmission group control has both a send counter and a receive counter for each end of a multiple-link transmission group.

TRANSMISSION GROUP WRAP ACKNOWLEDGMENT

Because the TG sequence numbers wrap around from 4095 to 0, it is possible for PIUs from a new sequence number group to be intermixed with PIUs from the previous group. This can happen if PIUs from the previous group are being held in the re-FIFO list. To prevent duplication or confusion of sequence numbers from one group to the next, transmission group control at the receiving end sends a special acknowledgment when it has received a PIU with TG sequence number 4095 and has been able to pass it on to explicit route control. After transmission group control on the sending side transmits a PIU with TG sequence number 4095, it suspends transmission until it receives an acknowledgment from the receiving end. This acknowledgment consists of a PIU with an FIDF header. The acknowledgment is assigned a sequence number, so if it is duplicated because of a BTU retransmission, duplicates can be discarded. In addition to the normal send and receive counters, transmission group control also maintains send wrap acknowledgment and receive wrap acknowledgment counters. The wrap acknowledgment PIU is transmitted ahead of any other PIUs in the priority list so that transmission delays will not occur because of transmission group control waiting to receive the acknowledgment before resuming transmission.

TRANSMISSION GROUP SWEEP

As part of transmission over a transmission group with multiple links, an acknowledgment is returned indicating whether or not a PIU has been transmitted successfully. If the transmission is not successful, it is attempted again, using another link in the group. This retransmission is one possible cause for PIUs arriving out of sequence.

As an additional precaution against confusing PIUs from one sequence group with those of another, a process called a *transmission group sweep* is used. In a TG sweep, transmission group control in the sending node waits until all previously transmitted PIUs have been successfully received before transmitting another PIU. A TG sweep is performed before a PIU with TG sequence number 0 is transmitted. A TG sweep is performed again after the PIU with TG sequence number 0 is sent. This ensures that PIUs from one sequence group do not overlap with PIUs from another. It also ensures that the PIU with TG sequence number 0 is the first PIU received in a sequence group. In this way transmission group control in the receiving node knows that a new sequence group has started. A TG sweep will also be performed for any PIU that has the TG Sweep Indicator in the FID4 header set to 1. This ensures that the PIU is not received ahead of any PIUs that were previously transmitted. The TG Sweep Indicator is used primarily for certain network control messages.

TH HEADER CONVERSION

Transmission group control is responsible for the conversion of TH headers that is required if the route includes a node that does not support explicit route and virtual route processing. When transmitting to this type of node, transmission group control converts the TH header from an FID4 header to an FID0 or FID1 header. If the SNA Indicator is set to zero, an FID0 header is used; if it is set to one, an FID1 header is used. When receiving a BTU from this type of node, transmission group control converts the FID0 or FID1 header to an FID4 header before passing it on to explicit route control. Because of the more limited information that is carried in the FID0 and FID1 header, if this type of node is included in the route, no virtual route sequencing or virtual route pacing can take place over that route.

ERROR HANDLING

Transmission group control is also responsible for certain forms of error checking and handling that are performed within the path control layer. If a transmission error occurs on a multiple-link transmission group, data link control notifies transmission group control that it is attempting error recovery. Transmission group control then passes the BTU to data link control for transmission over another link. If an error occurs on this link, the process is repeated until the BTU is successfully transmitted or until all links in the group have been tried.

If transmission group control receives a PIU from explicit route control that exceeds the maximum BTU length for the link over which it is to be transmitted, transmission group control converts the PIU into the format of a special error message that is transmitted in place of the original PIU. Transmission group control also performs validity checking on each BTU that is received before the BTU is processed by data link control. This includes checking that FID and Data Count Field values are valid, that minimum PIU length requirements are met, and that the PIU length in total corresponds to the length of the BTU as it was received by data link control.

VIRTUAL ROUTE PACING

Transmission group control and virtual route control cooperatively provide the virtual route pacing services. The goal of virtual route pacing is to control the flow of data between the two end subarea nodes of a virtual route. This data flow is controlled in a way that minimizes both transmission delays and congestion along the route. Virtual route pacing is based on limiting the number of PIUs that can be sent by the node on one end of the virtual route before an acknowledgment is received from the other end. The number of PIUs that can be sent before receiving an acknowledgment is called the *pacing window size,* and the pacing acknowledgment is called a *pacing response.*

Each virtual route has associated with it a *minimum window size* and a *maximum window size.* These values apply to transmissions in either direction along the route. There is also a *current window size* for each transmission direction. When a virtual route is activated, the window size in each direction is initially set to the minimum window size.

NORMAL FLOW

Virtual route control also maintains a *pacing count* for each transmission direction, indicating the number of PIUs that can be sent before a pacing response is received. The pacing count is initially set to the current window size, and as each PIU is sent, the pacing count is reduced by one. If the pacing count reaches zero before a pacing response is received, no further PIUs are transmitted in that direction along the virtual route until a pacing response is received. When a pacing response is received, the pacing count is increased by the current window size. This allows any remaining PIUs in the current pacing group plus the next pacing group to be sent before another pacing response is received. A pacing response is not sent until the node on the receiving end of the virtual route is able to handle what remains in the current pacing group plus the next pacing group.

The first PIU sent as part of a window, or pacing group, has the virtual route pacing request bit in the FID4 header set to one, causing the PIU to act as a *VR pacing request.* A *VR pacing response* consists of a BTU that consists only of an FID4 header with no BIU. The virtual route pacing response bit in this header is set to one. A VR pacing response is sent as a nonsequenced, supervisory message (VR Sequence and Type Indicator = 01) and is sent at network priority. One pacing response is sent for each pacing request that is transmitted when the receiving-end subarea node is able to handle another pacing group.

If the pacing count reaches zero before a pacing response is received, the last PIU transmitted (the one that causes the pacing count to reach zero) has the VR Pacing Count Indicator set to one. This notifies the receiving-end subarea node that no more PIUs will be sent until a pacing response is received. If necessary, virtual route control at the receiving end can then take implementation-specific action to expedite sending the pacing response.

CHANGING WINDOW SIZE

For each PIU that is sent along a virtual route, virtual route control sets the Virtual Route Change Window Indicator to zero, which constitutes a request to increase the window size. As the PIU passes along the virtual route, any node that detects congestion can change the indicator back to one. But if there is no congestion, the indicator will remain zero when the PIU reaches the subarea node on the receiving end of the virtual route. When virtual route control at the receiving end sends back a pacing response, it sets the Virtual Route Change Window Reply Indicator based on the Change Window Indicators it has received. If they have all been zero, the indicator in the pacing response is set to zero, which indicates that the window size should be increased.

When a pacing response is received, the current window size is increased by one if all of the following conditions are met:

- The Virtual Route Change Window Reply Indicator is zero.
- The pacing count has reached zero.
- The maximum window size has not been reached.

If the pacing count has not reached zero, no delays are currently being incurred by a wait for a pacing response, and the window size is not increased. Window size will thus gradually be increased as long as there is no congestion along the route. When a point is reached where there are no transmission delays incurred by waiting for pacing responses or when the maximum window size is reached, the window size stops increasing.

Figure 18.4 illustrates the pacing process. The window size is initially set to three, so that three PIUs can be sent before receiving a response. After the three PIUs are sent, node A stops transmission on this virtual route until a pacing response is received. Since the pacing response does not arrive until after all the PIUs in the pacing group have been sent, there is a pacing delay. The

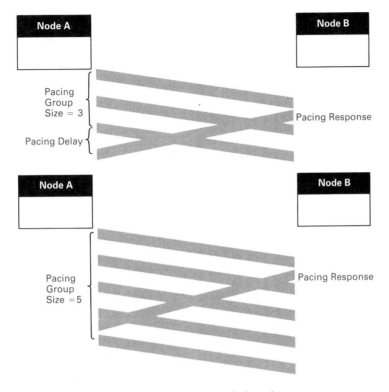

Figure 18.4   Increasing window size.

use of the Virtual Route Change Window Indicator and Virtual Route Change Window Reply Indicator will cause window size to increase until it reaches five. Here the pacing response is received before the entire pacing group has been transmitted, so window size is not increased further.

MODERATE CONGESTION

If moderate congestion is detected at any node along the virtual route, transmission group control at that node will change the Virtual Route Change Window Indicator to one in each PIU it is transmitting in the direction of the congestion. Once these PIUs reach the receiving subarea node, virtual route control sets the Virtual Route Change Window Reply Indicator in the next pacing response to one, requesting a decrease in the window size. When the pacing response is received, the window size is decreased by one. This process continues, with window size gradually decreasing, until no more congestion is encountered or the minimum window size is reached.

SEVERE CONGESTION   If transmission group control detects severe congestion, it has a way of more quickly reducing window size. It sets the Virtual Route Reset Window Indicator to one in each PIU being sent in the opposite direction, back to the sending-end subarea node. When the sending-end subarea node receives a PIU with the Virtual Route Reset Window Indicator set to one, virtual route control sets the current window size to the minimum window size. If the pacing count is currently greater than the minimum window size, the pacing count is also set to the minimum window size.

PATH CONTROL BOUNDARY FUNCTION   If a session involves a peripheral node at one end or the other, boundary function support is used for the portion of the route that extends from the subarea node to the peripheral node. The path control components in boundary function and in the peripheral node provide for routing messages from the subarea node to the peripheral node and vice versa. Boundary function is responsible for the conversion between network addresses and local addresses and for the conversion between FID4 headers and either FID2 or FID3 headers.

Boundary function can also break a BIU into segments before transmission to the peripheral node. The path control layer in the peripheral node is then responsible for reassembling the BIU. Peripheral node support for the reassembly function is optional. If the reassembly function is not supported, any segmented BIUs that are received are rejected. Peripheral nodes can also segment BIUs that they are sending. Segmented BIUs received by boundary function at the path control level are routed in their segmented form to boundary function for transmission control in that node. Since boundary function does not perform segment assembly, the segments are then passed on in their segmented form to their destinations and are reassembled by the receiving half-sessions.

SUMMARY   The path control layer consists of three components: virtual route control, explicit route control, and transmission group control. Virtual route control provides virtual route pacing, virtual route sequencing, and segmenting of BIUs. Explicit route control provides subarea-to-subarea routing. Transmission group control provides transmission group sequencing, blocking of PIUs, transmission prioritization, and header conversion. Virtual route sequencing provides for end-to-end sequencing of PIUs sent across a virtual route, using send and receive counters.

A BIU can be segmented into several PIUs by using the Mapping Field in the TH to identify the segments. A primary function of path control is to route messages from one node to the next along the route they travel. The destination address and explicit route number in the TH are used in combination with a routing table maintained at each node to determine the address of the next sub-area node along the route and the number of the transmission group to be used for transmission to that node. Multiple PIUs can be blocked together to form a single BTU. This is done to reduce transmission overhead incurred by data link control. PIUs can be assigned different priorities to control the sequence in which they are transmitted across a transmission link. PIUs for a particular transmission group are placed in a priority list based on the Network Priority and Transmission Priority fields in the TH. PIUs are removed from the priority list for transmission based on priority and time of arrival. The Expedited Flow Indicator in the TH can be used to allow PIUs to bypass transmission queues.

For transmission groups consisting of multiple links, transmission group sequencing is used to ensure that PIUs are processed on the receiving side in the same sequence that they were sent. Out-of-sequence PIUs are held in a re-FIFO list until the PIUs are received that allow them to be processed in the correct sequence. To ensure that PIUs from one sequence group are not confused with PIUs from the next, a special acknowledgment, consisting of a PIU with an FIDF header, is sent after a PIU with TG sequence number 4095 has been received and processed. A TG sweep is performed before and after transmitting a PIU with TG sequence number 0. In a TG sweep the sending node waits until all previously transmitted PIUs have been received and processed before sending another PIU.

Virtual route pacing controls the flow of data between the two end subarea nodes of a virtual route in a way that minimizes both transmission delays and congestion along the route. Pacing window size is the number of PIUs that can be sent from the sending end before a pacing response is received. The pacing count indicates the remaining number of PIUs that can be sent before receiving a pacing response. The Virtual Route Pacing Request and Response fields are used to indicate whether congestion is encountered along the virtual route. If no congestion is encountered, the pacing window size is gradually increased until it reaches the maximum window size or no transmission delays occur. If congestion is encountered, pacing window size is gradually decreased until it reaches minimum window size or no further congestion is encountered. If severe congestion is encountered, the Virtual Route Reset Window Indicator can be used to reduce window size more quickly.

The path control layer boundary function supports the routing of messages between a subarea node and a peripheral node, including the necessary header conversion. Boundary function can also segment a BIU into several PIUs before transmission to a peripheral node.

PART **IV** NAUs: TRANSMISSION AND
DATA FLOW CONTROL

19 TRANSMISSION CONTROL

The two chapters in this part of the book discuss the first two layers that make up the NAU portion of SNA. In this chapter we examine the lowest NAU layer: the transmission control layer (see Fig. 19.1). We begin this chapter by examining the header that is appended to each message unit by transmission control. We then describe the major functions performed by the transmission control layer, including sequencing, cryptography, and session-level pacing. We will begin by looking at the message units that pass to and from transmission control and their relationship to the request/response header.

BIU FORMAT

The unit of data that passes back and forth between the data flow control layer and the transmission control layer is the *request/response unit* (RU). Various parameters are also passed between the layers along with the RU. When a message and its associated parameters are sent down from data flow control, transmission control uses the information supplied in the parameters to construct a *request/response header* (RH), which it appends to the RU. The RU and RH together constitute a *basic information unit* (BIU). An outgoing BIU is passed from transmission control to path control, where a *transmission header* (TH) is added to form a *path information unit* (PIU). This process is illustrated in Fig. 19.2. On the receiving side, transmission control uses the information it finds in the RH for various control purposes, as well as for passing parameters up to the data flow control layer. Path control can segment the BIU to form several PIUs, as shown in Fig. 19.3. When the BIU is segmented, the first segment contains the request/response header.

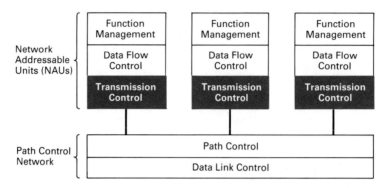

Figure 19.1   The Transmission Control layer.

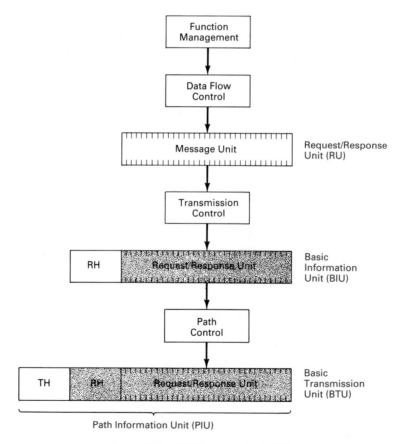

Figure 19.2   BIU format—single PIU.

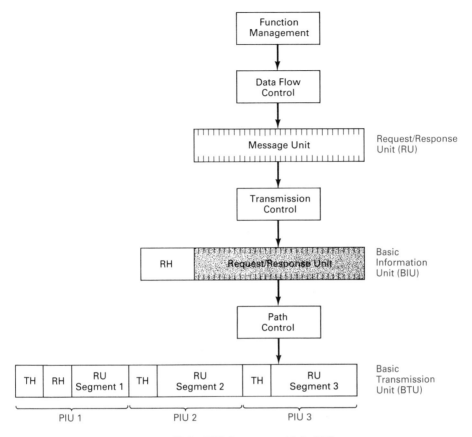

Figure 19.3   BIU format—multiple PIUs.

REQUEST/RESPONSE HEADER   A request/response header is always three bytes (24 bits) in length, though not all of the bits are currently used. The unused bits are included in the header so that new control functions can be added in the future without requiring changes to SNA hardware and software that is already installed. In some cases the transmission control layer creates a BIU that contains only an RH and has no associated RU. These BIUs are used to perform control functions.

The exact format for an RH depends on whether it is appended to a request or a response. The format for a request header is shown in Fig. 19.4; the format of a response header is shown in Fig. 19.5. Box 19.1 provides descriptions of each of the bits in request/response headers. A comparison of Figs. 19.4 and 19.5 shows that a response header is similar in format to a request header but that many of the bits that have meaning for a request do not have meaning for a response.

	Bit 0	Bit 1	Bit 2	Bit 3	Bit 4	Bit 5	Bit 6	Bit 7
Byte 0	Request/ Response Indicator (0)	RU Category			Format Indicator	Sense Data Included Indicator	Begin Chain Indicator	End Chain Indicator
Byte 1	Definite Response 1 Indicator		Definite Response 2 Indicator	Exception Response Indicator			Queued Response Indicator	Pacing Indicator
Byte 2	Begin Bracket Indicator	End Bracket Indicator	Change Direction Indicator		Code Selection Indicator	Enciphered Data Indicator	Padded Data Indicator	

Figure 19.4   Request header format.

A given request may or may not be followed by an associated response; the sender specifies in the request header whether or not a response is required. This is done by setting the appropriate bits in the Response Indicators contained in the request header. These bits can indicate any one of the following:

- No response requested
- Response requested only if an error is detected
- Mandatory response requested

The Exception Response Indicator in a response is set to one if the response is negative and to zero if the response is positive. A positive response indicates that the request unit was successfully received and processed. A negative response indicates that an error was encountered. A negative response can also contain information that describes the error.

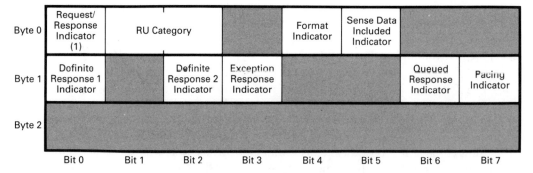

	Bit 0	Bit 1	Bit 2	Bit 3	Bit 4	Bit 5	Bit 6	Bit 7
Byte 0	Request/ Response Indicator (1)	RU Category			Format Indicator	Sense Data Included Indicator		
Byte 1	Definite Response 1 Indicator		Definite Response 2 Indicator	Exception Response Indicator			Queued Response Indicator	Pacing Indicator
Byte 2								

Figure 19.5   Response header format.

BOX 19.1 Request/response header bits

- **Request-Response Indicator.** This bit indicates whether the RU is a request or a response.

- **RU Category.** An incoming or outgoing RU has one of four possible destinations: session control (which is part of transmission control), data flow control, function management, or network control. Network control RUs are not used by logical units. The RU Category bits define an RU's destination as follows:

00	Function management
01	Network control
10	Data flow control
11	Session control

- **Format Indicator.** This bit indicates the format of the RU. For RUs destined for session control, network control, or data flow control, the bit is always set to one. For RUs destined for function management that are part of an LU-to-LU session, this bit indicates whether or not an FM header is present. A one indicates that it is present, a zero that it is not. For function management messages that are part of an SSCP-to-SSCP, SSCP-to-PU, or SSCP-to-LU session, a value of 1 indicates the presence of a network service header and field formatting. A value of 0 indicates no network service header and character coding. (This will be covered in more detail later in the chapters on function management.)

- **Sense Data Indicator.** Occasionally an error will be detected during a session; for example, information may have been received out of sequence, or a response may not correlate with a request. Under these circumstances, the Sense Data Indicator is turned on to indicate that information about the nature of the error (sense data) is included in the RU.

- **Chaining Control Indicators.** Data flow control has the ability to connect or *chain* several request units so that they will be transmitted together. When data flow control sends a request unit to transmission control, it also sends parameters indicating whether the RU is the first, middle, last, or only unit in a chain. Transmission control encodes this information in two Chaining Control Indicators, the Begin Chain Indicator and End Chain Indicator. Possible values are as follows:

BCI	ECI	Interpretation
1	0	First RU in chain
0	0	Middle RU in chain
0	1	Last RU in chain
1	1	Only RU in chain

(Continued)

BOX 19.1 *(Continued)*

- **Form of Response Indicators.** When a request is issued, the source of that request can specify that no response is necessary, that a response is necessary only if an error (exception condition) is recognized, or that a response to the request is always necessary. The type of response expected is indicated in a combination of one-bit indicators: the *Definite Response 1 Indicator, Definite Response 2 Indicator,* and *Exception Response Indicator.* If all three indicators have a value of 0, no response is expected. If the Exception Response Indicator has a value of 1 and the Definite Response Indicators have a value other than 00, only a negative response is expected if an error or exception condition is detected. If the Exception Response Indicator has a value of 0 and the Definite Response Indicators have a value other than 00, a response is always expected.

- **Queued Response Indicator.** The Queued Response Indicator indicates whether the response to this message can be enqueued in the transmission control queues (value of 1) or whether the response is to bypass the queues (value of 0).

- **Pacing Indicator.** A method of flow control called session-level pacing can be implemented by transmission control to be sure that a receiving node is not flooded with more requests than it can handle in a given time period. This method specifies a maximum number (N) of request units that can be issued before a response is received. When a source node sends a request with its Pacing Indicator set, it is asking permission to send another group of N requests to the destination node. When the destination node has buffer space or time to handle another group of requests, it issues a response with the Pacing Indicator turned on. The source node can then send another group of up to N requests.

- **Bracket Control Indicators.** Data flow control has the ability to group a sequence of request chains and their responses into a processing unit called a bracket. The Begin Bracket and End Bracket Indicators are used to mark the beginning and end of a bracket. The first request in the first chain in the bracket has a value of 1 in the Begin Bracket Indicator. The first request in the last chain in the bracket has a value of 1 in the End Bracket Indicator.

- **Change Direction Indicator.** This bit is set to one during half-duplex communication to tell the receiving node that it can now transmit.

- **Code Selection Indicator.** One bit is allocated in the RH to indicate which of two preselected character codes (for example, EBCDIC or ASCII) is being used.

- **Enciphered Data Indicator.** The Enciphered Data Indicator is used to indicate whether or not the data in the associated RU are encrypted. A value of 1 means they are encrypted, 0 that they are not.

- **Padded Data Indicator.** The Padded Data Indicator indicates whether the RU has been padded to the next higher multiple of eight bytes before encryption. A value of 1 indicates that it is padded.

TRANSMISSION CONTROL ELEMENTS

As discussed earlier, various types of sessions take place as part of an active network. Session types include PU-to-SSCP sessions, LU-to-SSCP sessions, and LU-to-LU sessions. A single node might be involved in several concurrent LU-to-LU sessions. The transmission control functions for each session are handled by a separate component called a *transmission control element* (TCE). The transmission control layer on each end initiates a separate transmission control element for each session that is started.

Figure 19.6 illustrates the use of multiple TCEs to support concurrent sessions. In this figure a host processor contains one SSCP, one physical unit, and two logical units, each of which is participating in multiple concurrent LU-to-

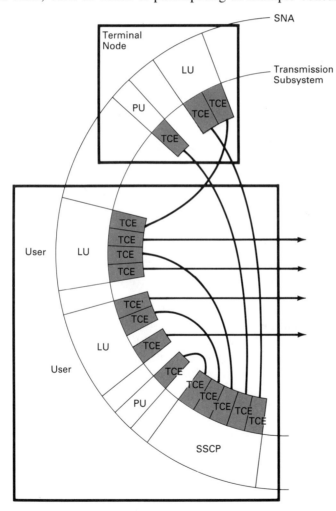

Figure 19.6 Multiple Transmission Control Elements.

LU sessions. The figure also shows one terminal node that is involved in an LU-to-LU session with the host node. Although this illustration shows only three logical units, 16 TCEs are active in the two nodes shown. This number would be higher if we were to show the other nodes that are in session with the host computer. Each TCE performs transmission control layer functions for the session in which it is participating.

TCE COMPONENTS

Each TCE is divided into two components: the *connection point manager* (CPM) and the *session control component*. These components interact with the data control layer, with the path control layer, and with each other.

CONNECTION POINT MANAGER

The routine management of messages traveling between the data control layer and the path control network is done by the connection point manager component of the TCE. Primary functions provided by the CPM include formatting and verifying request/response headers, controlling message sequencing, handling cryptography, and controlling session-level pacing.

ASSEMBLING AND DISASSEMBLING REQUEST HEADERS

A primary responsibility of the connection point manager is to assemble the request/response headers for outgoing RUs and to disassemble the headers for incoming RUs. As we stated earlier, much of the information required to build the RH does not originate in the transmission control layer. Instead, it is passed in the form of parameters to the connection point manager from the data flow control layer. RUs can be originated by many different SNA components. Some RUs are originated by components that operate above the transmission control layer; other RUs are created by the transmission control layer itself. It is desirable, however, that the request/response headers be assembled and disassembled at a single centralized point. The SNA system architects chose the connection point manager as this centralized point. Each higher-level SNA component that creates an RU passes parameters along with it that contain the information that will be necessary to format the RH later.

MESSAGE SEQUENCING

Earlier we described how SDLC uses a sequence-numbering scheme in transmitting frames. The SDLC sequence numbers are used to control the sequencing of frames that are transmitted over an individual data link. When a transmission group with multiple links is used, path control provides transmission group sequence numbers to control the sequencing of BTUs sent over the transmission group. In both these cases, sequencing is dealt with at the level of transmission from one node to the next. Another set of sequence numbers is used by the layers above the data link control and path control layers to provide *end-to-end* sequence control of request/response units.

When the data flow control layer passes a normal flow request unit down to the connection point manager in a TCE, it passes a 16-bit sequence number as a parameter along with the RU. The CPM passes this sequence number, along with the BIU that it creates, down to the path control layer. The path control layer then uses the sequence number in constructing the transmission header (TH) that it attaches to the BIU to create a basic transmission unit (BTU). Data flow control adds one to the sequence number for each subsequent RU that it creates. The maximum value for a sequence number is 65535, after which the value wraps around to 0.

In normal data flow, a response to a request carries the same sequence number as the original request. On the receiving end, transmission control checks the sequence number from the transmission headers of the requests and responses that it receives to ensure that RUs are being passed up to data flow control in the same sequence in which they were sent.

These sequence numbers, along with information that identifies the session, provide a unique identifier for each request and response unit (unique within each group of 65,535 RUs). This identifier serves three primary purposes:

- **Response Correlation.** The sequence number allows each response to be correlated with the request that elicited it. This is particularly important when an error occurs during the transmission of a request. When an error occurs, an *exception response* is transmitted by the receiving TCE that contains a sequence number that identifies the request in which the error occurred.

- **Failure Recovery.** When a transmission line or other system component fails, a method of recovering without loss of data is needed. The techniques used to recover from failures all employ sequence numbers.

- **Sequence Checking.** As messages are received, the sequence numbers are checked to ensure that the messages have been received in the same sequence in which they were sent.

Expedited messages bypass the queues that are used in normal data flow. Since expedited messages are not directly associated with other requests or responses, they are not numbered sequentially in the same manner as RUs involved in the normal data flow. However, an expedited RU is ordinarily assigned a number that acts as a unique identifier for that RU.

CRYPTOGRAPHY OPTION   The connection point manger also implements the SNA *cryptography option,* which can be used to provide security for data being transmitted across the network. When the cryptography option is employed, data are *enciphered* by the sending node before being transmitted. The receiving node then *deciphers* the data, converting them back to their original form. The CPM enciphers outgoing request units before it passes them to path control and deciphers incoming RUs after receiving them from path control.

The three possible cryptography options are no cryptography, selective cryptography, and mandatory cryptography. If mandatory cryptography is specified, all RUs for that session are encrypted. If selective cryptography has been specified, RUs are encrypted only if the Enciphered Data Indicator parameter that is passed to transmission control is set to one. It is the responsibility of the network user to cause the Enciphered Data Indicator parameter to be set.

Cryptography Algorithm and Key

The cryptography option involves the use of a *cryptography algorithm* and a specific *cryptographic key.* The algorithm can be known publicly, but the keys must remain secret in order for the enciphered data to be secure. SNA uses the Data Encryption Standard (DES) algorithm published by the National Bureau of Standards. The specific cryptographic keys used for different sessions are provided by IBM's Programmed Cryptography Facility, a program product to which SNA has an interface.

When a session that specifies cryptography is initiated, the SSCP obtains a key to be used for the session from the Programmed Cryptography Facility. Each logical unit that supports cryptography has a master cryptographic key. The SSCP enciphers two versions of the session cryptographic key, one version using the primary LU master key and another version using the secondary LU master key. The SSCP then passes both enciphered master keys to the primary LU as part of session initiation. The primary LU sends the version enciphered with the secondary LU's master key to the secondary LU as part of bind processing. In this way the session cryptography key is sent to both LUs in enciphered form and thus remains secure.

Cryptography Processing

After receiving the session cryptographic key, the secondary LU enciphers an eight-byte test value and sends that value back to the primary LU in its bind response. The primary LU then deciphers the test value and transforms it by inverting the bits of the first four bytes. The primary LU then enciphers the transformed value and sends it to the secondary LU as part of a CRV (Cryptographic Verification) request. The secondary LU deciphers the returned test value and again inverts the bits of the first four bytes. It compares the result to the original test value. If both are the same, both LUs have successfully enciphered and deciphered the value and are properly prepared to exchange enciphered data during the session. The test value that was initially generated by the secondary LU is then used as the cryptography *session seed value* for this session. The session seed value is used in enciphering the data in each RU that is to be enciphered. Box 19.2 describes the enciphering process, which is called *block chaining with cipher-text feedback*.

SESSION-LEVEL   The final major function performed by the connection
PACING   point manager is session-level pacing. Session-level
     pacing is used to control the rate at which requests
are sent within a particular session so that message units do not arrive faster than the receiving LU can accept them. This type of pacing is applied to each session separately, in contrast with virtual route pacing, which is concerned with the total traffic on a particular route.

When a session is initiated, the number of requests that the receiving LU is able to accept at one time is defined. This number is called the *window size* or *pacing-group size* and specifies the maximum number of requests the sending LU should send before receiving a *pacing response* from the receiving LU. The connection point manager in the sending LU's TCE maintains a *pacing count*

BOX 19.2   The enciphering process

1. The RU is padded, if necessary, to make its length a multiple of eight bytes. The last padding byte contains a binary count of the number of padding bytes added. When padding bytes are added, the Padded Data Indicator in the request header is set to one.

2. An exclusive-OR operation is performed on the first eight bytes of the RU using the session seed value as the argument. The result of the exclusive-OR operation is then enciphered using the session cryptographic key.

3. An exclusive-OR operation is performed on each remaining group of eight bytes in the RU using the enciphered value of the previous eight bytes as the argument of each operation. The result of each exclusive-OR operation is then enciphered using the session cryptographic key.

4. The result of all exclusive-OR and enciphering operations is finally transmitted from one LU to another, where the inverse of the above procedure is performed by the receiving LU to decipher the received message.

that indicates how many requests it can send before receiving a pacing response. Initially the pacing count is set to the window size. Each time a request is sent, the pacing count is decremented by one. When a pacing response is received, the pacing count is increased by a value equal to the window size. The receiving LU transmits a pacing response when it is ready to receive another group of requests. If the pacing count maintained by the sending LU has not reached zero by the time it receives a pacing response, the sending LU continues sending request units without pause. If the pacing count drops to zero, the sender stops sending requests until it receives a pacing response.

Pacing Request and Pacing Response

When the sending LU transmits the first request in a pacing group, it turns on the Pacing Request Indicator in the request header. This indicates to the receiver that it should notify the sending LU when it is able to receive the next pacing group after the group currently being transmitted. When the receiving LU is ready to receive another pacing group, it sends a pacing response. The pacing response takes the form of any response that has the Pacing Response Indicator in the response header turned on. If no response is ready to be transmitted at the time that a pacing response is required, an *isolated pacing response* (IPR) is sent. An isolated pacing response consists of a BIU that has only a response header with no associated request unit. In the response header, the Response Indicator, Begin Chain Indicator, End Chain Indicator, and Pacing Indicator are all set to one; both Definite Response Indicators are turned off.

A normal response is used as a pacing response only if it has been removed from the pacing queue and is ready to be transmitted or if its Queued Response Indicator indicates that the message is bypassing the pacing queue. This prevents a deadlock situation from developing, where each LU in an LU-to-LU session is waiting for a pacing response from its partner and are thus both unable to transmit messages from their pacing queues.

Two-Stage Pacing

Session-level pacing can take the form of either one-stage or two-stage pacing. One-stage pacing is always used when both session partners are subarea nodes. If a session involves a peripheral node, two-stage pacing can be used. In two-stage pacing, pacing is applied separately between the two subarea nodes and between boundary function in the subarea node and the peripheral node. Stage 1 pacing controls the pacing of requests sent to boundary function. Stage 2 pacing controls the pacing of requests sent from boundary function. Pacing requests and responses flow independently in each stage, and each stage has its own window size, determined at session binding time.

Pacing also operates independently for the two directions in which data flow within a session. Pacing can take place in both directions, in only one direction, or in neither direction. If a peripheral node is involved, either one- or two-stage pacing can be used in either direction, and the same form of pacing need not be used in both directions.

Figure 19.7 illustrates the possibilities for two-stage pacing in an LU-to-LU session involving a peripheral node. When request units are sent from the primary LU to the secondary LU, stage 1 pacing (point 1) controls the flow of requests from the primary LU to boundary function. Stage 2 pacing (point 2) controls the flow from boundary function to the peripheral node. For transmission in the opposite direction, stage 1 pacing (point 3) controls the flow of requests from the peripheral node to boundary function, and stage 2 pacing (point 4) from boundary function to the primary LU. Four pacing parameters are defined as part of session binding for each LU-to-LU session:

- Primary send pacing-group size
- Primary receive pacing-group size
- Secondary send pacing-group size
- Secondary receive pacing-group size

The primary send pacing-group size acts as the window size for the flow indicated at point 1, the secondary receive pacing-group size defines the window size for point 2, secondary send pacing-group size specifies the window size for point 3, and primary receive pacing-group size defines the window size for point 4. When one-stage pacing is used, the appropriate send and receive pacing-group sizes are set to the same value. For example, if one-stage pacing is used for requests sent from the primary LU to the secondary LU, the primary send pacing-group size and secondary receive pacing-group size are set to the same value. A pacing-group size of zero means that pacing is not applied. If pacing is not applied, the sending LU continues to send requests without pause. Care must be taken when this option is specified to ensure that the receiver is able to accept an uninterrupted flow of data.

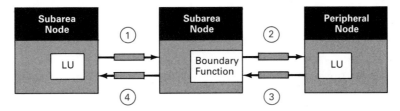

Figure 19.7　Two-stage pacing.

SESSION CONTROL COMPONENT

As we mentioned earlier, the second component of the TCE is called the session control component. The primary functions of session control are to establish and terminate sessions and to aid in the recovery from catastrophic errors. When a catastrophic error occurs, session control clears the original data flow and resynchronizes the new data flow as the recovery from the error takes place. Resynchronization includes the setting of sequence number counters to appropriate restart values and reinitializing the information that correlates requests and responses.

A number of commands are used by session control for controlling its functions. Box 19.3 summarizes these commands. They are discussed further in later chapters that examine session initiation and synchronization point processing.

SUMMARY

Transmission control is the lowest layer in the NAU component of SNA. It communicates with data flow control by means of request/response units (RUs) and parameters. For outgoing

---

BOX 19.3 Session control commands

SDT   The SDT command (Start Data Traffic) is used to start data traffic flowing in both directions within a session. The SDT command is sent by a primary station to a secondary station.

CLEAR   The CLEAR command (Clear) is used to reset session values for brackets, pacing, and sequence numbers. It also stops normal data traffic until an SDT command is issued. The CLEAR command is sent by a primary LU to a secondary LU.

RQR   The RQR command (Request Recovery) is used to request a primary LU to initiate and direct recovery procedures by sending a CLEAR command or by deactivating the session. The RQR command is sent by a secondary LU to a primary LU.

STSN   The STSN command (Set and Test Sequence Numbers) is used to test and/or reset and resynchronize sequence numbers as part of session resynchronization processing. The STSN command is sent by a primary LU to a secondary LU.

CRV   The CRV command (Cryptographic Verification) is used when session-level cryptography is specified as part of the process that sets the session seed value. The CRV command is sent by a primary LU to a secondary LU.

RUs, it adds a request/response header (RH) to the RU to form a basic information unit (BIU). The BIU is the message unit that is passed back and forth between transmission control and path control.

Transmission control initiates a transmission control element (TCE) for each session in which a node participates. Each TCE consists of a connection point manager (CPM) and a session control component. The CPM is responsible for assembling and disassembling the request/response header, message sequencing, cryptography, and session-level pacing. Session control is responsible for establishing and terminating sessions and for aiding in recovery from catastrophic errors. Transmission control uses parameters that are passed from data flow control in formatting the RH. Information from the RH is passed in the form of parameters to data flow control on the receiving end. Data flow control assigns a sequence number to each RU that it passes to transmission control. Transmission control passes this number in the form of a parameter to the path control layer, where it is inserted into the transmission header (TH). The sequence number is used to ensure that RUs are passed to data flow control in the same sequence in which they were sent. Expedited messages, which bypass the pacing queues, are assigned unique identifiers rather than sequence numbers.

Session-level pacing controls the rate at which requests are sent within a session so that they do not arrive faster than the receiving LU can accept them. One-stage pacing is used when both session partners are subarea nodes. Two-stage pacing can be used if one partner is a peripheral node. With two-stage pacing, pacing is handled separately between the two subarea nodes and between boundary function in one subarea node and the peripheral node.

20 DATA FLOW CONTROL

This chapter discusses the functions of the data flow control layer. Data flow control is the central layer of an NAU, as illustrated in Fig. 20.1. Data flow control communicates with both function management and transmission control by passing back and forth request/response units (RUs) and parameters. Data flow control functions include processing a series of messages as a chain, processing a series of messages and responses as a bracket, determining and controlling the send/receive mode, assigning sequence numbers to RUs, interrupting data flow on request, and processing session status and error recovery.

CHAINS

Often a group of request units is related in such a way that it is convenient to handle them together as a single unit rather than in the form of individual request units. A *chain* is a group of request units treated as one entity for the purposes of error recovery. Chaining is the concern of the data flow control layer and is independent of any blocking, deblocking, or segmenting of RUs that is performed in the lower-level path control network layers.

When data flow control chains several requests, error recovery is applied to the chain as a whole rather than to individual RUs. If any one of the RUs cannot be processed by the receiving logical unit, the entire chain is discarded and an appropriate error response is sent. When data flow control passes to transmission control an RU that is part of a chain, it also passes parameters that indicate the position of the RU within the chain. Transmission control uses these parameters to set the Chaining Indicators in the request header that it creates. As discussed in Chapter 19, these indicators tell whether the RU is the first RU in a chain, a middle RU, the last RU in a chain, or the only RU in a chain. Only normal-flow request units can be grouped into chains. Responses and expedited-flow requests must be sent as single-unit chains.

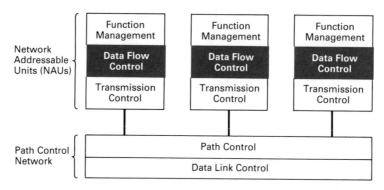

Figure 20.1   The Data Flow Control layer.

There are three different types of chains, as described in Box 20.1. Notice that chain types are categorized according to the type of response that is expected:

- No-response chains
- Exception-response chains
- Definite-response chains

BRACKETS

A series of related normal-flow chains and their associated responses can be grouped together into a larger unit called a *bracket*. Bracketing is typically used when several request units are all related to a particular transaction or work unit. As with chains, data flow control passes parameters to transmission control, which then sets the Bracket Control Indicators in the request header to the appropriate values. As discussed in Chapter 19, the first request unit in the first chain in the bracket is marked with the Begin Bracket Indicator; the first request unit in the last chain in the bracket is marked with the End Bracket Indicator.

BRACKET INITIATION

When brackets are used within a session, one of the participating half-sessions is designated during session binding as *first speaker* and the other as *bidder*. The first speaker is always allowed to start a bracket without requesting permission simply by sending an RU with the Begin Bracket Indicator on. If the bidder wishes to start a bracket, it must send a BID command to the first speaker. If the first speaker sends back a positive response, the bidder can begin sending the bracket. If the response is negative, the bidder must wait.

The first speaker can later send an RTR (Ready to Receive) command to

BOX 20.1   Chain types

- **No-Response Chains.** No response is expected to any RU in the chain. The Form of Response Indicators in the request header for each RU in the chain are set to the values corresponding to no response (see Chapter 19).
- **Exception-Response Chains.** A response is sent only if an error condition is detected. The Form of Response Indicators for each RU in the chain are set to exception-only response.
- **Definite-Response Chains.** A positive or negative response must be sent after the last RU in the chain is received. If an error is detected for an earlier RU, a negative response is sent. The Form of Response Indicators for the last RU in the chain are set to indicate a definite response; for all other RUs in the chain, these indicators are set to specify an exception response.

the bidder, granting permission for the bidder to begin sending a bracket. Also, when the first speaker sends a negative response, it can indicate through the use of sense code data whether or not it will send an RTR command later. If an RTR is expected, the bidder can wait to receive that command or can send another BID command.

The bidder can also attempt to start a bracket by sending a request unit with the Begin Bracket Indicator on, rather than sending a BID command. If the first speaker sends a positive response, the bidder continues sending the bracket; if a negative response is received, the bidder must wait for an RTR or can try again at a later time. The first speaker can send an RTR at any time, whether or not the bidder has requested permission to begin a bracket. If the bidder is ready to start a bracket, it sends a positive response and begins sending the bracket; if not, it sends a negative response.

**BRACKET
TERMINATION**

There are two different rules that control how brackets are terminated. Which rule to use is specified as part of session binding.

- **Rule 1: Conditional Termination.** The conditional termination rule is controlled by the type of response requested by the last chain in the bracket: definite response, exception-only response, or no response. If the response type indicates exception-only or no response, the bracket is terminated when the last request unit in the last chain is sent. If the response type requests a definite response, the bracket is terminated when a positive response is received for the last request unit in the last chain. If the response to the RU is negative, the bracket is continued. If there is a negative response to an earlier RU in the last chain, the sender can either terminate or continue the bracket. To terminate the bracket, the sender either sends a CANCEL command with the End Bracket Indicator on or sets the response type on the last RU in the chain to exception-only or no response. To continue the bracket, the sender either sends a CANCEL command with the End Bracket Indicator off or sends the last RU in the chain as a definite response.

- **Rule 2: Unconditional Termination.** Under the unconditional termination rule, a bracket is terminated whenever the last request unit of the last chain is processed.

REQUEST/RESPONSE MODES   Because of SNA's great flexibility, data flow control procedures need to be applied to an extremely wide variety of applications, each with its own special characteristics and needs. To meet these needs, different modes of operation are defined for the interaction of requests and responses. The four possible modes, which are described in Box 20.2, are as follows:

- Immediate-request mode
- Delayed-request mode
- Immediate-response mode
- Delayed-response mode

BOX 20.2   Request/response modes

- **Immediate-Request Mode.** *Immediate-request mode* indicates that a logical unit can send only one request chain before receiving a response, or it can send a group of request chains provided that only the last chain in the group specifies definite-response type.

- **Delayed-Request Mode.** *Delayed-request mode* indicates that multiple request chains can be sent before receiving a response, each soliciting any form of response.

- **Immediate-Response Mode.** *Immediate-response mode* indicates that responses must be sent in the same order that request units are received.

- **Delayed-Response Mode.** *Delayed-response mode* indicates that responses can be sent in any order. With delayed-response mode, responses can be received in a different order from that in which the corresponding requests were sent.

The particular request and response modes used for normal flow data by a given session are determined as part of session initiation. The modes used for data flow in one direction are independent of, and may differ from, the modes used in the other direction.

REQUEST/RESPONSE CORRELATION   One of the functions of data flow control is to correlate requests and responses. Since it is possible for several requests to be sent before a response is received, data flow control must have a way of matching each response with the request or requests that elicited it. This is done using the sequence number field in the transmission header and a set of correlation tables. When a request is sent, data flow control assigns a sequence number to it and passes the number in the form of a parameter to transmission control, which in turn passes it down to the path control layer for insertion in the transmission header. On the receiving side, the number is passed in the form of a parameter, along with the RU itself, up to data flow control. This number takes the form of either a sequence number (normal-flow RUs) or a unique identifier (expedited RUs). When each response is sent, the response contains the same value in its Sequence Number Field as the request to which it is responding.

Data flow control maintains two sets of tables that are used for request/response correlation. One set handles messages sent in the normal flow, and the other set handles expedited messages. Each set consists of two tables, one for sending responses and the other for receiving responses. Each entry in a correlation table corresponds to a chain. The information kept for each entry includes selected request/response indicators, such as Begin Bracket, End Bracket, and Change Direction; sequence numbers for the first and last request units in the chain; the type of chain involved; and whether or not an RU has been sent or received.

When the first request unit in a chain is sent, an entry is added to the table for receiving responses; when the first request unit in a chain is received, an entry is added to the table for sending responses. Each new entry is added to the end of the appropriate table. Entries are deleted from a table when a response is sent or received, and the corresponding chain has been completely sent or received. If a response is sent before an entire chain has been processed, the entry is deleted when the last request unit in the chain has been sent or received. Entries can be deleted from the table in any sequence. The Sequence Number Field in the response determines to which entry in the table it correlates. A response to an entry is one that has a sequence number falling within the range defined by the sequence numbers of the first and last request units in the chain. The size of the correlation table depends on the type of response and the particular request/response mode that is being used. For example, if all chains require a definite response and the immediate-request mode is used, the correlation table will contain a single entry. This is because a response must be received (and the table entry deleted) before another request chain can be sent. For other response types and request/response modes, there can be a variable number of entries in the table.

SEND/RECEIVE MODES

Data flow control is also responsible for coordinating changes between sending and receiving mode as specified by the *send/receive mode* being used for a particular session. There are three possible send/receive modes that can be used for normal transmission: half-duplex flip-flop, half-duplex contention, and full-duplex. These modes control transmission at the session level and are independent of the transmission mode (half-duplex or full-duplex) used on the data links that physically implement the network.

Half-Duplex Flip-Flop

In half-duplex flip-flop mode, the two half-sessions each alternate sending and receiving. When the half-session that is sending reaches the end of the normal-flow request units it has to send, it turns on the Change Direction Indicator in the request header of the last request unit sent. When the receiving half-session receives the request unit with the Change Direction Indicator on, it begins transmitting.

There are some differences in this protocol depending on whether or not brackets are used. If brackets are not used, one of the half-sessions is designated as *first sender* as part of session initiation and the other as *first receiver*. The first sender begins the session by sending, and the two then alternate between sending and receiving based on the Change Direction Indicator.

If brackets are used, one half-session is designated as the *first speaker* during session initiation and the other as *bidder*. The Change Direction Indicator is used to alternate sending and receiving within a bracket. Between brackets, either half-session can send. If contention occurs (both attempt to send at the same time), the first speaker is the contention winner.

Half-Duplex Contention

With half-duplex contention mode, one half-session is specified during session initiation as *contention winner* and the other as *contention loser*. Either half-session can begin sending request units. If contention occurs, the contention winner can send a negative response to the contention loser, which must then wait until the end of a chain before attempting to transmit again. When transmission of a chain is complete, either half-session can attempt to send. The contention loser must queue any requests it receives while it is sending, so that it is able to process the requests if it receives a negative response from the contention winner. The contention winner can queue requests it receives while sending and process them rather than send a negative response. The Change of Direction Indicator can also be used as a way of avoiding contention.

Full-Duplex

With full-duplex mode, both half-sessions are able to send requests at the same time. The request/response flows in each direction operate independently, and any correlation between the two flows must take place at a level above data flow control.

SESSION STATUS

At times it may be necessary for a half-session to send session status information to its session partner. This can be done by data flow control in one of several ways. The status information can be included in a data request unit. An LU Status (LUSTAT) request, which travels in the normal data flow, can be used. A Signal (SIG) request, which uses the expedited flow, can be used when a LUSTAT cannot be sent, for example, while the half-session is receiving.

DATA FLOW INTERRUPTION

Under certain conditions it may be necessary for session data flow to be interrupted, either temporarily or in anticipation of session termination. When this happens, it is important for the interruption to be performed in an orderly manner. Data flow control provides several protocols that can be used to coordinate processing between half-sessions when implementing different types of interruptions.

Stop Bracket Initiation

One form of interruption that might be necessary is to stop a half-session from sending bracket initiation requests. In this protocol, one half-session sends a Stop Bracket Initiation (SBI) request, requesting that the other half-session stop sending requests to initiate a bracket. The other half-session responds with a Bracket Initiation Stopped (BIS) response, indicating that it agrees to stop sending bracket initiation requests. A BIS can also be sent even though an SBI has not been received, indicating that the half-session will be sending no further bracket initiation requests. This protocol can be used prior to session termination to ensure that any syncpoint requests have been processed before the session ends. If a syncpoint request is not processed, it is possible that protected resources may continue to be locked until the session is reactivated and resynchronized.

Quiesce

At times a half-session may wish to stop the other half-session from transmitting normal-flow requests. The reason for this might be that the half-session is getting low on a resource needed to process requests, or it might be because the half-session is preparing to terminate the session. The Quiesce protocol is then used to stop normal-flow transmission. Either half-session can "quiesce" its partner.

A half-session sends a Quiesce (QEC) request to the other half-session to tell it to stop sending normal-flow requests after it completes the chain it is currently sending. When the half-session completes the chain, it sends back a QC response, indicating it will send no more requests on the normal data flow. At a later point the original half-session can send a RELQ request to let the other half-session resume normal data flow transmission. Only normal-flow transmission is affected by Quiesce. While quiesced, a half-session can still receive normal-flow requests and respond appropriately.

Shutdown

The Shutdown protocol is typically used as a way of preparing for session termination. As with Quiesce, it is used to stop transmission of normal-flow requests. However, only the primary logical unit can initiate a shutdown. It does so by sending a Shutdown (SHUTD) request to the secondary half-session. The SHUTD request asks the half-session to stop sending normal-flow requests when a convenient point is reached. This, for example, might be at the end of a bracket. When such a point is reached, the half-session responds with a SHUTC response, indicating that no further normal-flow requests will be sent. The primary half-session can then later send a RELQ request allowing the secondary half-session to resume sending normal-flow requests.

The SHUTC response is sent on the expedited flow, which means it might bypass requests that were sent in the normal flow. If the secondary half-session needed to retransmit a normal-flow request because of an error condition, it would not be able to do so after the SHUTC had been sent. To avoid this situation, the secondary half-session can send a CHASE request. The CHASE request asks that the primary half-session respond to all previous requests before responding to the CHASE. Thus when the secondary half-session receives the response to the CHASE, it can be sure it will receive no further responses requiring retransmission on the normal data flow, and it can then safely send the SHUTC.

SUMMARY

Data flow control is the central layer among the three major layers that make up the NAU component of SNA. Data flow control communicates with both function management and transmission control by passing back and forth request/response units (RUs) and parameters. A chain is a group of RUs treated as one entity for error recovery purposes. Data flow control passes parameters to transmission control that indicate whether an RU is the beginning, middle, end, or only RU in a chain. A chain can be a no-response chain, an exception-response chain, or a mandatory-response chain; this is also indicated in the parameters passed by data flow control. A bracket is a series of related chains and their associated responses that are grouped as one work unit. Unrelated requests and responses are not transmitted during the processing of a bracket. The first speaker half-session can always initiate a bracket. The bidder half-session can request permission to start a bracket with a BID command or by sending a request with the Begin Bracket Indicator on. The first speaker can grant permission for the bidder to initiate a bracket by sending a positive response when the bidder requests permission or by sending an RTR command. Bracket termination can be either conditional or unconditional. With unconditional termination, a bracket is terminated after the last request in the last chain is processed. With conditional termination, it is possible to continue the bracket if an error occurs during the processing of the last chain.

Data flow control is responsible for correlating responses with the specific requests that elicited them. This is done by using the Sequence Number Field in the TH and a set of correlation tables. An entry is included in a correlation table for each chain sent or received. When a response is sent or received, an entry is removed from its table. The table entry to remove is identified by the value in the Sequence Number Field.

Send/receive mode for normal transmission can be either half-duplex flip-flop, half-duplex contention, or full-duplex. With half-duplex flip-flop mode, the two half-sessions alternate sending and receiving. The Change of Direction Indicator in the RH is used to signal the receiving half-session that it can begin sending. If brackets are used, the Change Direction Indicator is used to alternate sending and receiving within a bracket. With half-duplex contention mode, one half-session is designated as the contention winner and the other as the contention loser. Either half-session can begin sending requests. If contention occurs, the contention winner sends either a positive or negative response to the contention loser. If negative, the contention loser must wait until the end of a chain before attempting to transmit again. With full-duplex mode, both half-sessions can send requests at the same time.

The Stop Bracket Initiation protocol is used to stop a half-session from sending bracket initiation requests. The Quiesce protocol is used to stop a half-session from sending normal-flow requests after it completes the chain it is currently sending. The Shutdown protocol is used to stop a half-session from sending normal-flow requests when a convenient point is reached. When the normal flow has been quiesced or shut down, a RELQ command can be sent, allowing the half-session to resume sending on the normal flow.

PART V

NAUs: FUNCTION MANAGEMENT

21 END-USER SERVICES

The purpose of SNA is not to make the job of the typical systems analyst or application programmer more complex. On the contrary, it is designed to provide application developers with flexibility and ease in the performance of their jobs by providing a set of easy-to-use, high-level functions to the end users of the network. In this part of the book we examine the services that are provided by the uppermost of the five major SNA functional layers. These are the services that are closest to the end users of the SNA network.

DISTRIBUTED SOFTWARE   Nodes throughout a network can implement a variety of facilities that must work together in a coordinated fashion. A peripheral node may or may not have storage devices. It may or may not have substantial computing or processing capability. If it has storage or computing capabilities, these might be employed in a wide range of manners to the benefit of the other devices and users on the network. Most of the valuable ways of using distributed intelligence require that the machines at each end of an SNA session cooperate with each other in a precisely defined manner. One device might be editing or formatting data on the basis of characters sent to it by the device at the other end. One device might be compressing data so that they can be sent more economically and the other expanding them to their original form. One might encipher data for security purposes, and the other must decipher them. A peripheral storage device might store panels for display on a terminal as a part of a dialog, and another machine might specify which panels are to be used, possibly even sending the data to be inserted in the panels.

The software modules that are used for functions such as managing a database or controlling a time-sharing service are highly complex and are likely to become more elaborate in the future as the application development process is further automated. Before the advent of distributed intelligence, these software modules all resided entirely in a central computer. Now, increasingly, there are good reasons to distribute certain functions of the software to peripheral machines. We can speak of distributed dialogs, distributed storage, and distributed database operations. For example, at one time a logical unit might be connected to a database management system. At another time it might be using personal computing facilities. At still another time it might be sending data requiring tight security controls, possibly including cryptography. Coordinating and providing these different services and facilities are among the primary tasks of the uppermost layer of SNA.

As we have already seen, the highest major layer of SNA is the function management layer. As shown in Fig. 21.1, the function management layer can be divided into two sublayers: the *NAU services manager* and *function management data services*. These components provide a broad range of services, some of which are related to sessions and others to the control and management of the network as a whole. The major function management services are listed in Box 21.1. *End-user services* are involved with the exchange of data between end users via an LU-to-LU session. *Session network services* are involved with various aspects of network management and control. We begin this chapter by examining the functions provided by end-user services. Chapter 22 discusses the formats of the various function management message headers that are used as part of end-user services. Session network services are covered in later chapters in this part.

FUNCTION MANAGEMENT COMPONENTS

The various software or firmware components that provide function management services are shown in Fig. 21.2. Notice that the function management layer contains different components, depending on whether

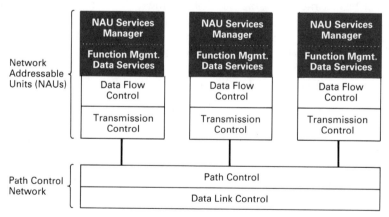

Figure 21.1   The Function Management layer.

BOX 21.1 Function management services

End-User Services

- Session presentation services
- Application-to-application services

Session Network Services

- Session services
- Configuration services
- Maintenance and management services
- Network operator services

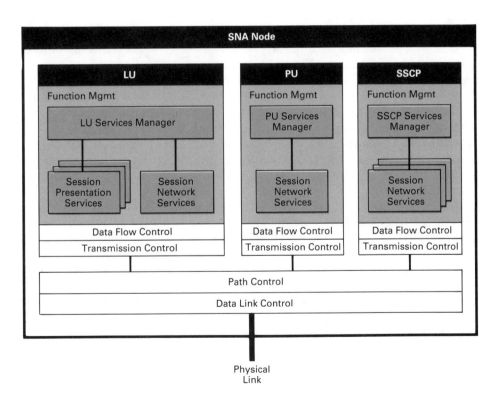

Figure 21.2 Function management components.

the NAU is an LU, a PU, or an SSCP. Each NAU has a single *services manager* component. In addition, there is a *session presentation services* or *session network services* component for each half-session active in the NAU. Session presentation services components are used for LU-to-LU sessions. Since a single LU can often support several LU-to-LU sessions, it might contain several session presentation services components. Session network services components are used for SSCP-to-SSCP, SSCP-to-LU, and SSCP-to-PU sessions.

END-USER SERVICES

End-user services focus on the interface between the end user, which might be an application program or a terminal user, and the logical unit that represents that end user to the SNA network. The two end users involved in a session might have different requirements and capabilities for processing the data being interchanged. End-user services provide support for data transformations and for any processing that is needed to transmit the data efficiently across the SNA network and to appropriately display the data.

As shown in Box 21.1, there are two categories of end-user services: *session presentation services* and *application-to-application services*. Session presentation services are primarily concerned with data formatting and with the display of data to the end user. Application-to-application services provide for processing synchronization, particularly when application programs in different nodes are communicating. The LU services manager and session presentation services component, in combination, provide these services.

We will next examine session presentation services in detail. First we look at the structure of the request/response unit and examine the different types of data stream formats that are supported as part of session presentation services. After that we examine the *data compression* and *data compaction* session presentation services. We conclude this chapter by discussing the synchronization function provided by application-to-application services.

REQUEST/RESPONSE UNIT STRUCTURE

As we have already seen, the basic message unit that is transmitted across the SNA network is the *request/response unit* (RU). Various headers and trailers are appended to the RU and are later removed from it as the RU moves up and down through the various functional layers of the sending and receiving nodes and any intermediate nodes the RU passes through. As discussed in Chapter 19, RUs that flow in LU-to-LU sessions are divided into the following three categories, according to the SNA components that originate and receive the RU:

- Function management data (FMD)
- Data flow control
- Session control

Network control RUs constitute a fourth RU category that are used only in PU-to-PU sessions using the expedited data flow. FMD request units (FMD RUs) are in turn divided into two major categories: those that are used to perform network services and those that carry user data.

NETWORK SERVICES FMD RUs

Network services RUs are used for functions such as initiating and terminating sessions, recovering from errors, and sending responses to data transmissions. Each control RU has a specific, well-defined format. The formats of control RUs are described in the *Systems Network Architecture Format and Protocol Reference Manual: Architectural Logic* (SC30-3112).

Network services RUs can carry data in either of two formats: character-coded data and field-formatted data. The Format bit in the RH that is attached to the RU indicates whether a network services RU is character-coded or field-formatted. A character-coded RU carries data in the form of a character string; a field-formatted RU carries data in the form of fields, each of which contains data in a specified format, such as binary codes, counts, flags, or symbolic names. Network services RUs are discussed in detail in Chapter 23.

FMD-RUs THAT CARRY USER DATA

The general formats of FMD RUs that carry user data are shown in Fig. 21.3. An FMD RU that carries user data can contain *data,* one or more *function management headers* (FMHs), and *string control bytes* (SCBs). Any of

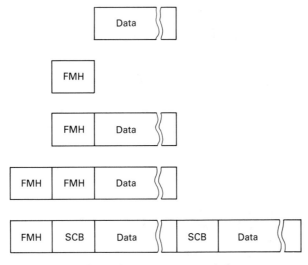

Figure 21.3   Request/response unit formats.

these elements can be omitted for a particular RU or can occur in any combination. Function management headers are used as part of end-user services for functions such as specifying a device (display terminal, printer, etc.) used to display data or controlling the way data are displayed or processed. String control bytes are used to implement data compression and data compaction functions. The structure of the RUs that are passed between end users and the use of function management headers and string control bytes depend on the type of LU-to-LU session taking place. Box 21.2 reviews the different LU types that we introduced in Chapter 8. Function management headers and string control bytes are examined in detail later in this chapter.

DATA STREAMS   The data portion of an FMD RU carries data using a particular type of *data stream*. With some logical unit types, the data stream that flows between the two logical units is defined by the architecture. For example, LU types 2 and 3 use the 3270 data stream, which is used to control 3270-type devices; LU types 1 and 4 use the SNA character string, which is a generalized data stream used to control the formatting of data for a variety of devices; and LU type 7 uses the 5250 data stream,

BOX 21.2   Logical unit types

LU Type	Capabilities
LU 0	Allows SNA formats and protocols to be augmented by user-defined formats and protocols using a user-defined data stream
LU 1	Supports application programs that communicate with a terminal that can implement multiple input/output devices using the SNA data stream
LU 2	Supports application programs that communicate with 3270 terminals or their equivalents using the 3270 data stream
LU 3	Supports application programs that communicate with 3270 printer devices or their equivalents using the 3270 data stream
LU 4	Provides peer-to-peer communication for certain types of devices using the SNA data stream
LU 6	Provides general peer-to-peer communication between application programs using a user-defined data stream
LU 7	Supports application programs that communicate with a 5250-type display terminal or their equivalents using the 5250 data stream

which is used to control 5250-type devices. With other logical units, such as LU types 0 and 6, any data stream can flow between the two logical units. With these LU types, the choice of a data stream is made by the user and can be any of the three data streams described or can be some other type of data stream defined by the user.

STRUCTURED FIELDS

A data stream can consist of a continuous string of characters, a sequence of *structured fields,* or a combination of the two. The use of structured fields is allowed by some LU types, and various methods are used to indicate that the data portion of an FMD RU contains structured fields. The use of structured fields allows the receiving LU to decompose a message into its component fields without having to examine each byte.

Figure 21.4 shows the data portion of an RU that carries two structured fields. Notice that each structured field begins with a two-byte length field, which allows the beginning of the next field to be immediately identified. Following the length field, the structured field contains a one- or two-byte identifier field. The identifier field identifies the structured field as containing a particular format of data or a particular control function. This identifier also defines the format of the rest of the structured field. A structured field can contain either data or a command. A few structured field commands are listed and described in Box 21.3. An RU might contain a single structured field, more than one structured field, or only a portion of a structured field. However, a single structured field cannot span more than one RU chain.

We will next examine more closely the two most common data stream types used in LU-to-LU sessions: the SNA data stream and the 3270 data stream.

SNA DATA STREAM

The SNA data stream is always used with LU types 1 and 4, and it can optionally be used with LU types 0 and 6. The SNA data stream uses a set of *SNA character string* (SCS) controls that are intermixed with user data. The SCS controls relate primarily to the formatting of data for visual display and specify

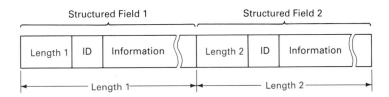

Figure 21.4   Structured field format.

BOX 21.3   Structured field commands

- **Read Partition.** Requests the LU to send a description of its device characteristics
- **Query Reply.** Sends information about device characteristics
- **Load Programmed Symbols.** Sends information about the character set to be used during the session
- **Request Recovery Data.** Requests the secondary LU to send data needed to restart a print job
- **Recovery Data.** Sends the restart data needed for a print job
- **Restart.** Indicates that a restart is in progress and that a certain number of pages and lines should be skipped before starting to print
- **Set Checkpoint Interval.** Sets the number of pages to be processed between checkpoints
- **SCS Data.** Indicates that the data that follow contain SNA character string (SCS) controls

such functions such as spacing, tabs, and new lines. When LU-to-LU sessions use SCS controls, certain bit configurations in the EBCDIC character set define control functions. These control function values lie in the range of from X'00' through X'3F' plus the value X'FF'. The other EBCDIC values are used to represent data.

Certain of the control codes are followed by parameters that either more specifically define the function to perform or to supply numeric values, such as the number of lines to move in a positioning function. An SCS control code, and the parameters following it, can span RUs but must be completed within an RU chain. Box 21.4 lists the SCS controls and the values assigned to each. Those followed by ellipses have one or more parameters following them. Certain SCS controls are used to set modes of device operation, to define the data to be used in a particular way, or to provide communication between a device operator and an application program. However, most relate to the formatting of data being displayed.

3270 DATA STREAM LU types 2 and 3 are specifically designed to use the data stream format associated with the 3270 family of devices. The 3270 data stream can be used with LU types 0 and 6 if appropriate end-user programming is provided to comply with the formatting conventions. This data stream format is designed to support

BOX 21.4   SNA character stream control functions

SCS Control Function	Code (hexadecimal)
Backspace	16
Bell	2F
Carriage Return	0D
Customer Use	1B, 3B
Device Control	11,12, 13, 3C
Enable Presentation	14
Expanded Backspace	36
Expanded Space	E1
Form Feed	0C
Graphic Escape	08 . . .
Horizontal Tab	05
Indent Tab	39
Index Return	33
Inhibit Presentation	24
Interchange Separator	1C, 1D, 1E, 1F
Line Feed	25
New Line	15
Null	00
Presentation Position	34 . . .
Program Operator Communication	17 . . .
Repeat	0A
Required Form Feed	3A
Required New Line	06
Required Space	41
Secure String ID Reader	0450
Select Left Paten	04C1
Select Magnetic Encoder	046n
Select Right Paten	04C2
Set	28 . . .
Shift In	0F
Shift Out	0E
Start of Format	2BC3
Subscript	38
Substitute	3F
Superscript	09
Switch	2A
Syllable Hyphen	CA
Transparent	35 . . .
Unit Backspace	1A
Vertical Channel Select	04
Vertical Tab	0B
Word Underscore	23

the various functions provided by the 3270 family of terminal devices, including the control of display characteristics, such as color and highlighting.

Outbound Data Stream

Figure 21.5 shows the basic format of a message being sent from an application program to a terminal using the 3270 data stream. The first byte of an outbound 3270 data stream contains a command. The command specifies such information as whether the application program is writing to or reading from the terminal, whether to erase the screen before writing on it, or whether structured fields are being used in the data stream. Box 21.5 lists the various 3270 command codes.

For write commands, the second byte in the data stream contains a write control character (WCC). The WCC is used to specify such functions as sounding an alarm at the terminal, unlocking the keyboard, or copying the contents of the display screen to a printer. The data portion of the data stream consists of a combination of orders and actual data characters to be displayed. Data values in the range $X'00'$ to $X'3F'$ are interpreted as orders. Orders specify information about the data in the data stream and how they should be displayed, including functions such as these:

- Identifying attribute information within the data stream when formatted screens are used
- Specifying positioning of data or the cursor on the screen
- Erasing data or providing fill characters
- Specifying the use of a graphic character from an alternate character set

A structured field format can also be used with the 3270 data stream. The use of structured fields is specified by the Write Structured Fields command code. This command code is immediately followed by a series of structured fields. These structured fields can contain commands, including both 3270 command codes and the commands listed earlier in the section on structured fields. A structured field containing a write command will also include a write control character. Other structured field commands relate to the use of *partitions*. With 3270 devices the display area can be divided into different areas, called partitions. Data can then be sent to or read from a specific partition. Structured field command functions include creating, activating, and deleting partitions.

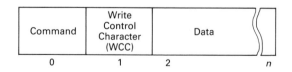

Figure 21.5   3270 data stream—outbound.

BOX 21.5 3270 command codes

Command	Value (hexadecimal)
Write	F1
Erase/Write	F5
Erase/Write Alternate	7E
Read Buffer	F2
Read Modified	F6
Read Modified All	6E
Erase All Unprotected	6F
Write Structured Fields	F3

Inbound Data Stream

Figure 21.6 shows the basic format of a data stream being sent from a 3270 terminal to an application program. The first byte is an attention identifier (AID). Generally, the AID indicates the method the terminal operator used to trigger the enter operation—pressing one of the attention keys on the keyboard, reading a magnetic stripe, or completing a light-pen operation. Following the AID is a two-byte field containing the current cursor position address. The data portion of the data stream consists of a combination of orders and data characters. An inbound data stream can also be in structured field format. In this case the AID byte contains the value X'88' followed by a structured field containing data from a specific partition.

Formatted Screens

The communication between an application program and a 3270 terminal can use formatted or unformatted screens. With unformatted screens, the data portion of the data stream is used in a free-form manner; with structured screens, the data portion is organized in the form of fields that have defined characteristics. Attributes are used to define the fields and their characteristics. A *field attribute* character marks the beginning of a field and specifies characteristics such as whether the field is to be displayed, whether data can be entered into

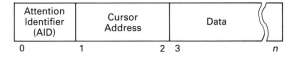

Figure 21.6 3270 data stream—inbound.

the field, and whether entered data must be numeric or alphabetic. *Extended field attributes* provide additional characteristics, including the use of color, highlighting, or an alternate character set. *Character attributes* specify the same characteristics as extended field attributes, but for an individual character rather than for an entire field. Various order values are used to identify the presence of field attributes, extended field attributes, and character attributes within the data portion of the 3270 data stream.

5250 DATA STREAM

The 5250 data stream is used by LU type 7 to support the 5250 family of terminals. The control functions supported by the 5250 data stream are similar to those for the 3270 data stream but are specifically oriented to the unique characteristics of 5250 equipment.

We continue our discussion of end-user services by discussing the data compression and data compaction functions that are optionally performed by session presentation services.

DATA COMPRESSION AND COMPACTION

Data compression and *data compaction* techniques can be used by session presentation services to provide for more efficient data transmission across the network. These techniques can be used by LU type 1 and 4 sessions using the SNA data stream. Both techniques are designed to reduce the number of bits that are transmitted. Data are compressed or compacted by the sending half-session and then restored to their original form by the receiving half-session.

When data compression is used, a sequence of consecutive occurrences of a single character is replaced by a control code and a count of the number of times the character occurred. The control code and count are contained in a *string control byte* (SCB) that replaces the repetitive string of characters in the data stream. A *prime compression character* is defined to identify the default character being replaced. A string of prime compression characters is identified by an SCB alone. A repetitive string of a character other than the prime compression character is identified by an SCB followed by the character being represented by the SCB. The prime compression character is normally the space (X'40'); however, this value can be changed by including the appropriate information in the function management header.

When data compaction is used, two characters of data are represented in a single byte. This is done by defining a set of eight-bit values that can be represented by four bits. Characters that are being represented by four bits are called *master characters*. A compaction table defines the values of the master characters; this table is transmitted from one half-session to the other via a function management header. Pairs of master characters are compacted into a single byte. SCB codes are then used to mark the beginning and end of a block of data that has been compacted. Box 21.6 shows the format of the SCB. The first two SCB bits specify the function code, and the remaining six bits contain a count field. Codes 01 and 11 specify data compression; code 10, data compaction. Code 00 is used to locate the next SCB when neither compression nor compaction applies.

When a half-session sends compressed or compacted data, it must first send a function management header with an appropriate indicator turned on. The compression indicator (CMI) indicates that SCBs for either prime-character or nonprime-character compression can follow. The compaction indicator (CPI) indicates that SCBs for compacted data can follow. The sending half-session must then insert SCBs as required into the data stream that follows.

APPLICATION-TO-APPLICATION SERVICES

Synchronization is the primary service provided by the application-to-application services category of end-user services.

BOX 21.6   SCB format

SCB Code (bits 0–1)	Count (bits 2–7)	Interpretation
00	nnnnnn	No duplicate characters were replaced. Count = number of bytes to next SCB.
01	nnnnnn	Prime compression character replaced. Count = number of occurrences of character replaced. The next byte is the next SCB.
11	nnnnnn	Nonprime compression character replaced. Count = number of occurrences of character replaced. The next byte is the value of the character replaced. The byte following that is the next SCB.
10	nnnnnn	Data compacted. Count = number of compacted bytes between this SCB and the next one.

SYNCHRONIZATION   The synchronization function provides a protocol for coordinating events between two or more communicating application programs. As introduced in Chapter 8, synchronization services are particularly useful for transaction processing applications where multistep actions performed by different programs are necessary to complete a unit of work.

Resources allocated to a transaction processing application program are defined as either *protected* or *unprotected*. For protected resources, a record is kept of any changes that are made to the resource. When the processing of a unit of work is completed, the two half-sessions agree to *commit* the changes to protected resources, thus creating a *syncpoint*. All changes made up to the syncpoint are considered permanent, and the record of changes made up to that point is discarded. A record is then kept of any new changes that are made following the syncpoint. If agreement is not reached to commit the changes, or if a session failure occurs before commitment is complete, changes are automatically backed out up to the previous syncpoint, and the unit of work can be restarted. Synchronization can involve more than one session; however, the individual application programs must coordinate synchronization processing when multiple sessions are involved.

Commit Protocols

Either of two protocols can be used for commit processing: *one-phase commits* and *two-phase commits*. In a one-phase commit, one half-session sends a request for the other half-session to commit to the completion of the current unit of work. This request takes the form of an RU that has the Definite Response Indicator 2 in the request header set to one. If the other half-session sends a positive response, the commitment is considered complete, and a new syncpoint is then established. In a two-phase commit, one half-session sends a Prepare to Commit request to the other. This request takes the form of either a specific function management header or a LUSTAT request containing the appropriate status value. The Prepare to Commit request asks the receiving half-session to send a Request to Commit request at the end of the current chain. When the Request to Commit request is sent, the original half-session sends a positive or negative response, as appropriate.

With either protocol, if a session failure occurs after a Request to Commit request has been sent but before a response is received, the half-session that sent the Request to Commit request is not able to determine if the new syncpoint was established before the failure occurred. In this case protected resources must be held until the session is reactivated and resynchronized. The two-phase commit protocol allows a choice of which half-session sends the request to commit and thus must hold locks on protected resources in the event of a failure.

Session Reactivation

If a session using synchronization processing fails, resynchronization takes place when the session is reactivated. After the session is activated, but before any data are sent, a Set and Test Sequence Number (STSN) request is sent. The STSN RU and its response cause the two half-sessions to exchange sequence numbers corresponding to their most recent syncpoint. If both numbers are the same, the half-sessions are in synchronization and processing can start. If they do not agree, one half-session must roll back changes to a previous syncpoint so that they do agree.

SUMMARY

Function management provides two groups of services: end-user services and session network services. End-user services include session presentation services and application-to-application services. Session network services include session services, configuration services, maintenance and management services, and network operator services. Each NAU contains a services manager component. LU-to-LU half-sessions each contain a session presentation services component; other half-sessions contain a session network services component. These components are involved in providing function management services.

Data are sent between logical units using a particular type of *data stream*. A data stream can consist of a continuous string of characters, a sequence of structured fields, or both. Structured fields are used to send variable-length messages in a way that makes individual fields easy to identify. Data streams supported by SNA include the SNA data stream, the 3270 data stream, and the 5250 data stream. The SNA data stream is used by logical unit types 1 and 4 and provides generalized control over data formatting. The SNA data stream employs SNA character string (SCS) controls intermixed with data. The 3270 data stream is used with logical unit types 2 and 3 for transmitting data to and from a 3270-type terminal. The 5250 data stream is used with logical unit type 7 and supports the 5250 family of terminal devices. Logical unit types 0 and 6 support any desired data stream.

Data compression and data compaction can be used to reduce the number of characters transmitted across the network. With data compression, a repetitive string of characters is replaced by a control code and a count of the number of times the character was repeated. With data compaction, selected eight-bit characters are represented by four-bit values. Two characters are then condensed into a single byte. When data compression or compaction is used, string control bytes (SCBs) are used to carry the information (control codes, counts, etc.) needed to restore the data to their original form when they are received.

Synchronization allows two or more application programs to coordinate the state of the resources they control. A record is kept of all changes made to protected resources. When a unit of work is completed, the two half-sessions agree to commit changes made to this point, thus creating a syncpoint. If agreement is not reached or a problem occurs, changes are backed out up to the previous syncpoint.

22 THE FUNCTION MANAGEMENT HEADER

In Chapter 21 we saw that an RU can contain one or more function management (FM) headers. Different FM headers serve different purposes, some of which were described in the Chapter 21 sections that discussed data compression and compaction and synchronization services. The currently defined FM headers are of types 1, 2, 3, 4, 5, 6, 7, and 10.

FM headers 1, 2, and 3 are used with LU type 1 and 4 sessions that use the SNA data stream. The remaining FM headers (types 4, 5, 6, 7, and 10) are used with LU type 6 sessions. LU type 0 employs RUs whose formats are determined by agreement between the two session partners, and function management headers are not used for this LU type. The remaining LU types employ the two equipment-specific data streams—the 3270 data stream and the 5250 data stream—in which control codes define the functions being performed; these LU types also do not use function management headers. In this chapter we look at the functions of all the various FM headers and examine the data each contains.

FM HEADER 1

FM header 1 (FMH-1) is used to control the flow of data to a particular *destination* within an LU. A destination normally represents the *medium* used to present data. A destination might be a device, such as a display terminal or a printer; a data set residing on a direct-access storage volume; or a data stream being accepted as input by an application program. An FMH-1 is also used to indicate what type of data stream follows the header and whether data compression or compaction has been used. FMH-1 headers are used in LU type 1 and 4 sessions that use the SNA data stream.

A key concept related to an RU's destination is that of a *stack*. At times it may be necessary for SNA to interrupt transmission to one destination in order to send data to another destination. Transmission to the original destination is resumed thereafter. For example, while data are being sent to a printer, it might be necessary to interrupt the printing operation in order to send a message to an operator's console device. This can be done by *suspending* the original destination and later *resuming* it. Both the sending and receiving LUs maintain a stack that contains information about destinations. An entry that describes the active destination is at the top of the stack. When a destination is suspended, its entry is pushed down in the stack. Information for the new active destination is then added to the top of the stack. When transmission to the active destination ends, that destination's entry is removed from the stack. If there is a suspended destination, it can be reactivated, making the suspended destination the active destination again. A stack can have one, two, or three levels, meaning that there can be zero, one, or two suspended destinations.

When the FMH-1 is being used to control the destination of an RU, there are several functions it can perform. These are described in Box 22.1. Figure 22.1 shows the format of a function management header 1. The first two bytes have the same format for all FM headers. The first byte always contain the header's length. The second byte always contains a bit that indicates whether another FM header follows this one and an identifier whose value identifies the particular type of FM header this is.

The Medium Select and Logical Subaddress fields identify the specific destination described by this FMH-1. The Stack Reference Indicator determines

BOX 22.1   FM header 1 functions

BEGIN	Identifies a new destination
END	Terminates the use of the active destination at the end of the current chain
BEGIN/END	Identifies a new destination to be used only for the duration of the current chain
END-ABORT	Immediately terminates the use of the current destination
SUSPEND	Causes the currently active destination to be suspended and pushes down that destination's stack entry
RESUME	Causes a suspended destination's stack entry to pop up in the stack and makes that destination active
CONTINUE	Provides information about the data stream that follows, such as the use of compression or compaction, without affecting the destination

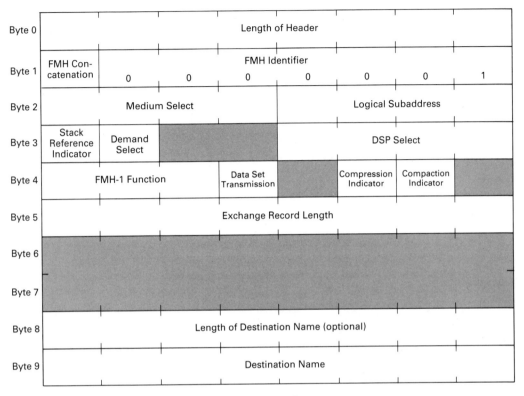

Figure 22.1   FM header 1 format.

whether the sender's or receiver's send stack is affected when a stack is involved in the operation. The Demand Select field specifies whether the receiver
is able to substitute a new destination to replace the specified destination. The
DSP Select field identifies the particular type of data stream that follows. Although the data that follow an FMH-1 always use the SNA data stream, the
DSP Select field gives additional information about the data stream—whether it
contains structured fields, a word processing document, a document being interchanged, and the like.

The FMH-1 Function field identifies the particular function this header
represents, such as Begin, End, or Suspend. The Data Set Transmission field
specifies further information about the data stream format. The Compression
Indicator and Compaction Indicator, as described earlier, indicate whether data
compression or data compaction was applied to the data that follow. The Exchange Record Length field specifies the record length of the data that follow,
to be used by the receiver to deblock the data. The Length of Destination Name
and Destination Name fields can be used to provide a destination name that

corresponds to a logical component in the receiving LU. The formats of all the various function management headers are not contained in the main *Architectural Logic* reference manual (SC20–3112); they are described in detail in *SNA Sessions Between Logical Units* (GC20–1868).

FM HEADER 2

FM header 2 (FMH-2) is used to specify a data management activity to be performed using the data that follow. FMH-2 headers are used in LU type 1 and 4 sessions that use the SNA data stream. An FMH-2 can be used only when a destination is active and thus must be preceded, either immediately or in an earlier RU, by a Begin, Begin/End, or Resume FMH-1. The FMH-2 data management functions can be performed on a number of data set organizations:

- Sequential
- Addressed direct (uses record number for retrieval)
- Keyed direct (uses key for retrieval)
- Keyed indexed

Box 22.2 lists some of the functions that can be specified with the FMH-2. Data sets can be created and deleted, and through the query function a data set can be sent from the FMH-2 receiver to the FMH-2 sender. Records can be added, replaced, or deleted. Also, copies of a record can be added to a data set or used to replace records in the data set. The Note and Note Reply functions are used to request and then to send the location of the next available record. A compaction table or a prime compression character value can be sent using an FMH-2. The Peripheral Data Information Record FMH-2 is used to send operator requests for services such as mounting forms or making copies. The Execute Program Offline FMH-2 provides the name of a program to be executed when the LU-to-LU session ends.

In addition to using an FMH-2 to specify an operation to be performed, it might also be necessary to use an FMH-2 to specify a location identifier or a password. For a data set operation, the location identifier is a volume serial number; for a record operation, it is a record identifier. The FMH-2 that specifies a function to be performed is known as the *root FMH-2*. An FMH-2 that carries the identifier or password is an *extension FMH-2*.

Figure 22.2 shows the general format of the FMH-2. The first two bytes and the Stack Reference Indicator serve the same purpose as for the FMH-1. The Function field indicates the specific function to be performed. The remaining bytes are used to provide information needed to perform the specified function. The content and format for this information vary with the function being performed.

BOX 22.2 FM header 2 functions

Function Category	Functions
Data set functions	Create Data Set
	Delete Data Set
	Erase Records
	Query Data Set
	Delete All Data Sets
Record functions	Add Record
	Replace Record
	Add Duplicate Records
	Replace Duplicate Records
	Erase Record
	Note
	Note Reply
Compression/compaction	Send Compaction Table
	Send Prime Compression Character
Operator communication	Peripheral Data Information Record
Program scheduling	Execute Program Offline
Extension information	Password
	Record ID
	Volume ID

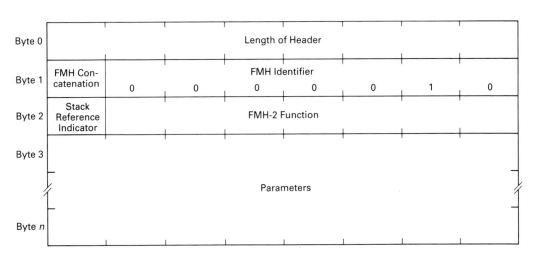

Figure 22.2 FM header 2 format.

FM HEADER 3   *FM header 3* (FMH-3) is used to carry information that applies to all destinations for both session partners. In some cases the information is the same as that contained in an FMH-2, but it applies to all destinations rather than only one. FMH-3 headers are used in LU type 1 and 4 sessions. Box 22.3 lists the functions performed by the FMH-3. A request can be sent for a compaction table to be returned. A compaction table or prime compression character value, applying to all destinations, can be sent. The Series ID FMH-3 is used preceding and following a sequence of FM headers to identify them as a series and to give the series a name. The Status Information FMH-3 provides user-defined status information about a series of FM headers, a user application program, or a data set with a given data set name.

Figure 22.3 shows the format of the FMH-3. As with the FMH-2, parameters following the Function field provide information needed to perform the function. The content and format of this information vary with the specific function being performed.

FM HEADER 4   As mentioned earlier, FM headers of types 4, 5, 6, 7, and 10 are used by LU type 6 sessions in which communication between application programs takes place. *FM header 4* (FMH-4) is used to describe the data stream contained in the RU. It is used by a particular type of transaction program called a *logical message services* (LMS) program. With LMS, data are processed by an LMS transaction program in both the sending and receiving nodes. In the receiving node an LMS program adds messages it receives to appropriate queues and passes messages from the queues to the appropriate transaction processing programs.

FMH-4 uses a data stream format in which the data portion of the RU contains *field-formatted records*. With a data stream that contains field-formatted records, the data consist of a series of transmission fields. These transmission fields correspond to the fields in a stored logical record. Normally, the

BOX 22.3   FM header 3 functions

- Query for Compaction Table
- Send Compaction Table
- Send Prime Compression Character
- Series ID
- Status Information

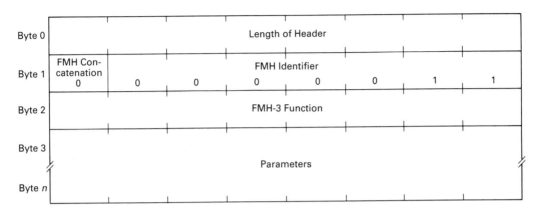

Figure 22.3   FM header 3 format.

receiver maintains a *map* that describes the formats of the fields in a stored logical record. The map can be used to help in associating transmission fields with stored logical record fields. Specific field-formatted record types have different ways of recognizing the end of each transmission field. Three formats are currently defined for transmission fields:

- Fixed fields without field separators (FFR-FNI)
- Fixed fields with field separators (FFR-FS)
- Fixed fields with or without field separators (FFR-FS2)

The FMH-4 header indicates which of these formats is used in the data portion of the RU. The order of the fields in the RU normally determines the correspondence between transmission fields and stored logical record fields. With the FFR-FNI format, the method used to identify the end of each transmission field is user-defined. With FFR-FS, a separator character, contained in the FMH-4, is used to mark the end of each transmission field. With FFR-FS2, either a separator character is used to terminate a field, or the maximum length of the field, as defined by the receiver's map, defines the end of the field.

Figure 22.4 shows the format of the FMH-4. The various length fields indicate the length of the fields that follow them. The Block Transmission Type field indicates whether FFR-FNI, FFR-FS, or FFR-FS2 data follow. The Flags field indicates whether or not a block data transform is included in the FMH-4. The Block Name, Block Data Transform, and Version Identifier fields are used by the receiver to process the block of data that follows the FMH-4.

FM HEADER 5   *FM header 5* (FMH-5) is used to attach and detach transaction programs needed to process the data stream that follows. It is also used to notify the session partner of changes in

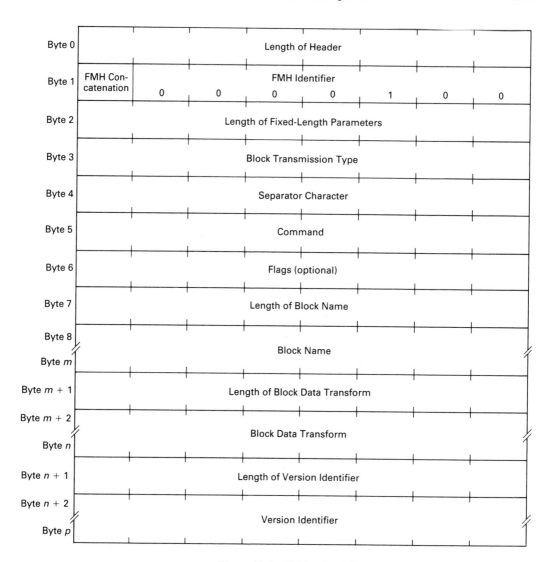

Figure 22.4   FM header 4 format.

the data stream's characteristics. There are three functions for which an FMH-5 can be used. The three FMH-5 types associated with those functions are described in Box 22.4.

When a program is to be attached, it is specified by name in the FMH-5. It is also possible to specify that certain resources be acquired by the destination program before it is attached. The sender of the FMH-5 can also specify the name of a transaction program to be used to process any replies sent by the

BOX 22.4　FM header 5 function types

Attach	Specifies a destination program to be attached by the session partner
Data Descriptor	Notify the session partner of changes in data stream characteristics
Reset Attached Program	Notify the session partner to detach the currently attached transaction program

destination program. However, when the sender specifies a program to process replies, the destination program is not required to use that program. Resources can also be named that must be acquired by the program before it can be attached. An access code can optionally be specified that must be validated before the destination program is attached. Finally, a queue name can be specified in order to associate a queue with the destination program. The sending transaction program can thus build up a queue of data and then name the destination transaction program that is to process them.

Both the Attach and Data Descriptor FMH-5s can be used to provide information about the data stream contained in the RU. Flags are used to indicate whether an interchange unit spans more than one RU chain, whether it has terminated, and whether other than the session partners can access the interchange unit queue. The FMH-5 specifies the data stream profile being used. Currently, the only profile supported is that of a user-defined data stream. A deblocking algorithm can also be specified. The algorithm is used to determine the amount of data passed to the transaction program when it executes a Read function to the half-session. Here are two possible algorithms:

- An RU chain is passed as a unit.
- Variable-length records are deblocked and passed to the transaction program. Variable-length records begin with a two-byte length field.

Figure 22.5 shows the format of the FMH-5. Box 22.5 contains a matrix that indicates which fields are included in each of the three FMH-5 types. The length fields associated with the Destination Program Name, Primary Resource Name, Return Destination Program Name, Return Primary Resource Name, Queue Name, and Access Code can be either one or two bytes in length. The Length of Length Field indicates whether they are one or two bytes in length in this particular FMH-5.

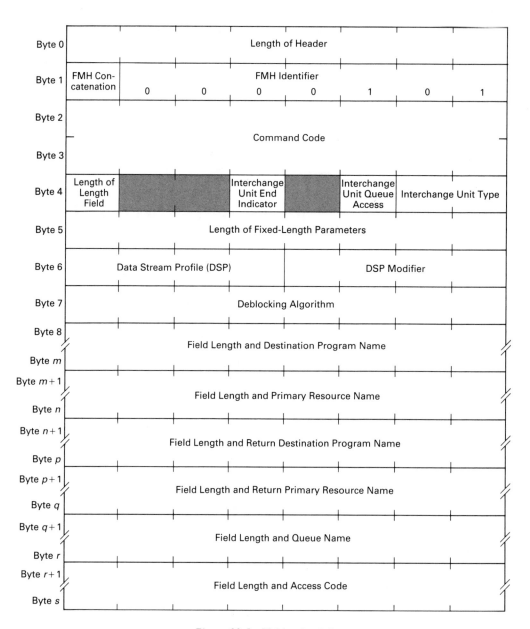

Figure 22.5   FM header 5 format.

FM HEADER 6   *FM header 6* (FMH-6) is used to send information,
                         including commands, messages, and data, to the
transaction program attached to the session partner. A general format for the
FMH-6 has been defined by SNA. However, the specific contents of the param-

BOX 22.5   FM header 5 field matrix

Field	Attach	Descriptor	Program
Length of Header	X	X	X
FM Concatenation	X	X	X
FMH Identifier	X	X	X
Command Code	X	X	X
Length of Length Fields	X	X	X
Interchange Unit End Indicator	X	X	
Interchange Unit Queue Access	X		
Interchange Unit Type	X	X	
Length of Fixed-Length Parameters	X	X	X
Data Stream Profile (DSP)	X	X	
DSP Modifier	X	X	
Deblocking Algorithm	X	X	
Destination Program Name	X		
Primary Resource Name	X		
Return Destination Program Name	X		
Return Primary Resource Name	X		
Queue Name	X		
Access Code	X		

eter fields and their meaning to the destination transaction program is implementation-specific. Figure 22.6 shows the general format of the FMH-6. An FMH-6 can contain fixed-length parameters, variable-length parameters, or both. For variable-length parameters, the length fields can be either one or two bytes in length. Transaction programs that exchange FMH-6s must share a consistent definition of the meaning of the various parameters used.

FM HEADER 7

FM header 7 (FMH-7) is used to send error information from one session partner to another. The information provided both identifies the cause of the error and describes the appropriate corrective action. An FMH-7 is followed by an Error Recovery Procedure (ERP) message. Typically, an FMH-7 and ERP message are sent by the data receiver following a negative response. An FMH-7 and ERP message can also be used by half-sessions to exchange information when an abort occurs so that appropriate backout actions can be taken. The FMH-7 and ERP message are sent as a single RU chain. Figure 22.7 shows the format of the FMH-7.

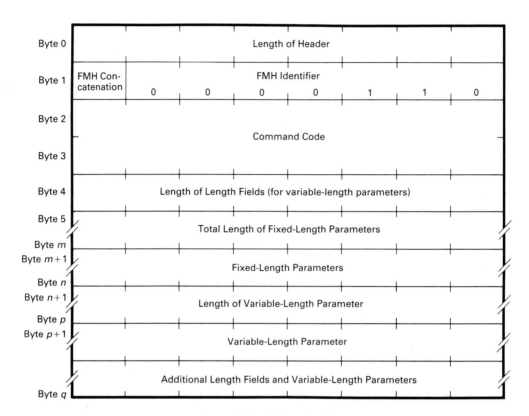

Figure 22.6   FM header 6 format.

Various sense codes have been defined within SNA corresponding to specific error conditions. The Sequence Number Field identifies the particular chain where the error occurred.

FM HEADER 10   *FM header 10* (FMH-10) is used to request that the session partner send a request for commit when it reaches the end of the chain it is currently receiving. At the end of the chain, the receiving partner then attempts to create a syncpoint by sending a request for commit (RH with Definite Response Indicator 2 on) if all its protected resource changes can be committed. If the resource changes cannot be committed, the receiving partner returns a negative response followed by an FMH-7 and ERP message. The FMH-10 is typically used by applications where resources from multiple LU type 6 sessions are being synchronized. Figure 22.8 shows the format of the FMH-10. The Command Modifier field specifies the values that are expected in the End Bracket and Change Direction fields in the RH in the request for commit returned by the receiver of the FMH-10.

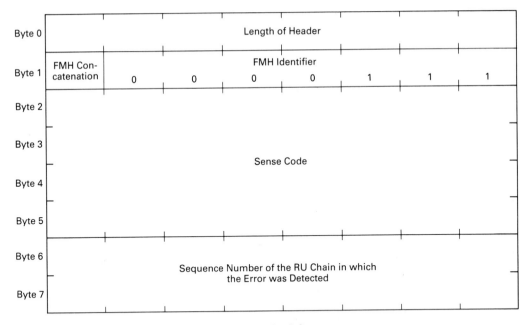

Figure 22.7 FM header 7 format.

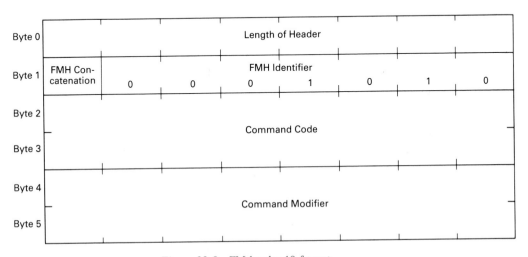

Figure 22.8 FM header 10 format.

SUMMARY   Function management headers are used only in LU type 1, 4, and 6 sessions. FM headers 1, 2, and 3 are used in LU type 1 and 4 sessions. An FM header 1 is used to control the flow of data to a particular destination within an LU. It can be used to start, end, suspend, or resume transmission to a particular destination. It also can provide information about the data stream that follows, including whether data compression or compaction was used, the record length, and the data stream profile type. An FM header 2 is used to specify a data management activity to be performed using the data that follow. Data management activities include creating, erasing, deleting, and transmitting a data set; adding, replacing, and erasing records; and determining the next available record location. An FM header 2 can also be used for control functions, including sending a compaction table or prime compression character, sending operator requests, and specifying a program to be executed when the session finishes. An FM header 3 is used to transmit information that applies to all destinations. This includes requesting and sending a compaction table, sending a prime compression character, giving a series ID to a sequence of FM headers, and providing status information about a series of FM headers, a user application program, or a data set.

FM header types 4, 5, 6, 7, and 10 are used only in LU type 6 sessions. An FM header 4 is used to describe the data stream that follows. It is used with logical message services (LMS) transaction programs. An FMH-4 indicates the type of field-formatted records that follow and provides data transform information to be used to process the block of data following the FMH-4. An FM header 5 is used to attach and detach transaction programs. It can specify the name of the transaction program to be attached by the receiver (destination program), resources to be acquired before the destination program can be attached, the name of a program to be used to process replies sent by the destination program, resources to be acquired before the program can be attached, an access code to be validated before the destination program is attached, and the name of a queue to be associated with the destination program. An FMH-5 can also specify information about the data stream that follows, including interchange unit information, the data stream profile being used, and a deblocking algorithm for variable-length records. An FM header 6 is used to send information to the transaction program attached to the session partner. The information consists of either fixed- or variable-length parameters and is implementation-specific. An FM header 7 is used to send error information from one session partner to the other. It is followed by an Error Recovery Procedure (ERP) message. The FMH-7 contains a sense code and the sequence number of the chain where the error was detected. An FM header 10 is used to request that the session partner send a request for synchronization when it reaches the end of the chain currently being processed. The FMH-10 specifies the values to be used for the End Bracket and Change Direction fields in the RH in the request for a syncpoint.

23 SESSION SERVICES

In this chapter we begin an examination of session network services. The functions provided by this component of the function management layer can be divided into four categories: session services, configuration services, maintenance and management services, and network operator services. The various categories of session network services deal primarily with SSCP-to-SSCP, SSCP-to-LU, and SSCP-to-PU data flows and are provided by a combination of the NAU services manager components and the session network services half-session components, shown in Fig. 23.1. Services in the session services category are responsible for initiating and terminating LU-to-LU sessions. The data flows involved in the initiation and termination activities are, for the most part, SSCP-to-LU and SSCP-to-PU flows. The components that perform initiation and termination processing are the LU and SSCP services managers and session network services half-session components.

NETWORK SERVICES RU FORMAT

Initiation and termination of LU-to-LU sessions is accomplished through a sequence of control RUs that pass between the LUs and SSCP or SSCPs involved. These RUs belong to the *network services* class of RUs. Network services RUs have an RU category of FMD in their RH header, and, as discussed in Chapter 21, can be either field-formatted or character-coded. A field-formatted RU consists of a three-byte network services (NS) header, followed by other fields that vary according to the specific RU type. Figure 23.2 shows the format of the NS header. The PU or LU Service field indicates whether the requested service relates to a PU, an LU, or either. The Cross-Domain Indicator denotes whether the request is used on a same-domain session (SSCP–PU or SSCP–LU) or a cross-domain session (SSCP–SSCP). The Network Services Category identifies to which of the four network services cat-

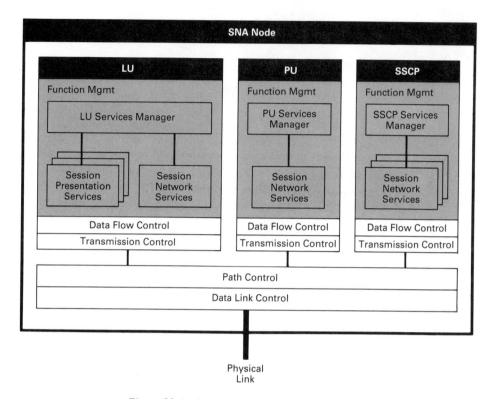

Figure 23.1   Function Management components.

egory the RU belongs. The particular function of the RU is specified by the
Request Code field. The format of the rest of the RU is defined for each request
code within each network services category. Character-coded RUs consist of
character strings that can be translated into a field-formatted form. A translation
protocol is provided in the session network services component in the SSCP.

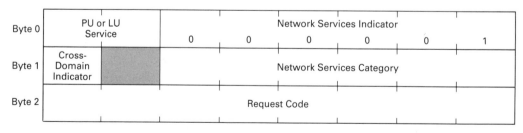

Figure 23.2   NS Header format.

SESSION INITIATION DATA FLOWS

We begin by looking at several alternative methods that can be used to initiate an LU-to-LU session within a single domain. We also examine the data contained in the control RUs involved in session initiation. Figure 23.3 illustrates the flow of RUs involved in initiating an LU-to-LU session at the request of the secondary LU. The numbers in the diagram relate to the request RUs that are transmitted during session initiation, and the dashed arrows represent responses. The steps in the process are as follows:

1. The secondary LU (LU A) sends an Initiate Self RU to the SSCP, requesting that a session be set up between LU A and LU B.
2. The SSCP sends a Control Initiate RU to the primary LU (LU B), requesting it to activate a session with LU A.
3. LU B sends a Bind RU to LU A, which contains information about the rules and protocols to be observed during the session. If LU A agrees to the rules and protocols, it returns a positive response. At this point the session is activated.
4. LU B sends a Session Started RU to the SSCP, indicating that the session is active.
5. LU B sends LU A a Start Data Traffic RU, which enables the two half-sessions to send and receive data RUs.

Figure 23.4 shows another possibility for session initiation. Here the primary LU sends the Initiate Self RU that begins the process. After the SSCP receives the Initiate Self RU from the primary LU, the remainder of the session initiation process is the same as in the previous example.

Figure 23.5 shows a third alternative for session initiation. Here the session initiation process is begun by an LU that does not itself take part in the

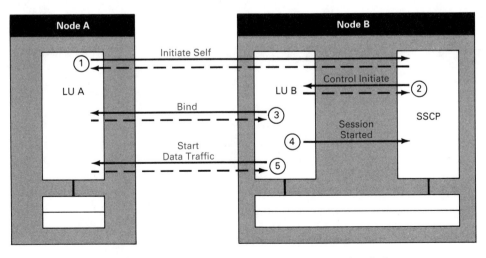

Figure 23.3   LU-to-LU session initiation by secondary LU.

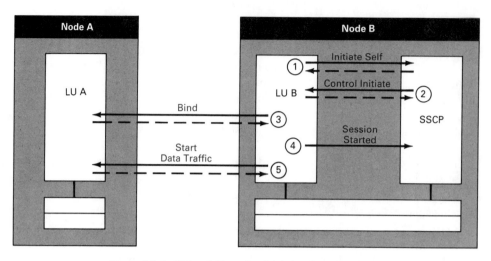

Figure 23.4   LU-to-LU session initiation by primary LU.

session. In this example, LU C sends an Initiate Other RU to the SSCP; the Initiate Other RU specifies the names of the two LUs that will participate in the session. An LU that will participate in the session can also begin session initiation with an Initiate Other RU by naming itself as one of the session LUs.

**SESSION
INITIATION RUs**

We next describe the general contents of the control RUs that are involved in session initiation. The complete formats for the various control RUs we will discuss are described in the *Systems Network Architecture Format and Protocol Reference Manual: Architectural Logic* (SC30–3112). There are a number of

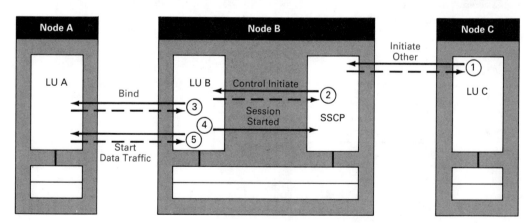

Figure 23.5   LU-to-LU session initiation by other LU.

functions that are performed as part of the session initiation process. These functions are introduced in Box 23.1 and will be discussed in detail as we look at each of the control RUs involved in session initiation.

INITIATE SELF, An Initiate Self (INIT—SELF) or an Initiate Other
INITIATE OTHER (INIT—OTHER) request is sent to begin session initiation. As discussed earlier, an Initiate RU is sent by an LU to its SSCP. The major pieces of information that are contained within an Initiate RU are listed at the beginning of Box 23.2. Each of these pieces of information is contained in one or more formatted fields within the data portion of the RU. Box 23.2 also lists the major functions the SSCP performs in processing an Initiate Self or Initiate Other RU.

CONTROL INITIATE The Control Initiate (CINIT) request is sent from the SSCP to the primary LU. It requests the primary LU to activate a session with the specified secondary LU by sending it a Bind request. Box 23.3 lists the information that can be contained in a CINIT. The primary LU can change certain parameters before including them in the Bind request. If a requester ID or password is included, the primary LU can use them to verify the authority of the end user or LU that initiated the session initiation process. The virtual route information includes a list of virtual routes that can be used for this session, derived by the SSCP from the class-of-service name.

BOX 23.1   Session initiation functions

- Checking that the initiating LU has the appropriate authority to initiate the requested session
- Converting network names to network addresses
- Determining the virtual route to be used for the session, based on mode name and class of service
- Checking that an LU is able to support another concurrent session where concurrent sessions are involved
- Determining the protocols and rules to be used for the session and, in particular, determining the transmission services (TS), function management (FM), and presentation services (PS) profiles
- Creating a session control block that contains information to be used throughout the session

BOX 23.2 The initiate self and initiate other RUs

Initiate Self and Initiate Other RU Data

- **LU Names.** The name of the other LU to participate in the session. (For Initiate-Other, the names of both LUs are specified.)
- **Primary LU.** Identification of primary and secondary LU
- **Mode Name.**
- **Class-of-Service Name.** (Optional)
- **Requester ID.** Identifies the end user requesting the service (optional)
- **Password.** (Optional)
- **Queuing Action.** Action to be taken for the request if the other LU is unavailable (optional)
- **User Request Correlation.** A user-defined identifier for the request (optional)

Initiate Self and Initiate Other SSCP Processing

- **Resolve LU Name.** The name of the other LU, or of both LUs for an Initiate Other, is translated from an uninterpreted name to a network name. (An uninterpreted name is a name by which an LU is known to another LU or its SSCP. Interpretation of an uninterpreted name yields a network name.) The network name is then translated into a network address. If the LU in question is able to support multiple sessions and already has an active session in progress, the SSCP sends a Request Network Address Assignment (RNAA) RU to the PU for that LU. The PU returns the network address to be used for this session.
- **Verify Paths.** The SSCP determines that the necessary connection exists between the SSCP and the LUs that will participate in the session. If necessary, configuration services are used to establish the connection. For a cross-domain session, a check is made that the appropriate SSCP-to-SSCP session is active.
- **Verify Authority.** If a requester ID or password is provided, the SSCP uses it to verify that the requesting end user and LU have the proper authority to access the other LU.
- **Verify Availability.** The SSCP checks to be sure the LU needed to establish the session is available.
- **Queue an Initiate Request.** If an LU is not available and queuing has been specified, the SSCP queues the Initiate request. Subsequent changes in the LU's availability are reported to the SSCP through a Notify RU, allowing the SSCP to complete processing of the Initiate request at a later time.

BOX 23.2   *(Continued)*

- **Verify Class-of-Service Name.** If a class-of-service name is specified, it is checked for validity. If class of service is not specified, the mode name is used to derive a class-of-service name.
- **Select Bind Parameters.** Parameters to be included in the Bind request are selected on the basis of mode name.
- **Assign an Identifier.** An identifier known as the PCID is assigned to this particular initiation procedure if a cross-domain session is being initiated.

BIND

The Bind (BIND) request is sent from the primary LU to the secondary LU to activate an LU-to-LU session between them. The secondary LU checks the parameters in the Bind request to see whether it can support the protocols and options that have been selected for this session and uses this to determine the response it makes to the Bind request.

Activation of a session through the processing of a Bind request and its

BOX 23.3   Control initiate RU data

- Network addresses of primary and secondary LUs
- Bind parameters
- Secondary LU name
- Requester ID
- Password
- User data
- Device characteristics
- Session cryptography key, encrypted with the primary LU's master cryptography key
- Session cryptography key, encrypted with the secondary LU's master cryptography key
- Mode name
- Class-of-service name
- Virtual route information

response is not actually performed by session services. Instead, the Bind request is processed by the common session control manager subcomponent of the PU services manager. After the primary LU formats the Bind request, the LU services manager passes it to the PU services manager in that node. A list of possible virtual routes to be used for the session being activated is passed along with the Bind request. The common session control manager within the PU services manager is then responsible for creating a session control block (SCB) for the primary-LU half-session and for seeing that a virtual route is assigned to the session; this virtual route is then used to send the Bind request to the secondary LU. On the receiving side, when the Bind request arrives, it is sent to common session control in the PU services manager. The common session control subcomponent in the receiving node then creates an SCB for the secondary-LU half-session.

SESSION CONTROL BLOCK

The SCB that is created and used by each half-session contains variables that define the options and protocols that are used for the session, as well as pointers to additional information used for the session. Much of the information contained in the Bind request is stored in the SCB. SCBs are created when a session is activated and deleted when the session is deactivated. If a session involves boundary function support, an SCB is also created at the node providing boundary function processing. The SCBs are created as the Bind request is processed. The Bind response is also passed to each PU common session control manager component. If the response is positive, final session values are stored in the SCBs. If the response is negative, the SCBs are deleted.

VIRTUAL ROUTE ASSIGNMENT

In addition to creating SCBs, the common session control manager sees that a virtual route is assigned to the session being activated. To do this it invokes another subcomponent of the PU services manager, the *PC route manager*. The PC route manager contains both a virtual route (VR) manager and an explicit route (ER) manager. When a virtual route needs to be assigned to a session, the VR manager begins the process.

The VR manager uses the list of possible virtual routes that was developed based on the class-of-service name. It checks the routes in the list starting from the top and working successively downward. It first checks whether a VR control block (VRCB) exists for this virtual route. If it does, the VR manager next checks to see if the route is active. If the route is active, the VR route manager sets a pointer to that route in the list and returns it to the common session control manager with a positive response. If the route is not active, the VR manager checks to see if activation is under way from a previous request for route assignment. If activation is under way, an entry for this session is added to a list of sessions to be assigned to the route once the route becomes active. If activation is not under way, the VR manager moves on to the next route on the list.

If a VRCB does not exist, the VR manager creates one and attempts to activate the virtual route by requesting the ER manager to activate the explicit route associated with the virtual route. If ER route activation is not successful, the VR manager goes on to the next virtual route on the list. If route activation is successful, the VR manager communicates with the VR manager at the other end of the virtual route. The two VR managers then synchronize the two ends with respect to both the state of the virtual route and the parameters to be used when transmitting data across it. The communication that takes place between the two VR managers consists of an NC Activate Virtual Route (NC__ACTVR) request that is sent from one VR manager to the other and its associated response. Via this request and response, the two ends agree on a minimum and maximum window size, the initial virtual route sequence number, explicit route number, and return explicit route number. If the response to the NC__ACTVR request is negative, the VR manager moves to the next virtual route on the list. If the response is positive, a pointer is set, and control is returned to the common session control manager. If, after checking the entire list of virtual routes, no active virtual route is available to use for the session, the VR manager returns a negative response to the common session control manager.

EXPLICIT ROUTE ACTIVATION

As part of virtual route activation, the underlying explicit route that supports this virtual route must be activated. The VR manager activates an explicit route by passing an Activate Explicit Route (ACTIVATE__ER) request to the ER manager. If the explicit route is already active, the ER manager sends a positive reply (ER__ACTIVATED). If the explicit route is inoperative, the ER manager returns a negative reply (ER__NOT__ACTIVATED). An explicit route is inoperative if one or more of the transmission groups along the route is unavailable.

An explicit route can be operative but not active. An explicit route is operative if all the transmission groups along the route are operative. In this case the ER manager attempts to activate the route by sending an NC__ER__ACT request to the other end of the route. If the response to this is positive, the route has been activated, and the ER manager returns an ER__ACTIVATED to the VR manager. If the response is negative, the ER manager returns an ER__NOT__ACTIVATED.

NEGOTIABLE OR NONNEGOTIABLE BIND

Box 23.4 lists the information contained in the formatted fields in the data portion of a Bind request. The Type field indicates whether the Bind is negotiable or nonnegotiable. The Bind carries information

BOX 23.4   Bind RU data

- Bind type (negotiable or nonnegotiable)
- FM profile
- TS profile
- PS profile
- LU session type
- PS usage
- Cryptography options and key
- Primary-LU name
- User data
- User request correlation (URC) data
- Secondary-LU name

about the various protocols to be used during the session, including such things as request/response mode, send/receive mode, use of chains and brackets, pacing, sequence numbers, and maximum RU size. If the Bind is nonnegotiable, the secondary LU must be able to support all the protocols and options specified, in which case it sends a positive response. If the secondary LU is not able to handle one or more of the specified protocols and options, it must reply by sending a negative response. If the Bind is negotiable, the secondary LU need not immediately respond negatively to the Bind if it has incompatibilities with the parameters contained in the Bind request. Instead, the secondary LU can send a positive response that contains an altered version of the Bind parameters; these new Bind parameters represent the protocols and options that the secondary LU *is* able to support. If the primary accepts the altered parameters, it allows the session activation process to complete using the new Bind parameters. If the new Bind parameters are not acceptable to the primary LU, it sends an Unbind request back to the secondary LU, indicating a failure to activate the session.

PROFILES

Many of the parameters contained in the Bind request relate to options and protocols that are associated with various SNA functional layers. Profiles are defined for different layers that each specify a particular set of functions to be used during the session. The relationship between the different types of profiles and the functional layers is as follows:

- **Presentation Services Profile (PS Profile).** Defines the functions to be performed by session presentation services
- **Transmission Services Profile (TS Profile).** Defines the functions to be performed by the transmission control layer
- **Function Management Profile (FM Profile).** Defines functions to be performed by certain components of the function management layer and by the data flow control layer

The Bind request specifies the profiles to be used for the session and also defines associated usage fields that provide further information related to the protocols chosen. Some of the more important protocols related to each profile are listed in Box 23.5.

CRYPTOGRAPHY

The Bind also carries information that specifies whether cryptography is to be used, and if so, at what level. If cryptography is specified, the Bind contains the session cryptography key encrypted with the secondary-LU master cryptography key. The secondary LU then returns an encrypted session seed value in its Bind response. The cryptography option is discussed in Chapter 19.

SESSION STARTED

If the primary LU receives a positive response to the Bind request, it sends a Session Started (SESSST) request to its SSCP, notifying it that the session has been activated. The SESSST RU contains the names of the two LUs.

START DATA TRAFFIC

The primary LU sends a Start Data Traffic (SDT) request to the secondary LU in order to enable data transmission. The SDT RU contains only the request code that identifies that RU.

SESSION INITIATION FAILURES

Figure 23.6 illustrates the control flow that occurs when session initiation fails for some reason. If the secondary LU is not able to participate in a session when it receives the Bind request, it returns a negative response to the Bind. The primary LU then sends a Bind Failure request to the SSCP, thus notifying it of the failure to activate the session.

BOX 23.5   Profile protocols

TS Profile Protocols

- Maximum RU size
- Session level pacing, including initial pacing count values
- Use of sequence numbers
- Support of control RUs used for recovery, resynchronization, and cryptography

FM Profile Protocols

- Request/response mode
- Use of multiple RU chains
- Response type
- Use of data compression
- Use of FM headers
- Use of brackets, including initiation and termination options
- Send/receive mode, including contention winner
- Recovery responsibility
- Use of Quiesce and Shutdown
- One-phase or two-phase commit
- Use of an alternate code set
- Availability of sequence numbers for resynchronization

PS Profile Protocols

- Data stream format, including the use of SNA character string controls, structured fields, or 3270 data stream
- Types of FM headers allowed
- Type of destination media supported, such as display, printer, data processing media, or word processing media

BIND FAILURE   As shown in Fig. 23.6, when the response from the secondary LU to a Bind request is negative, the primary LU sends a Bind Failure (BINDF) request to its SSCP, notifying it of the failure to activate the session. The BINDF RU contains sense data and a reason

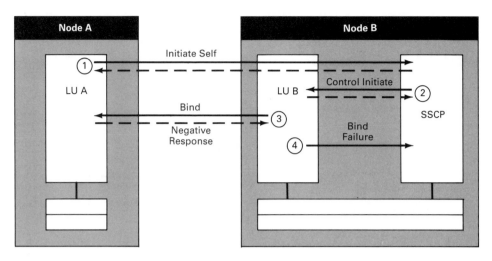

Figure 23.6   LU-to-LU session initiation—bind failure.

code that together identify the reason for the activation failure. The BINDF RU also contains the names of the two LUs.

**CROSS-DOMAIN
SESSION
INITIATION**

When an LU-to-LU session involves two domains, additional steps are involved in session initiation. In the example in Fig. 23.7, the primary LU is LU B, and the secondary LU is LU A; the two LUs reside in different domains. The steps in the session initiation process are as follows:

1. LU A sends an Initiate Self RU to SSCP C requesting a session with LU B in another domain. (An Initiate Other RU could also be used to request session initiation.)

2. SSCP C sends a Cross-Domain Initiate to SSCP B, describing the session initiation request. After receiving a response from SSCP B, SSCP C sends a response to LU A.

3. The SSCP associated with the secondary LU (SSCP C) sends to the SSCP for the primary LU (SSCP B) a Cross-Domain Control Initiate RU with information related to the protocols and rules to be used for the session.

4. The SSCP that receives the Cross-Domain Control Initiate sends a Control Initiate RU to the primary LU.

5. The primary LU sends a Bind request to the secondary LU.

6. If the response to the Bind is positive, the primary LU sends a Session Started RU to its SSCP.

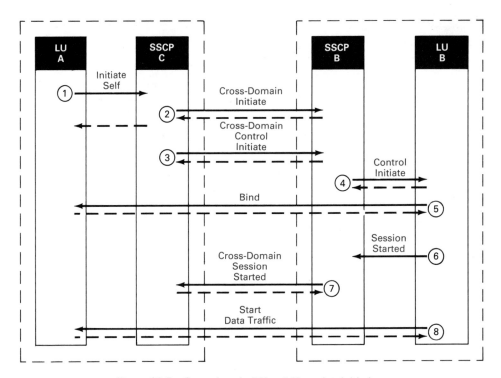

Figure 23.7   Cross-domain LU-to-LU session initiation.

7. That SSCP sends a Cross-Domain Session Started RU to the other SSCP.

8. The primary LU sends a Start Data Traffic RU to the secondary LU, which starts data flowing.

CROSS-DOMAIN INITIATE

A Cross-Domain Initiate (CDINIT) request is sent from the originating SSCP to the destination SSCP when the two LUs are in different domains. It contains the same major pieces of information as the Initiate Self and Initiate Other RUs, except for the User Request Correlation field. In addition, it contains the PCID that has been assigned to this initiation procedure and the network address of the originating LU. (As part of Initiate Self or Initiate Other processing for a cross-domain session, an identifier known as the procedure correlation identifier, or PCID, is assigned to identify the initiation procedure.) The second SSCP uses the information in the CDINIT to perform the functions described for the Initiate RU that are related to this SSCP's LU.

As part of the response to the CDINIT RU, the SSCP returns information generated by its processing, which can include the LU's network address, LU availability, a class-of-service name, verification of the mode name, requester

ID or password, and information about queuing status. Once CDINIT processing is complete and its response is returned, both SSCPs have complete information on network names and addresses for both LUs, status of the LUs and the initiation process, the mode name, class-of-service name, requester ID, password, and user data.

CROSS-DOMAIN CONTROL INITIATE The Cross-Domain Control Initiate (CDCINIT) request is sent from the SSCP for the secondary LU to the SSCP for the primary LU. It contains information needed for the Control Initiate RU that the SSCP sends to the primary LU. The information contained in the CDCINIT RU is listed in Box 23.6. The SSCP for the primary LU can modify some of the parameters from the CDCINIT before including them in the Control Initiate request it issues. The changes allowed are the same as those allowed during Bind processing.

CROSS-DOMAIN SESSION STARTED For a cross-domain session, the primary SSCP sends a Cross-Domain Session Started (CDSESSST) request to the secondary SSCP, notifying it of the successful session initiation. The CDSESSST RU contains the names of the two LUs that are involved in the session.

CROSS-DOMAIN SESSION INITIATION FAILURE Figure 23.8 demonstrates the sequence of RUs that flow when one of the LUs is unable to participate in a session at the time that it receives the Bind request. Following the negative response to the Bind request, the primary LU sends a Bind Failure RU to its SSCP. This SSCP sends a Cross-

BOX 23.6   Cross-domain control initiate RU data

- Network addresses for the two LUs to be involved in the session
- Bind parameters selected as part of the processing of the Initiate RU
- Session cryptography key, if the cryptography option has been selected
- LU or device characteristics
- PCID for this initiation procedure

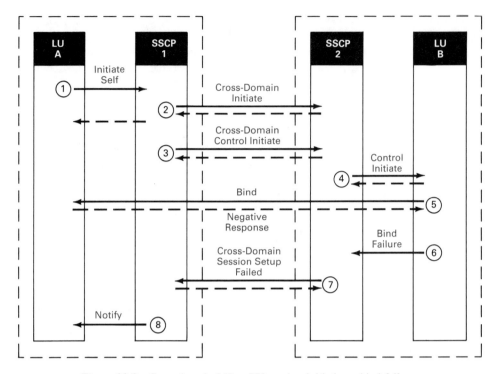

Figure 23.8   Cross-domain LU-to-LU session initiation—bind failure.

Domain Session Setup Failed RU to the other SSCP, which in turn sends a Notify RU to the secondary LU.

CROSS-DOMAIN   For a cross-domain session, the primary SSCP sends
SESSION SETUP   a Cross-Domain Session Setup Failed (CDSESSSF)
FAILED   request to the secondary SSCP to notify it of the fail-
                          ure. The CDSESSSF RU carries the same informa-
tion as the BINDF. The secondary SSCP then sends a Notify RU to its LU,
passing the status information on to the secondary LU.

CROSS-NETWORK   Session initiation is even more complex when it in-
SESSION   volves several SNA networks that are interconnected
INITIATION   via SNA Network Interconnection (SNI) gateway
                           nodes. Figure 23.9 illustrates the session initiation
process when the two LUs are in different networks. The processing is similar
to cross-domain session initiation, with some additional steps added to handle

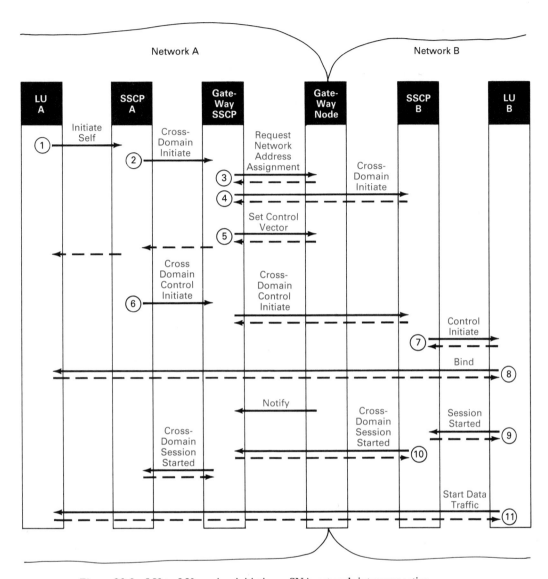

Figure 23.9 LU-to-LU session initiation—SNA network interconnection.

the name and address translations that are required to interconnect the two networks.

1. LU A sends an Initiate RU to its SSCP, requesting that a session be initiated. The Initiate RU specifies the alias name by which LU B is known within LU A's network. We will assume this alias name is LU X in the remainder of the steps.

2. SSCP A sends a Cross-Domain Initiate to the gateway SSCP—the SSCP that it perceives as the owner of LU X.

3. The gateway SSCP recognizes LU X as not being part of network A and uses a name translation function that identifies it as LU B belonging to SSCP B in network B. The name translation function also provides the name by which LU A is known in network B, plus the mode and class-of-service names to be used in network B that correspond to those specified in the Initiate request. The gateway SSCP then sends a Request Network Address Assignment (RNAA) RU to the gateway node, requesting alias addresses to be used for LU A and LU B. The gateway node assigns an alias address to be used in network A to represent LU B and one to represent LU A in network B. These addresses are returned to the gateway SSCP in the response.

4. The gateway SSCP sends a Cross-Domain Initiate to SSCP B, using translated names for LU A, mode name, class-of-service name, and the alias address for LU A. LU B's actual name is used. SSCP B returns LU B's address in its response.

5. The gateway SSCP now has alias names and addresses and real names and addresses for both LUs, as well as the information needed to select a virtual route between LU A and the gateway node. This information is sent to the gateway node via a Set Control Vector RU. The gateway SSCP then responds to the Cross-Domain Initiate sent by SSCP A, and SSCP A responds to LU A. These responses use the alias address for LU B.

6. The SSCP for the secondary LU, in this case SSCP A, then sends a Cross-Domain Control Initiate, containing the various session parameters, to the gateway SSCP. The gateway SSCP translates LU A's name and address from real to alias and LU B's from alias to real and sends the RU on to SSCP B.

7. SSCP B sends a Control Initiate to LU B, requesting LU B to activate a session with LU A.

8. As part of Bind processing, a virtual route between LU B and the gateway node is chosen. LU B sends a Bind request to LU A. When the Bind request passes through the gateway node, the LU names and addresses are converted between real and alias, as appropriate for use in network A. Also, a virtual route between the gateway node and LU A is selected for the session. The gateway node also provides name and address translation for the Bind response, and sends a Notify to the gateway SSCP, indicating that the session has been activated.

9. Assuming that LU B receives a positive Bind response, LU B sends a Session Started RU to its SSCP. (If the response were negative, LU B would send a Bind Failure RU to SSCP B.)

10. SSCP B sends a Cross-Domain Session Started RU to the gateway SSCP. The gateway SSCP translates names and addresses in the RU and passes it on to SSCP A. (In the event of bind failure, a Cross-Domain Session Setup Failed RU would be sent instead, and SSCP A would send a Notify RU to LU A.)

11. LU B, as the primary LU, sends a Start Data Traffic RU to LU A, with the gateway node providing address translation for the transmission header. Normal data transmission then begins, with the gateway node continuing to provide address translation for all transmission headers.

With SNA Network Interconnection, the gateway SSCP and node provide the necessary translation functions for LU names and addresses, mode name, and class-of-service name, both within RUs and in the transmission header. In this way neither of the LUs involved in the session nor their SSCPs are ever aware that the session is crossing network boundaries.

SUMMARY   Session services are responsible for initiating and ter-
                       minating LU-to-LU sessions. Processing is done by
the LU and SSCP services manager and session network services half-session components. Session services, as part of session network services, uses network services RUs, which contain network services header. Session initiation functions include checking the authority of the initiating LU, converting network names to network addresses, determining the virtual route to be used, activating a virtual route and an explicit route, checking that the concurrent session limit is not exceeded, determining the protocols and rules to be used for the session, and creating session control blocks. For cross-domain session initiation, the initiation processing is split between the two SSCPs involved. For cross-network sessions, the gateway SSCP and gateway node determine alias addresses to be used and provide conversion between real and alias network names and addresses in both control RUs and transmission headers.

The Initiate Self RU requests that a session be established with the LU specified in the request. The Initiate Other RU requests that a session be established between the two LUs specified in the request. Processing of an Initiate request includes converting LU names to network addresses, verifying that the proper SSCP-LU sessions exist, verifying the availability of the requested LUs, deriving or verifying class-of-service name, selecting Bind parameters, and assigning a PCID to cross-domain requests. A Cross-Domain Initiate RU passes session initiation information to the second SSCP in a cross-domain request so that both SSCPs are able to perform the necessary initiate processing. A Cross-Domain Control Initiate RU is sent from one SSCP to the other to provide the information needed for the Control Initiate RU. A Control Initiate RU requests the primary LU to activate a session with the specified secondary LU. It carries information needed by the primary LU for Bind processing.

A Bind request is used to activate an LU-to-LU session. As part of Bind processing, session control blocks (SCBs) are created, a virtual route and an explicit route are assigned, and agreement is reached on the protocols and rules to be used during the session. The protocols and rules include the specification of a transmission services (TS) profile, a function management (FM) profile, and a presentation services (PS) profile.

24 SESSION TERMINATION AND OUTAGE NOTIFICATION

In this chapter we continue our examination of session services. First we examine the contents of the control RUs and the RU data flows that take place when sessions are terminated within a single domain, across domains, and across SNA networks. We then look at the data flow that occurs when the session deactivation process fails. We examine a process called *cross-domain takedown* that is used to terminate all of the sessions between two SSCPs. We conclude by discussing an error notification procedure known as *session outage notification*.

SESSION TERMINATION

When an LU-to-LU session has completed, session services perform the processing needed to terminate the session and to release the various resources associated with it. Figure 24.1 shows the basic control flow used to terminate a session when both LUs are in the same domain. In this example, LU B, the secondary LU, initiates session termination.

1. LU B sends a Terminate Self request to the SSCP, identifying the other LU in the session to be terminated.
2. The SSCP sends a Control Terminate request to the primary LU, telling it to deactivate its session with the specified secondary LU.
3. The primary LU sends an Unbind request to the secondary LU.
4. Assuming that a positive response to the Unbind RU is received, both LUs send a Session Ended RU to the SSCP, notifying the SSCP that the session has been successfully deactivated.

Generally, the RUs used for session termination carry less information than those involved in session initiation. Information typically included is that

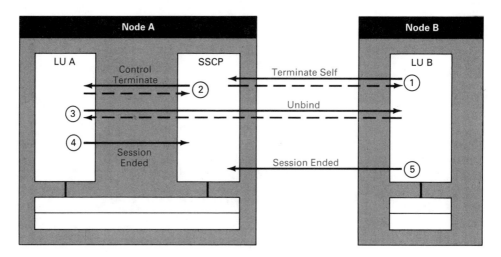

Figure 24.1   Session termination.

needed to identify the particular session being terminated, the reason for termination, and information about any actions to be taken.

TERMINATE SELF,   Box 24.1 lists the information that can be included in
TERMINATE OTHER   a Terminate Self (TERM__SELF) request and also
                      lists some of the functions the SSCP performs in processing a Terminate Self RU. In addition to TERM__SELF, a Terminate Other request can be used to start session termination. A Terminate Other request names both LUs that are involved in the session to be terminated. If the session being terminated is a cross-domain session, the processing is split between the two SSCPs involved, with each SSCP handling the functions related to its LU.

The Type field contains information that specifies the session or sessions to be terminated and the type of termination to take place. The TERM__SELF RU can request termination of one specific session, or for an LU-to-LU that supports parallel sessions, it can request termination of multiple sessions. If a specific session is being terminated, the session can be identified through the names of the LUs involved, their network addresses, or a User Request Correlation value assigned when the session was initiated. If multiple sessions are involved, the Type field can be used to specify the sessions to terminate. A subfield within Type can be used to specify whether active, pending active, queued sessions, or some combination of those should be terminated. Another subfield specifies termination based on whether the partner LU to the LU that issued the TERM__SELF RU is the primary LU in the session, the secondary LU, or either. The Type field is also used to specify the type of termination to

BOX 24.1   Terminate RU

Terminate RU Data

- Type
- Reason
- Notification specifications
- Network names, network addresses, or user request correlation from session initiation
- Requester ID
- Password
- User request correlation from termination request

Terminate RU SSCP Processing

- Using the requester ID and password, if provided, to verify the authority of the requesting LU and end user to request termination of the session
- Resolving an uninterpreted name into a network name and network names into network addresses
- Generating an identifier, known as PCID, for this termination procedure if the session is a cross-domain session
- Sending control RUs required, such as Control Initiate, Cross-Domain Terminate, and Cleanup, and sending a response to the TERM_SELF

take place: orderly, forced, or cleanup. If termination is orderly, the primary LU is allowed to perform end-of-session processing before deactivating the session. If termination is forced, the primary LU must begin deactivation processing immediately. If termination is cleanup, the SSCP(s) involved provide cleanup processing for the primary and secondary LUs and, if necessary, boundary function support.

The Reason field indicates whether termination has been requested by the network user or network manager and whether it is normal or abnormal. The Notify field indicates whether the LU issuing the TERM_SELF is to be notified when termination is complete.

CONTROL
TERMINATE

A Control Terminate (CTERM) request is sent to the primary LU by its SSCP, requesting that the LU deactivate a specific session. Box 24.2 lists the infor-

BOX 24.2   Control terminate RU data

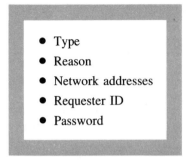

- Type
- Reason
- Network addresses
- Requester ID
- Password

mation carried in the CTERM RU. The Type field indicates whether the termination is orderly, forced, or cleanup. The network addresses identify the particular LU-to-LU session being terminated. If a requester ID and password are included, they can be used to verify the authority of the LU or end user requesting the termination.

UNBIND   An Unbind request is sent from the primary LU to the secondary LU during session deactivation. As with Bind and session activation, Unbind and session deactivation are accomplished by the common session control manager in the PU rather than by session services in the LU and SSCP. Unbind contains a code that identifies the reason for the deactivation, and for certain failure conditions Unbind also contains sense data. If the response to the Unbind is positive, the SCBs for both half-sessions are discarded. If a peripheral node is involved, boundary function support for the session is also deactivated, and the boundary function SCB is discarded.

Once the session is deactivated, the VR manager is notified that the virtual route assigned to this session is no longer needed. A virtual route can be shared by several sessions. When all the sessions using the virtual route have been deactivated, the virtual route is deactivated. The underlying explicit route, however, is not deactivated if no sessions are using it. An explicit route is deactivated only if one of its transmission groups becomes inoperative.

SESSION ENDED   If the response to the Unbind request is positive, each LU sends a Session Ended (SESSEND) RU to its SSCP, notifying the SSCP that the session has been deactivated. The SESSEND RU contains either names or addresses to identify the session being deactivated and can contain a code identifying the cause of the termination and whether either LU will restart the session. If one of the session partners resides in a peripheral node, boundary function actually sends the SESSEND.

CROSS-DOMAIN SESSION TERMINATION

Figure 24.2 illustrates the control flow used when a cross-domain session is terminated. LU A initiates the termination process. LU B is the primary LU.

1. LU A sends a Terminate Self request to its SSCP.

2. This SSCP sends a Cross-Domain Terminate request to the other SSCP, notifying it of the request to terminate.

3. The primary LU's SSCP sends a Control Terminate request to its LU.

4. The primary LU sends an Unbind request to the secondary LU.

5. If the Unbind is successful, each LU sends a Session Ended RU to its SSCP.

6. A Cross-Domain Session Ended request is then sent from one SSCP to the other to confirm that the session has been deactivated.

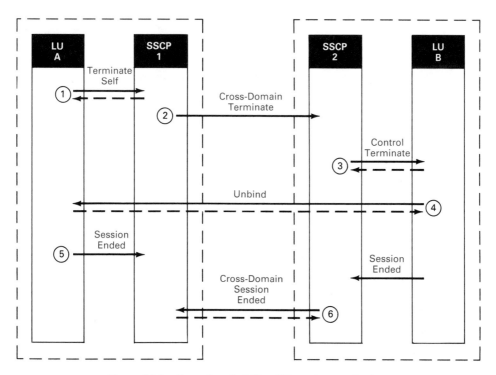

Figure 24.2   Cross-domain LU-to-LU session termination.

CROSS-DOMAIN   For cross-domain sessions, a Cross-Domain Termi-
TERMINATE   nate (CDTERM) request is sent from the SSCP that
                     receives the TERM request to the other SSCP in-
volved in the session. It is used to notify the other SSCP of the request for
termination and to provide the information the SSCP needs to perform its part
of the termination processing.

Box 24.3 lists the information carried in a CDTERM RU. It provides
much the same information as the TERM request, with the addition of the PCID
that was generated as part of TERM processing. The Reason field also contains
additional information about the cause of the termination.

CROSS-DOMAIN   Through the CDSESSEND RU and its response, both
SESSION ENDED   SSCPs are notified that the termination procedure has
                     been successfully completed. The CDSESSEND RU
contains similar information to the SESSEND, plus the PCID that identifies the
termination procedure. The CDSESSEND can be sent by either SSCP or by
both. It is sent if the SSCP receives a SESSEND and has not received a
CDSES—SEND from the other SSCP.

SNA NETWORK   Figure 24.3 shows the control flow used for session
INTERCONNECTION   termination when a session crosses networks using a
SESSION   gateway node. LU B in network B is the primary
TERMINATION   LU. The session is being terminated by LU A in net-
                         work A.

BOX 24.3   Cross-domain terminate RU data

- Type
- PCID that identifies the termination procedure
- Reason
- Network names or addresses or the PCID generated when the session was initiated
- Requester ID
- Password

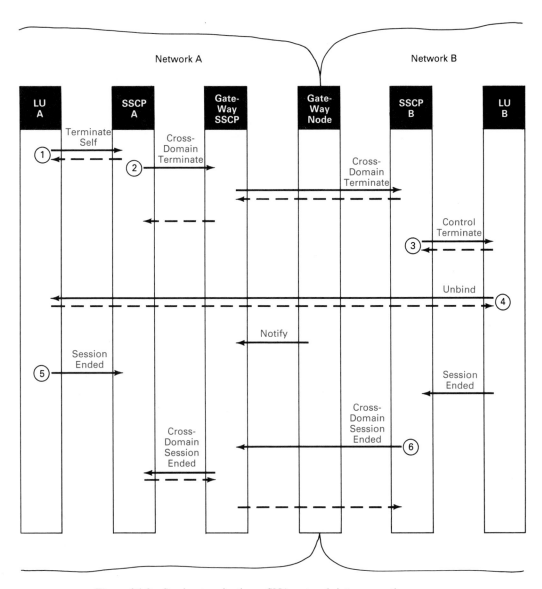

Figure 24.3   Session termination—SNA network interconnection.

1. A Terminate request is sent from an LU to its SSCP.

2. This SSCP sends a Cross-Domain Terminate request to the gateway SSCP. The gateway SSCP routes the Cross-Domain Terminate request to the SSCP in the other network. As with session initiation RUs, the gateway SSCP translates the network names and addresses in control RUs, and the gateway node translates the addresses contained in transmission headers.

3. The SSCP in network B sends a Control Terminate to the primary LU.

4. The primary LU sends an Unbind request to the secondary LU. When the response to the Unbind passes through the gateway node, the node discards its information about this session and returns to the address pool the alias addresses assigned to it so that they can be used for another session. It also sends a Notify RU to the gateway SSCP so that the gateway SSCP knows it can discard its information about the session. In this way gateway resources are free to be reassigned even if the Cross-Domain Session Ended RU fails to reach the gateway SSCP.

5. Each LU sends its SSCP a Session Ended RU.

6. One SSCP sends a Cross-Domain Session Ended to the gateway SSCP, which passes it on to the other SSCP.

SESSION TERMINATION FAILURE

Figure 24.4 shows the control flow used when session termination processing fails. If the primary LU receives a negative response to the Unbind request, it sends an Unbind Failure RU to its SSCP. If this is a

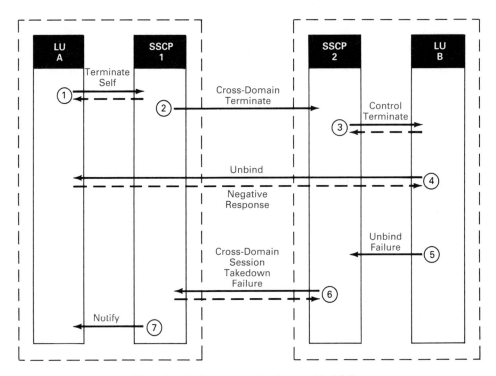

Figure 24.4 Session termination—unbind failure.

cross-domain session, the SSCP sends a Cross-Domain Session Takedown Failure RU to the other SSCP, and the second SSCP sends a Notify RU to the secondary LU.

UNBIND FAILURE   The Unbind Failure (UNBINDF) request contains a reason code and sense data describing the failure. It also contains either names or network addresses to identify the session involved. For a cross-domain session, the primary LU's SSCP sends a Cross-Domain Session Takedown Failure (CDSESSTF) request to the secondary LU's SSCP, notifying it of the failure. The CDSESSTF RU contains the same information as the UNBINDF RU, plus the PCID that identifies this termination process. The receiving SSCP then sends a Notify RU to the secondary LU, notifying it of the termination failure.

CROSS-DOMAIN   In addition to initiating and terminating individual
TAKEDOWN   sessions, it is also possible to terminate all cross-domain sessions involving a particular pair of SSCPs. This is known as a *cross-domain takedown* procedure. Figure 24.5 shows the control flow involved in a cross-domain takedown.

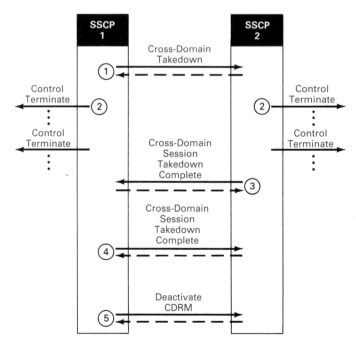

Figure 24.5   Cross-domain takedown.

1. The process begins when one SSCP sends another SSCP a Cross-Domain Takedown request.

2. Following this, each SSCP terminates all LU-to-LU sessions involving the two domains in question, with each SSCP terminating sessions where that SSCP's LU is the primary LU. The sessions are terminated in the normal manner, with the termination process started by the SSCP sending a Control Terminate request to the primary LU.

3. After all sessions have been terminated, the SSCP that received the Cross-Domain Takedown request sends a Cross-Domain Takedown Complete request to the other SSCP.

4. That SSCP then sends a Cross-Domain Takedown Complete request back to the other SSCP. It also sends a Deactivate CDRM RU to deactivate the SSCP-to-SSCP session.

CROSS-DOMAIN TAKEDOWN RU
The Cross-Domain Takedown (CDTAKED) RU contains a PCID that identifies the takedown procedure, a Type field, and a Reason field. The Type field is used to indicate the types of sessions that are affected by the takedown (active, pending active, or queued). The Type field also indicates the action to take for active or pending active sessions (quiesce or terminate orderly, forced, or cleanup) and the action to take for queued sessions (hold or purge). The Reason field provides information about the source of the Takedown request and why it was issued.

CROSS-DOMAIN TAKEDOWN COMPLETED
The Cross-Domain Takedown Completed (CDTAKEDC) request contains the PCID for the takedown process and also a status code that indicates whether all session terminations were successful.

DEACTIVATE CDRM
The Deactivate CDRM (DACTCDRM) request, like Bind and Unbind, is issued by the common session control manager in the PU rather than by session services. It contains information about the reason for the deactivation.

SESSION OUTAGE NOTIFICATION
Session termination might result from reaching a normal end point to the session, or it might be caused by a failure within the network. When a network failure occurs, a procedure called *session outage notification* is used to terminate all sessions that are affected by the failure. A number of types of network failures can affect sessions; some of the more important ones are listed in Box 24.4.

BOX 24.4　Types of network failures

- **Route Inoperative.** The failure of a transmission group causes all explicit routes that use that transmission group to become inoperative and, in turn, the virtual routes supported by those explicit routes to become inoperative. Sessions using the virtual routes must then be deactivated.
- **Virtual Route Deactivation.** A particular virtual route can be explicitly deactivated, affecting sessions using that route.
- **Route Extension Inoperative.** The portion of a route between a subarea and a peripheral node might become inoperative, affecting sessions using the route extension.
- **SSCP Session Deactivation.** An SSCP-to-PU or SSCP-to-LU session might be deactivated, affecting other sessions involving the PU or LU.

When a network failure occurs, the network notifies the common session control manager within the affected PUs. The common session control manager determines which sessions are affected and, for LU-to-LU sessions in which it is participating, sends an Unbind request to its half-sessions. Depending on the specific cause of the failure, sessions can sometimes be restarted. For example, with virtual route outage, sessions can often be restarted using a different virtual route.

SUMMARY　　　　　Session termination deactivates the LU-to-LU session and frees the resources it has been using. If no other active sessions are using the virtual route assigned to the deactivated session, the virtual route is deactivated. For cross-network sessions, alias addresses are freed.

A Terminate Self RU requests the termination of a specific LU-to-LU session or of several sessions. A Terminate Other RU requests the termination of a specific session. Termination can be orderly, forced, or cleanup. Functions that are part of termination processing include verifying the authority of the requester to terminate the session, translating names into network addresses, and generating a PCID for cross-domain termination requests. A Cross-Domain Terminate RU passes termination information from one SSCP to the other so that both are able to perform their part of termination processing. A Control Terminate RU requests the primary LU to deactivate a specified LU-to-LU session. An Unbind RU is used to deactivate the session. As part of session deactivation, system control blocks are discarded, the virtual route is deactivated if no other session is using it, and alias addresses and other network resources are freed. A cross-domain takedown is used to terminate all LU-to-LU sessions involving a specified pair of SSCPs. Each SSCP terminates the LU-to-LU sessions where its LU is the primary LU.

Session outage notification is a procedure used to terminate all sessions affected by a particular failure. Failures that might lead to a session outage notification include route inoperative, virtual route deactivated, route extension inoperative, and SSCP session deactivated.

25 CONFIGURATION SERVICES

In this chapter we begin an examination of *configuration services,* the second category of session network services. Configuration services are concerned with the physical configuration of the network. These services are used to start up the network by activating the NAUs and links that implement the SNA system. Configuration services are also used to change the configuration of the network, to restart a portion of the network that previously failed, and to shut down the network.

CONFIGURATION SERVICES FUNCTIONS

The major function of configuration services is to activate and deactivate SNA network resources. Activation and deactivation of specific resources can occur automatically as part of network startup or shutdown, or it can be in response to operator commands or end-user requests. An SNA network resource is a logical resource (SSCP, LU, PU, link, link station) contained within a physical resource (host processor, controller, terminal). Physical resources must be powered on before their associated logical resources can be activated. Network activation and deactivation, as we will be seeing in this chapter and the next, are concerned with logical resources.

NETWORK ACTIVATION

SSCPs control the activation and deactivation of logical resources. By activating a resource, an SSCP gains control over the resource and makes it part of its domain. Figure 25.1 illustrates a simple domain and the resources under its control. We have given the various resources addresses according to the conventions used by ACF/NCP. Actual addresses will vary according to the SNA access method used and the sequence in which the resources are defined.

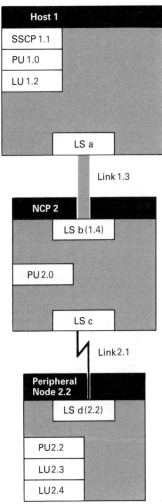

Figure 25.1   Domain resources.

Using the ACF/NCP conventions, the first part of the address identifies the subarea. Since the peripheral node shown in Fig. 25.1 is part of the subarea managed by NCP 2, it also has a subarea address of 2. The second part of the address is the element address. The element address for a PU in a subarea node is 0. The element address for the SSCP is 1. In a host node, LUs are assigned element addresses starting with 2; links are assigned addresses starting with the first available address after the LU addresses. After a link is assigned an address, the link station (LS) at the far end of the link is assigned an address one greater than the address assigned to the link (see LS b in Fig. 25.1). For an NCP a link to a node other than its SSCP is given the first available address, and the link station at the far end is then given an address that is one greater than that. In a peripheral node the PU is given the same address as the link station. LUs are assigned addresses starting one higher than the PU.

A typical activation sequence for the resources shown in Fig. 25.1 is listed here. This sequence assumes that physical units in the network have been powered on, the host has been loaded with operating system and SNA access method programs, and the programs have been started.

1. The SNA access method activates SSCP 1.1 and the physical units and links associated with the SSCP—PU 1.0 and Link 1.3.

2. Channel-attached communications controllers (NCP 2) are loaded with NCP.

3. PU 1.0 performs a channel contact on Link 1.3, which establishes an explicit route between SSCP 1.1 and NCP 2.

4. SSCP 1.1 activates an SSCP-to-PU session with PU 2.0. This causes an explicit route and a virtual route to be activated between SSCP 1.1 and PU 2.0.

5. SSCP 1.1 directs PU 2.0 to activate Link 2.1 and, if necessary, to load peripheral node 2.2. PU 2.0 activates the link and informs SSCP 1.1 whether it is necessary to load the peripheral node. SSCP 1.1 notifies the network operator if loading is necessary. After the loading, SSCP 1.1 activates an SSCP-to-PU session with PU 2.2, which also activates PU 2.2.

6. SSCP 1.1 activates SSCP-to-LU sessions with LU 2.3 and LU 2.4, thereby activating them.

RESOURCE HIERARCHY AND CASCADED ACTIVATION

In the activation procedure, resources are activated in a specific sequence, with higher-level resources being activated before lower-level resources. For example, the SSCP is activated before the NCP, NCP 2 before Link 2.1, and Link 2.1 before peripheral node 2.2. This sequence is known as the *SSCP resource hierarchy*. Figure 25.2 shows the domain we have been examining and its corresponding resource hierarchy. The resource hierarchy is defined when the resources are defined to the SNA access method. Once the hierarchy is defined, resource activation must follow the sequence of the hierarchy, moving from top to bottom.

It would be difficult for an operator to enter all the commands needed to activate a network and to enter the commands in the exact sequence required. To simplify the activation process, the SNA access methods allow entire subareas or portions of subareas to be activated by entering a single command, using a process called *cascaded activation*. When the network is defined, the resources to be activated as a group are specified. All the resources in the subarea can be activated automatically, or specific resources can be left unactivated. These can later be activated when required. For example, a particular resource might be activated only at a certain time of day.

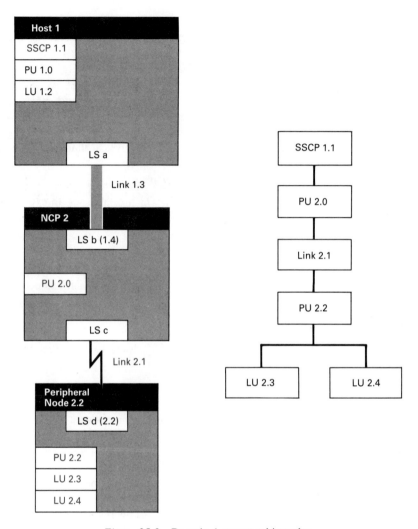

Figure 25.2   Domain 1 resource hierarchy.

Figure 25.3 shows the resource hierarchies for a more complex example that contains two interconnected domains. Note here that links between two subarea nodes are assigned link addresses and link station addresses in both directions. This is because both NCPs must activate the link between them and thus must each be able to address that link. Notice that there is a separate resource hierarchy for each SSCP in the network. Within each resource hierarchy there is a subhierarchy for each subarea. Links between subareas are represented in each subhierarchy using link station addresses that pertain to that subarea. For example, Link 4.6 is in the subhierarchy for NCP 4, and Link 5.1 is in the subhierarchy for NCP 5. Also, where a connection exists between domains, the SSCP from the other domain forms a subhierarchy in the first SSCP's hierarchy. So here SSCP 3.1 has a subhierarchy under SSCP 1.1, and vice versa. The SSCP subhierarchy contains all the LUs controlled by the SSCP. An SSCP subhierarchy is used when a cross-domain LU-to-LU session is to be activated. For example, if SSCP 1.1 needs to activate an LU-to-LU session with LU 4.5, it would know from its resource hierarchy that it needs to communicate with SSCP 3.1 in order to establish the session.

**RESOURCE
CONTROL**

The configuration of an SNA network is unlikely to stay exactly as it was originally specified. Planned addition and removal of network resources are required over time. Unplanned changes are also necessary when failures or performance problems occur within the network. As switched-link connections are made or broken, the associated resources are added to or removed from the hierarchy. The network definitions made to the SNA access method upon which the resource hierarchy is based can be changed dynamically through a process called *dynamic reconfiguration*. A dynamic configuration data set contains statements that alter the original configuration. An operator command then causes the configuration data set to be processed, thus associating the changes with the appropriate NCP. When the NCP is activated, the changes are reflected in its subhierarchy. The operator can later process another configuration data set to restore the original configuration.

Resource hierarchies can also be changed through the use of *shared control* of resources. Certain types of resources can be shared concurrently by up to eight SSCPs; other resources can be shared serially by different SSCPs at different times but may have only one SSCP in control at a given time. Some examples of both types of shared resources are listed in Box 25.1.

BOX 25.1   Examples of shared resources

Concurrent Sharing	Serial Sharing
The PU in an NCP subarea node	Switched links
A nonswitched SDLC link and the link station representing another NCP node	A PU, LUs, and link station in a peripheral node and the link between the peripheral node and its subarea node

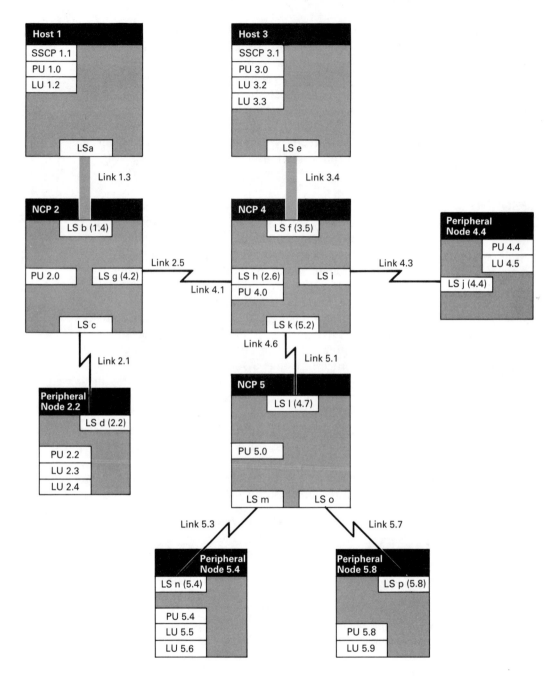

Figure 25.3   Resource hierarchies: two-domain network.

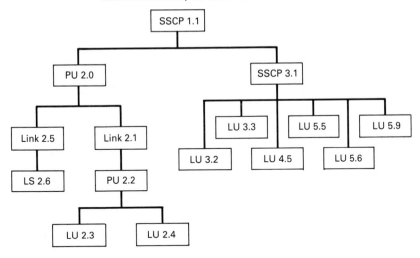

Resource Hierarchy for SSCP 1.1

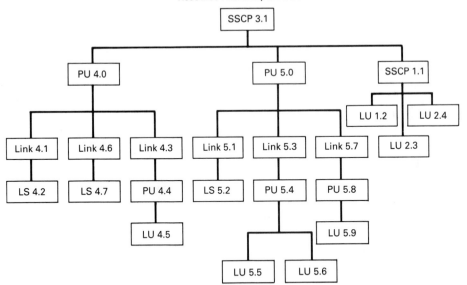

Resource Hierarchy for SSCP 3.1

Figure 25.3   (Continued)

Control over a PU or an LU is established when an SSCP activates an SSCP-to-PU or SSCP-to-LU session with it. Control over a link is established when the SSCP activates the link. Control over a link station is established when the SSCP issues a Contact request for that link station.

The resource hierarchies shown in Fig. 25.3 were based on SSCP 3.1 having established control over Link 4.3, PU 4.4, and LU 4.5. However, if the SSCP-to-PU and SSCP-to-LU sessions for these resources were deactivated, it would be possible for SSCP 1.1 to establish SSCP-to-PU and SSCP-to-LU sessions with them and thus to gain control over them. This would be done through Link 2.5 and PU 4.0. Once this was done, the resource hierarchies would appear as in Fig. 25.4. Now PU 4.0 appears as a subhierarchy under SSCP 1.1, with PU 4.4 and LU 4.5 resources belonging to SSCP 1.1. LU 4.5 is no longer part of the SSCP 3.1 subhierarchy under SSCP 1.1. However, in SSCP 3.1's hierarchy, LU 4.5 is now part of SSCP 1.1's subhierarchy. Shared control of NCP 4 is indicated by PU 4.0 appearing in both hierarchies. Likewise, the link between NCP 2 and NCP 4 (Link 2.5/Link 4.1) appears in both hierarchies.

NETWORK
ACTIVATION
CONTROL FLOWS

The control flow required for network activation depends on the configuration of the network. We will look next at typical control flows involved in activating different segments of a network. Figure 25.5 shows the control flow involved in activating a host node, a channel-attached NCP, and the link between them. The steps in the flow are as follows:

1. The SSCP sends an Add Link request to the PU in its node to get the network address for the link to be activated. The response provides the address.

2. The SSCP sends an Activate Link request to its PU, requesting that the channel link be activated.

3. The SSCP issues an Add Link Station request to get the network address of the link station in the NCP.

4. The SSCP issues a Contact request to its PU, requesting it to activate the link station in the NCP.

5. The link station in the host sends an Exchange Identification request to the link station in the attached subarea node, providing suggested parameters to be used with this link, such as the maximum number of bytes to be sent to the host at one time.

6. The link station in the subarea node sends back an Exchange Identification accepting the parameters related to the host and sending parameters related to the NCP's use of the link.

7. The link station in the host sends a Channel Contact request to the other link station, indicating acceptance of the parameters.

Resource Hierarchy for SSCP 1.1

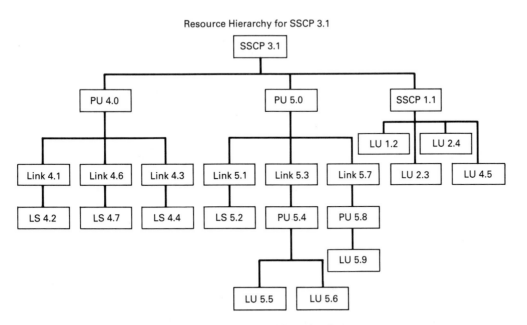

Figure 25.4   Resource hierarchy changes.

8. PU 1.0 notifies the SSCP that the link has been successfully activated by sending it a Contacted request.

9. The PU in the host node sends an NC Explicit Route Operative request to the subarea node PU, notifying it that the link is active and providing the addresses of other subarea nodes that can be reached using explicit routes that use this transmission group.

10. The subarea PU sends an NC Explicit Route Operative request to the host PU, providing addresses that can be reached from the subarea node using explicit routes that contain this transmission group.

11. SSCP 1.1 then sends an Activate PU request to PU 2.0, requesting that an SSCP-to-PU session be established between them. As part of the processing of this request, a virtual route and an explicit route are activated between Host 1 and NCP 2.

12. Once the SSCP-to-PU session has been activated, the SSCP sends a Start Data Traffic request to enable data transmission across the session.

13. The SSCP then issues a Set Control Vector request, sending the current date and time to PU 2.0.

We next examine the various control RUs used in this control flow.

ADD LINK

An Add Link (ADDLINK) request is sent by the SSCP to a PU to get the network address associated with a particular link identifier. The Add Link contains the link identifier, and the response to it contains the network address for that link.

ACTIVATE LINK

An Activate Link (ACTLINK) request can be sent by either an SSCP or a PUCP to the PU in the node attached to the link. The purpose of the request is to put the link in an active state. Certain links can be under shared control of several SSCPs. In this case the first Activate Link causes the link to be activated. When additional Activate Links are received from other SSCPs, these SSCPs are added to the list of control points for the link, and a positive response is sent back.

ADD LINK STATION

An Add Link Station (ADDLINKSTA) request is sent from the SSCP to the PU to get the network address of a link station. Again, the request contains an identifier, and the reply contains the network address that corresponds to the identifier. The Add Link Station request also specifies the types of FID headers that are supported by this link station.

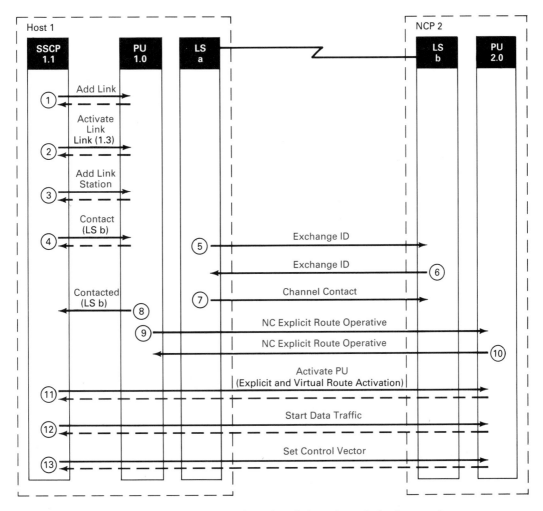

Figure 25.5 Activating a host node, channel, and channel-attached subarea node.

CONTACT   A Contact request is sent from an SSCP or a PUCP
                     to a PU, requesting the PU to contact the adjacent
link station specified in the request. (An adjacent link station is one at the far
end of a link attached to the PU's node.) Once contact is established, the two
link stations communicate with each other, exchanging parameters and information about protocols to be used for transmission across the link. This information might include identification of primary and secondary link station, trans-
mit/receive mode, segment assembly capability, and commands and responses
supported.

CONTACTED   Once the link stations have completed their exchanges, the PU sends a Contacted request back to the SSCP or PUCP. The Contacted RU provides information on the status of the adjacent link station and the attempt to contact it, as well as information on the IPL module that may need to be loaded in the adjacent node.

**NC EXPLICIT
ROUTE OPERATIVE**   Once a link and its link stations become active, the PUs on each end of the link exchange a pair of NC Explicit Route Operative (NC__ER__OP) requests. These RUs contain information about destination subarea addresses that can be reached from the node sending the NC__ER__OP RU (destination subarea addresses that are in the node's subarea routing table). For each destination subarea address there is an indication of which explicit route numbers are operative. The explicit route number for a destination subarea address is operative if all the transmission groups between the node sending the NC__ER__OP and the destination subarea node are active. The NC__ER__OP also lists the sending node as a destination subarea address with all explicit routes active.

When the PU receives the NC__ER__OP, it updates tables that keep track of which explicit routes are operative for the destination subarea addresses in its subarea routing table. The PU also modifies the NC__ER__OP so that it includes information only for those destination subarea address–explicit route number pairs that are in the node's subarea routing table and have also just become operative as a result of the transmission group's becoming operative. The resulting NC__ER__OP is then sent out to all adjacent subarea nodes that have an active link, except for the node that sent the original NC__ER__OP. This updating, modifying, and sending of the NC__ER__OP, called *fan-out propagation,* continues until there are no more entries left on the list of explicit routes that have become operative.

Figure 25.6 illustrates the fan-out propagation process, using a single destination subarea address (node A) and explicit route number (ERN 3) as an example. Initially, transmission groups a and b are not active, but transmission group c is active.

1. When a link in transmission group a is activated, node A sends node B an NC__ER__OP request, indicating that all explicit routes to node A are operative. Since node B has (A,3) in its subarea routing table, it changes the status of the entry for (A,3) to operative. Since transmission group b is not active, it does not send an NC__ER__OP request to node C.

2. When transmission group b is activated, node B sends node C an NC__ER__OP request, indicating that explicit route 3 to node A is operative. Node C then changes the status of the (A,3) entry in its subarea routing table.

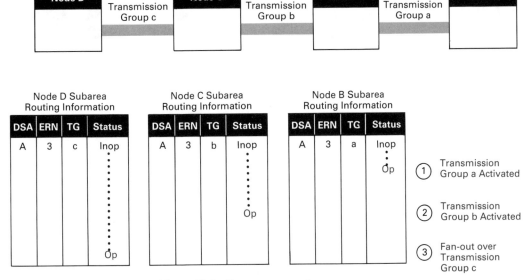

Figure 25.6   Fan-out propagation.

3. Node C, as part of fan-out propagation, sends an NC—ER—OP request to node D, indicating that explicit route 3 to node A is operative. Node D then changes the status of the (A,3) entry in its subarea routing table.

By the time all transmission groups along an explicit route have been activated, the exchange of NC—ER—OPs and their propagation will have informed all the nodes along the route of the operative status of that explicit route.

ACTIVATE   An Activate Physical Unit (ACTPU) request is sent
PHYSICAL UNIT   from the SSCP to the PU to activate the PU and to
                           establish an SSCP-to-PU session. As with a Bind re-
quest, when the ACTPU RU is sent, a virtual route and an explicit route are
activated, if required, between the SSCP and the PU. The route steps involved
in the virtual and explicit route activation are the same as described in Chapter
23 for Bind processing. The ACTPU specifies parameters and protocols to be
used for the SSCP-to-PU session. This includes an FM profile, a TS profile,
and an SSCP ID that can be used to validate the ACTPU.

ACTIVATING A   We will next see examples of the control flows used
PERIPHERAL NODE   to activate other types of network resources. Figure
                           25.7 shows the control flow used to activate a periph-

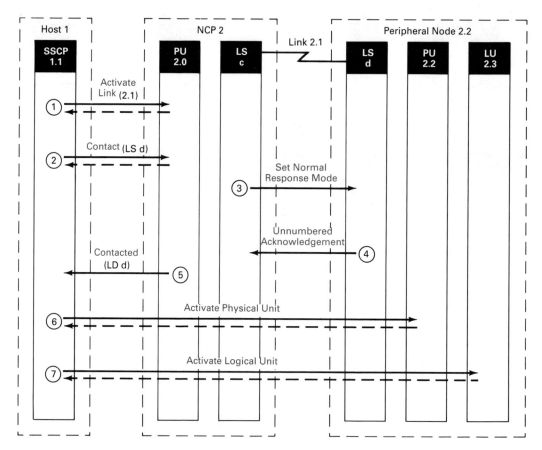

Figure 25.7   Activating a peripheral node.

eral node connected to an NCP via an SDLC data link. The steps in this control flow are as follows:

1. The SSCP sends an Activate Link request to the PU in the subarea node, requesting it to activate the link to the peripheral node.
2. The SSCP sends a Contact request to the PU in the subarea node, asking it to contact and activate the link station in the peripheral node.
3. The PU in the subarea node has its link station send a Set Normal Response Mode request to the link station in the peripheral node.
4. The link station in the peripheral node sends back a positive response in the form of an unnumbered acknowledgment.
5. The PU in the subarea node sends a Contacted RU to the SSCP, indicating that the link stations are prepared for communication.

6. The SSCP initiates an SSCP-to-PU session with the PU in the peripheral node by sending it an Activate Physical Unit request. As part of this, an explicit route and a virtual route are activated between the host node and the peripheral node.

7. The SSCP initiates SSCP-to-LU sessions with the LUs in the peripheral node by sending each LU an Activate Logical Unit request.

ACTIVATE LOGICAL UNIT

An Activate Logical Unit (ACTLU) request is sent from the SSCP to an LU to activate the LU and to establish an SSCP-to-LU session with it. Before an ACTLU RU can be validly processed, the SSCP must have established an SSCP-to-PU session with the PU in the LU's node. The ACTLU RU specifies both an FM profile and a TS profile; these are used to establish parameters and protocols for the session. The response to the ACTLU RU contains additional information about the session, including the capability of the LU to act as the primary or secondary session partner, whether parallel sessions are supported, maximum RU size, and resynchronization capability. If an LU supports parallel sessions, it will have one secondary-LU network address and more than one primary-LU network address. An ACTLU is sent only to the secondary-LU address. When the secondary-LU address is activated, the primary-LU addresses are as well.

ACTIVATING AN SDLC LINK

Figure 25.8 shows the control flow involved in activating a link between two subarea nodes. The steps in this control flow are as follows:

1. After NCP 4 has been loaded, the PUCP in NCP 4 activates Link 4.1 by sending an Activate Link request and a Contact request to the PU in NCP 4. Link activation can be performed by either the SSCP in Host 1 or the PUCP in NCP 4. In this example, link activation is performed by the PUCP.

2. SSCP 1.1 activates Link 2.5 by sending an Activate Link request and a Contact request to the PU in NCP 2.

3. The link stations then issue Exchange ID requests to exchange the parameters to be used for transmission. The response mode is set and acknowledged, and a Receive Ready request is sent indicating that the link stations are ready for transmission.

4. The PU in NCP 2 sends a Contacted request to inform the SSCP that the link and link stations are active and ready for transmission. The PU in NCP 4 does the same for the PUCP.

5. The PU in NCP 2 sends an NC Explicit Route Operative request to the PU in NCP 4, informing NCP 4 of the addresses of subareas that can be reached using explicit routes that contain this link.

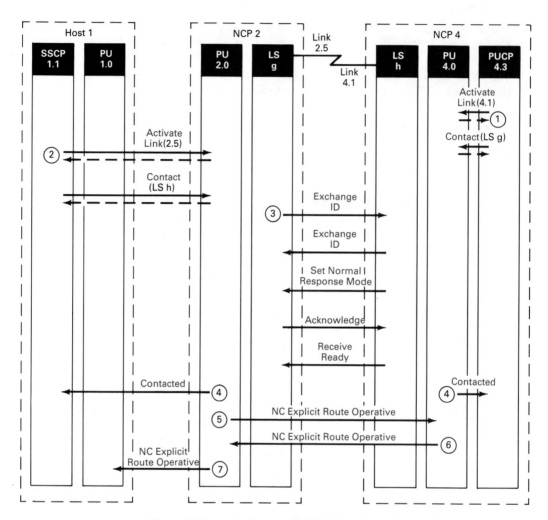

Figure 25.8   Activating an SDLC link between subarea nodes.

6. The PU in NCP 4 sends an NC Explicit Route Operative to the PU in NCP 2, providing subarea addresses that can be reached from NCP 4.

7. The PU in NCP 2 passes the information it received on to the PU in Host 1 via another NC Explicit Route Operative request.

NODE LOADING   As part of the processing performed in activating a node, it might be necessary to load a program into that node. For example, a PU type 4 node might need to be loaded with its copy of NCP. Program loading often takes place as part of the startup procedures executed before network activation begins. For some nodes loading takes place as part of activation.

When a link station is being activated with a Contact request, that station determines whether loading is required and indicates this in its response. This information is passed back to the SSCP or PUCP in the Contacted RU. If program loading is required, it is handled by an SSCP or a PUCP. A PU type 4 or 5 node is loaded by the SSCP. A PU type 1 or 2 node can be loaded by either the SSCP or the PUCP in the subarea node that provides boundary function support.

Node loading always involves three control RUs. An SSCP uses the IPL Initial, IPL Text, and IPL Final RUs to load a PU type 4 or 5 node; an SSCP uses the NS IPL Initial, NS IPL Text, and NS IPL Final RUs to load a PU type 1 or 2 node; and a PUCP uses the NC IPL Initial, NC IPL Text, and NC IPL Final RUs to load a PU type 1 or 2 node. In each case an IPL Initial RU signals that loading is to begin and identifies the adjacent link station address of the node to be loaded. A series of IPL Text RUs is then used to download the program text. An IPL Final RU indicates that loading is complete and passes the entry point of the load module. These RUs flow between the SSCP or PUCP and the PU in the node being loaded.

CONFIGURATION SERVICES AND NODE DATABASES   Information about network resources and their configuration is maintained in two major repositories: the *configuration services database* and the *node database*. The configuration services database stores information about each domain, the node database about each node.

There is a *node control block* for each node in the network. The node control block contains pointers to other control blocks that contain information pertaining to the node. This information includes explicit route lists, virtual route lists, transmission group lists, node resources, session control blocks, domain resources, SSCPs or PUCPs that have established control over this node, and routing table information. The node control block also contains information on the network address of the PU and the SSCP or PUCP, the address split being used, PU type, intermediate node-routing capability, maximum number of explicit routes and virtual routes, and explicit route to transmission group mapping type.

The configuration services database contains, for each domain, the node control block for the SSCP and a *domain resource list*. The domain resource list contains an entry for each resource—PU, LU, link, and link station—in the domain. The entries are organized by subarea and are hierarchically linked within each subarea. Figure 25.9 shows the hierarchy for a subarea. Each link entry points to the subarea PU entry. Each adjacent link station entry for a given link points to that link entry. (A multipoint link has multiple adjacent link sta-

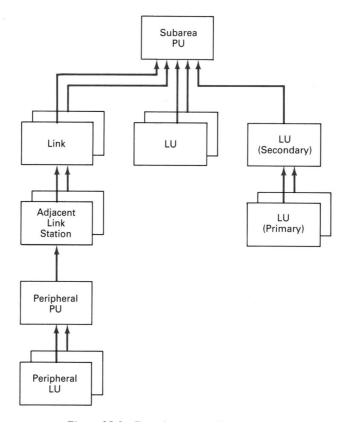

Figure 25.9   Domain resource list hierarchy.

tions; other link types have only a single adjacent link station represented on the list.) The resource entry for a peripheral PU points to the adjacent link station entry for the link station it contains. Peripheral LU entries point to the peripheral PU entry. Subarea LU entries point to the subarea PU entry. For an LU that supports multiple sessions, an entry for the secondary-LU network address points to the subarea PU entry. Other entries for that LU, which are for the primary-LU network addresses, point to the secondary-LU entry.

The information contained in a domain resource list entry varies with the type of resource it describes. At a minimum, the entry contains information about the state of the resource, its network name and address, a pointer to the next higher resource in the hierarchy, and any control RUs that are waiting for the resource to be activated. In addition, for PUs and LUs the entry contains the session ID for the SSCP-to-PU/LU session. For links and link stations the entry identifies switched links and whether the link is primary or secondary. For peripheral PUs and LUs the entry contains the local address. The entry also contains other fields specific to PU, link, and adjacent link station resources.

The node resource database contains a node control block and a *node resource list* for each node. The node control block contains the information described previously. The node resource list, like the domain resource list, is structured hierarchically. Figure 25.10 illustrates a node resource list hierarchy. PU and LU entries are hierarchically associated with the node control block. LUs that do not support parallel sessions are represented by a single entry. LUs that support parallel sessions have an entry for the secondary-LU address that points to the node control block. Primary-LU addresses are represented by entries that point to the secondary-LU entry. Link entries point to the PU entry, adjacent link station entries point to the link entry, boundary function PU entries

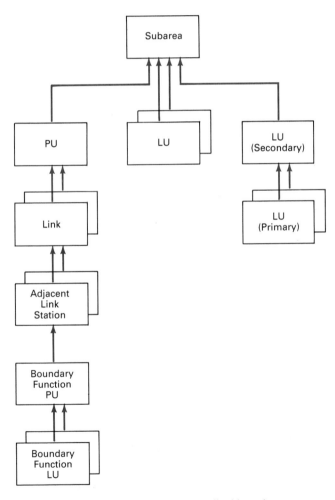

Figure 25.10   Node resource list hierarchy.

point to the adjacent link station entry, and boundary function LU entries point to the boundary function PU entry.

The node resource entries contain status information for the resource, its element address, and its hierarchical pointer. Other information varies with the type of resource. Links and link stations have information such as headers and options used, whether it is primary or secondary, whether it is a switched link, and a list of any control RUs waiting for the resource to be activated. For boundary function PUs and LUs the entry contains a local ID, a secondary receive pacing count, and the source of address assignments. The entry also contains information related to shared control of resources. It contains a share limit that determines the maximum number of SSCPs or PUCPs that can concurrently share control of the resource. It also contains a pointer to the list of SSCPs or PUCPs that currently have control of the resource. When a request is received that establishes control over the resource (ACTPU, ACTLINK, or CONTACT), the share limit is checked, and if the limit is exceeded, the request is rejected.

For shared-control resources, there can be an entry for a given resource in multiple domain resource lists. The resource will appear in the list for each domain in which the SSCP has established control over it. However, there is only one node resource list entry for a given resource. The node resource list entry reflects the overall status of the resource. If the resource has been activated by any one SSCP, it is considered active. A resource is not considered inactive until all SSCPs have deactivated it.

SUMMARY

Configuration services are responsible for activating and deactivating SNA network resources. Network resources in a given domain are structured according to an SSCP resource hierarchy. This hierarchy is defined when the resources are defined to an SNA access method. Cascaded activation allows an entire subarea or portion of a subarea to be activated with a single command. The resources are activated according to the resource hierarchy for the subarea, starting from the top and moving to the bottom. The resource hierarchy for an SSCP will change over time. As switched links are connected or broken, changes are made to the hierarchy. Dynamic reconfiguration can be used to alter the network configuration. Resource hierarchies can also be changed through shared control of resources. As SSCPs take or relinquish control of shared resources, corresponding changes take place in their resource hierarchies.

Network activation activities include assigning network addresses to links and link stations, activating links, contacting and activating adjacent link stations, putting explicit routes in operative status, activating physical units by establishing SSCP-to-PU sessions, activating logical units by establishing SSCP-to-LU sessions, and activating virtual and explicit routes. Network activation might also involve loading programs into subarea and peripheral nodes.

Information about network resources is kept in the configuration services database and the node database. The configuration services database consists of a node control block for each SSCP and a domain resource list for the SSCP's resources. The node database consists of a node control block and a node resource list for each node. Entries in these databases are updated as network resources are activated and deactivated and as changes are made to the network configuration.

26 SWITCHED LINKS AND NETWORK DEACTIVATION

Certain peripheral nodes might be attached to the network using switched communication facilities (e.g., a telephone line). This type of connection is known as a *switched link*. The connection is established when required and then terminated and broken when there are no longer any active sessions to support over the link. A node might connect to the network through different switched links at different times. The activation of the switched link is initiated by a *call*, which might originate either from the peripheral node to be attached or from the subarea node to which it will attach. The placing and answering of the call can be handled by either a manual or an automated procedure. In order for the switched link to be established, an SSCP-to-PU session must already be established for the subarea PU, and the peripheral node PU must be defined to the network and part of the SSCP's domain resource list.

SWITCHED-LINK ACTIVATION

Figure 26.1 illustrates the control flow required to activate a switched link. The steps involved are as follows:

1. The SSCP prepares the subarea PU for activating the link by sending either a Connect Out or an Activate Connect In request. If a Connect Out is sent, the subarea PU places the call. If an Activate Connect In is sent, the subarea PU prepares to receive a call, which is placed by the peripheral node.

2. After the call has been made and answered, the two link stations exchange information about the parameters and protocols to be used during transmission across the link.

3. The subarea PU notifies the SSCP via a Request Contact RU that a connection has been established with the peripheral node link station. The SSCP uses information from the Request Contact RU to update the domain resource list entry for the peripheral node.

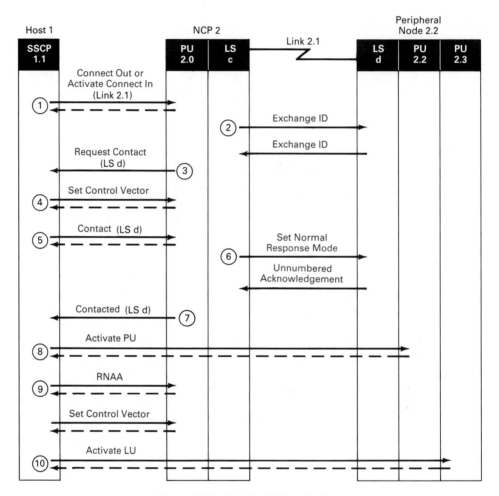

Figure 26.1   Switched link activation.

4. The SSCP sends the subarea PU information about the peripheral node link station, including the PU type, maximum number of BTUs to be sent before polling or sending to another station, error retry and recovery information, and the maximum BTU size.

5. The SSCP sends the subarea PU a Contact request, asking it to contact the peripheral link station.

6. The subarea PU causes the subarea link station to contact the peripheral link station, telling it to go into normal response mode.

7. Once the contact procedure between the link stations is completed, the subarea PU informs the SSCP via a Contacted request that the peripheral link station is ready to receive.

8. The SSCP activates an SSCP-to-PU session with the peripheral PU by sending it an Activate PU request. As part of the processing of the Activate PU request, an explicit route and virtual route are established between the SSCP and the peripheral node.

9. Since the network addresses in a peripheral node reflect the address of the subarea node and the link through which it is attached, the addresses for a peripheral node attached through a switched link are not determined until the particular switched link to be used has been selected. Then, as part of the activation process, network addresses are determined. As part of the Request Contact RU processing, the network addresses of the peripheral PU and the link station are updated in the domain resource list entry. Following the Activate PU, the SSCP sends the subarea PU the local addresses of all the peripheral node LUs in a Request Network Address Assignment RU. The PU determines network addresses for the LUs and returns them to the SSCP in its response. The SSCP then updates the domain resource list entries for the LUs to reflect these addresses. The SSCP also sends to the subarea PU a Set Control Vector request for each peripheral LU, containing a secondary receive pacing count and a scheduling priority.

10. The SSCP then sends each peripheral LU an Activate LU request to activate an SSCP-to-LU session with that LU.

Several of the control RUs used in switched-link activation serve the same function as they do in other types of network activation. There are, however, some control RUs unique to switched-link processing, which we will examine next.

CONNECT OUT

A Connect Out (CONNOUT) request is sent from the SSCP or PUCP to a PU, requesting the PU to initiate a procedure that will establish a connection over the specified link. The CONNOUT RU contains the address of the link over which to establish the connection and the local address of the adjacent link station at the far end of the link. The CONNOUT also indicates whether the call that establishes the connection will be placed manually or automatically. For an automatic call, the CONNOUT RU also contains the digits to dial and the number of times to retry the call if it is not completed successfully the first time. The CONNOUT RU also indicates if a CCITT X.21 direct call procedure is to be used.

ACTIVATE CONNECT IN

A Connect Out RU is used if the subarea PU is to place the call; an Activate Connect In (ACTCONNIN) request is used if the subarea PU is to receive the call. The Activate Connect In request causes the subarea PU to prepare the link specified in the RU to accept incoming calls.

REQUEST
CONTACT

Once the two link stations have successfully completed establishing a connection across a switched link and have exchanged information via Exchange IDs, the subarea PU notifies the SSCP or PUCP of the successful connect procedure by sending a Request Contact RU. The Request Contact (REQCONT) RU contains the information on parameters and protocols that was sent by the peripheral link station in its Exchange ID request. This information is then used to update the domain resource list entries for the link station and the PU.

REQUEST
NETWORK
ADDRESS
ASSIGNMENT

Once the SSCP has established an SSCP-to-PU session with the peripheral PU over a switched link, it sends a Request Network Address Assignment (RNAA) RU to the subarea PU in order to get network addresses for the peripheral LUs. The RNAA specifies the address of the peripheral link station, a count of the number of addresses to be assigned, and the local addresses of all the LUs in the peripheral node.

NETWORK
DEACTIVATION

As with network activation, network deactivation is also performed in a cascaded manner. For example, if a subarea node is deactivated, the various link stations, LUs, and peripheral nodes associated with it are also deactivated. Portions of a network might be deactivated because of a failure or problem and then later reactivated. Generally, when a resource is reactivated, resources subordinate to it in the hierarchy are also reactivated. However, it is possible to specify that a particular resource, and any of its subordinate resources, not be automatically reactivated.

When failures occur and a session outage notification procedure is employed, SSCP-to-PU, SSCP-to-LU, and SSCP-to-SSCP sessions may be affected. In that case the various SSCP sessions are deactivated, using the appropriate RU to deactivate each type of session. The loss of an SSCP, however, does not necessarily mean that all sessions within that domain are deactivated. When an NCP loses contact with its SSCP, it uses a process called *automatic network shutdown* (ANS) to deactivate, in an orderly manner, the resources controlled by the SSCP. LU-to-LU sessions are not deactivated, however, unless the LU in the subarea is no longer able to communicate with its session partner. Links to other subareas also are not deactivated, so that virtual and explicit routes that include this subarea can continue to be used.

As with network activation, the control flows involved in network deactivation vary, depending on the network configuration. We look next at the principle types of control flows involved in network deactivation.

DEACTIVATING A PERIPHERAL NODE

Figure 26.2 demonstrates the control flow used to deactivate a peripheral node and all of its resources. The steps in the flow are as follows:

1. The SSCP sends a Deactivate LU request to each LU in the peripheral node. This deactivates the SSCP-to-LU session and causes the SSCP to relinquish control of the LU.

2. The SSCP sends a Deactivate PU request to the peripheral PU. This causes the SSCP-to-PU session to be deactivated and the SSCP to relinquish control of the peripheral node.

3. The SSCP sends a Discontact request to the subarea PU, instructing it to break contact with the peripheral link station.

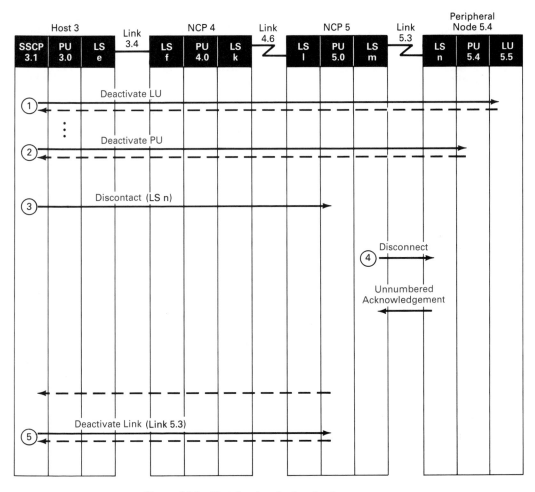

Figure 26.2 Peripheral node deactivation.

4. The subarea PU causes the local link station to initiate a procedure to break contact with the peripheral link station by sending it a Disconnect message. Once the link stations have completed the disconnect procedure, the subarea PU sends the SSCP a response to the Discontact RU.

5. The SSCP sends the subarea PU a Deactivate Link request, instructing it to deactivate the link to the peripheral node.

Next we will look at the principal control RUs used for network deactivation. We will discuss the functions they perform and describe the information they carry.

DEACTIVATE LOGICAL UNIT

A Deactivate Logical Unit (DACTLU) request is sent from an SSCP to an LU in order to deactivate the SSCP-to-LU session. This deactivation can be either a normal deactivation or part of a session outage notification. The DACTLU RU indicates the type of deactivation and a specific cause for it.

DEACTIVATE PHYSICAL UNIT

A Deactivate Physical Unit (DACTPU) request is sent from an SSCP to a PU in order to deactivate the SSCP-to-PU session. As with the DACTLU, a DACTPU RU indicates the type of deactivation and gives a specific cause for the deactivation.

DISCONTACT

A Discontact request is sent from an SSCP or a PUCP to a PU in order to have the PU deactivate link-level contact with a specified adjacent link station. Following a Discontact, the two link stations use a procedure to break contact that is specific to the particular data link control protocol used for the link. The Discontact contains the network address of the adjacent link station to be discontacted.

DEACTIVATE LINK

A Deactivate Link (DACTLINK) request is sent from an SSCP or a PUCP to a PU in order to deactivate a link by breaking the connection between a local link station and the link attached to it. Before a link can be deactivated, all the adjacent link stations on the link must have been discontacted. The DACTLINK RU contains the address of the link to be deactivated.

DEACTIVATING A SWITCHED LINK

Figure 26.3 illustrates the control flow involved in deactivating a peripheral node attached via a switched link. There are two differences between this control flow and the previous one. First, after each SSCP-to-LU session is deactivated via the Deactivate LU request, the SSCP sends the subarea PU a Free Network Address request for that LU. The LU network address that was assigned when the switched link was activated is now released and can be reassigned by the PU if this switched link is activated again. The second difference is that an Abandon Connection request is sent in place of the Deactivate Link request to deactivate the link to the peripheral node.

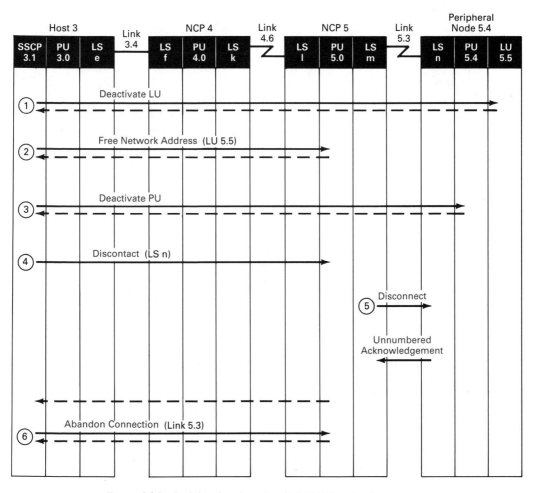

Figure 26.3 Peripheral node and switched link activation.

FREE NETWORK ADDRESS   A Free Network Address (FNA) is sent from an SSCP to a subarea PU, notifying it to remove certain entries from the node resource list and to free the network addresses assigned to them. Depending on the type of resources being freed, there is a target resource associated with the request. The relationship is shown in Box 26.1. The FNA RU can specify the network address of the target resource. It can also specify a list of network addresses of resources to be removed from the node resource list. If the FNA specifies a target resource but no list of network addresses, all resources associated with the target resource that match the relationship shown in Box 26.1 are freed. If the FNA specifies a list of network addresses but no target resource, the target resource is identified based on the relationship shown. When a positive response to the FNA is received, the SSCP also removes the resource from the domain resource list.

ABANDON CONNECTION   An Abandon Connection (ABCONN) request is sent from an SSCP to a subarea PU to deactivate a link after a switched link connection over that link has been broken. It causes the connection between the subarea link station and the link to be broken. The Abandon Connection RU specifies the network address of the link in question.

DEACTIVATING A SUBAREA NODE   Figure 26.4 shows the control flow used to deactivate a subarea node. It assumes that the subarea node has

BOX 26.1   Request/target resource relationship

Resource Being Freed	Target Resource
LUs identified by a network address that is used in an SSCP-to-LU session	PU
LUs identified as primary LUs where multiple sessions are supported	Secondary LU
BF.PU and adjacent link station	Link to BF.PU node and peripheral node
BF.LUs	BF.PU

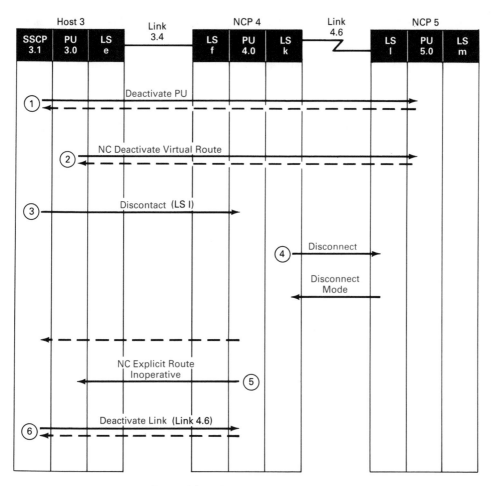

Figure 26.4 Subarea node deactivation.

no LUs or that all SSCP-to-LU sessions have already been deactivated. The steps in this control flow are as follows:

1. The SSCP sends the subarea PU a Deactivate PU request to deactivate the SSCP-to-PU session and relinquish control of the node.

2. Since all sessions between the SSCP and the subarea node have now been terminated, the host PU sends the subarea PU an NC Deactivate Virtual Route request, causing the virtual route that was being used for these sessions to be deactivated.

3. The SSCP sends a Discontact RU to the PU in NCP 4, instructing it to break contact with link station l in NCP 5.

4. The PU in NCP 4 causes local link station k to send a Disconnect request to link station l, causing the connection between them to be broken. Once the link stations have completed the disconnect procedure, the PU in NCP 4 sends a response to the Discontact RU to the SSCP, notifying it that the contact has been broken.

5. Since the link between NCP 4 and NCP 5 has been disconnected, any explicit routes containing that link are now inoperative. The PU in NCP 4 sends an NC Explicit Route Inoperative RU to the host PU, notifying it that the explicit route from the host to NCP 5 is now inoperative. If either NCP 4 or NCP 5 has links to other host or NCP nodes that are affected by the link being disconnected, NC Explicit Route Inoperative RUs are sent to them as well.

6. The SSCP sends a Deactivate Link request to the PU in NCP 4, instructing it to deactivate the link between NCP 4 and NCP 5.

DEACTIVATE VIRTUAL ROUTE

A Deactivate Virtual Route (DACTVR) request is used to deactivate a virtual route once it no longer has any active sessions using it. When the common session control manager in the PU at one end of a virtual route determines there are no active sessions using the virtual route, it notifies the virtual route manager in the PU of this fact. If this is the PU that originally sent the Activate Virtual Route RU that activated the route, it now sends a Deactivate Virtual Route request to the PU at the other end of the virtual route. If there are no active sessions at the other end of the route, the PU sends back a positive response, and the virtual route is deactivated. The deactivation can be either orderly, as described, or forced. If the deactivation is forced, the virtual route is deactivated even if there are active sessions using it. The active sessions are deactivated using the session outage notification procedure. The sending PU deactivates sessions at its end before sending the DACTVR RU. The receiving PU deactivates its sessions before sending back a positive response. The DACTVR RU indicates whether the deactivation is forced or orderly.

EXPLICIT ROUTE INOPERATIVE

When a transmission group becomes inoperative, either through normal deactivation or because of a failure, all explicit routes that use that transmission group must be deactivated. The PUs at each end of the transmission group determine the explicit routes that must be deactivated and then send NC Explicit Route Inoperative (NC__ER__INOP) requests listing these routes to the PUs in all adjacent subarea nodes. Each adjacent subarea node updates its subarea routing table to reflect the changed status of the routes and passes the NC__ER__ INOP RU on to its adjacent subarea nodes. This continues until all nodes involved in the inoperative explicit routes have been notified.

Each node that sends an NC__ER__INOP RU also sends an Explicit Route Inoperative (ER__INOP) request to the SSCP to notify the SSCP of the explicit routes that have become inactive. The virtual route manager in the PU is also notified so that it can deactivate any active virtual routes using the inoperative explicit routes.

The NC__ER__INOP and Explicit Route Inoperative RUs indicate whether the interruption to the route was controlled (the result of a Discontact) or due to a failure or other unexpected condition. They also include the network address of the PU that originated the RU and the transmission group number of the transmission group that failed or was deactivated. They also contain a list of the destination subarea addresses of explicit routes that have become inoperative. For each destination subarea address there is an indication of which explicit route numbers are now inoperative.

DEACTIVATING A CHANNEL-ATTACHED SUBAREA NODE

Figure 26.5 illustrates the control flow used to deactivate a subarea node that is channel-attached. The steps in this control flow are as follows:

1. The SSCP sends the subarea PU a Deactivate PU request, deactivating the SSCP-to-PU session and causing the SSCP to relinquish control of the subarea node.

2. Since all sessions between the SSCP and the subarea node have been terminated, the host PU sends the subarea PU a Deactivate Virtual Route request, deactivating the virtual route that was being used for the sessions.

3. The SSCP sends a Discontact request to the host PU, instructing it to break contact with the subarea link station.

4. The host link station sends the subarea link station a Channel Discontact RU, causing the connection between them to be broken.

5. The SSCP sends the host PU a Delete Network Resource request for the subarea link station. This allows the network address that had been assigned to the subarea link station when it was activated to be available for reassignment.

6. The SSCP sends the host PU a Deactivate Link request, instructing it to deactivate the link to the subarea node.

7. The SSCP sends the host PU a Delete Network Resource RU for the subarea link. This allows the network address that was assigned to the link when it was activated to be available for reassignment.

DELETE NETWORK RESOURCE

A Delete Network Resource (DELETENR) request is sent from an SSCP to a PU when a link or adjacent link station has been deactivated, causing the address assigned to it to become free for reuse. The Delete Network Resource RU contains the address to be released; upon receipt, the PU puts the address back into the pool of addresses available to be assigned.

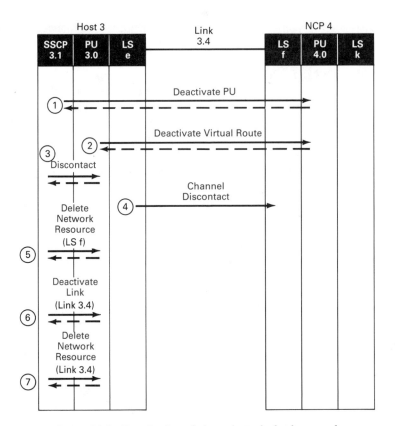

Figure 26.5   Deactivation of channel-attached subarea node.

SUMMARY

Switched links normally use dial-up communication facilities of a common carrier. Connections are established when required to support a session and are broken when the session ends. The activation of a switched link is initiated by a call, which might originate either from the peripheral node or the subarea node. The placing and answering of the call can be either manual or automated. Activating a switched link involves preparing for the connection, placing and answering the call, activating the peripheral link station and peripheral PU, assigning addresses to the peripheral LUs, and activating the peripheral LUs. As part of this process, virtual and explicit routes might be activated, and domain and node resource lists are updated.

Network deactivation is performed in a cascaded manner and can be either a normal deactivation or a deactivation that occurs in response to a network failure. When an NCP loses contact with its SSCP, it uses an automatic network shutdown procedure to deactivate resources in a controlled manner. LU-to-LU sessions and links to other subareas are not deactivated unless they have lost the ability to continue transmission. This allows as much network activity as possible to continue in the event of a failure. Network deactivation activities include deactivating SSCP-to-PU and SSCP-to-LU sessions, deactivating links and link stations, deactivating virtual routes, changing explicit route status to inoperative, freeing network addresses, and updating domain and node resource lists.

27 MAINTENANCE AND MANAGEMENT SERVICES

In this chapter we complete our examination of session network services by looking at maintenance and management services. The other category of session network services, network operator services, has not yet been defined from an architectural standpoint. It is currently only implementation-defined, as part of SNA products, and will not be discussed in this book. Maintenance and management services are used to determine if a link or node has failed, to identify the cause of a failure, to gather error statistics, and to gather test results. These services employ SSCP-to-PU and SSCP-to-LU sessions.

COMMUNICATION NETWORK MANAGEMENT

Maintenance and management services are implemented through a *communication network management* structure, illustrated in Fig. 27.1. Communication network management consists of two types of components: *communication network management applications* (CNMA) and *communication network management services* (CNMS). There is a CNMA component for each domain. The component is associated with a host LU. It communicates with the SSCP via an SSCP-to-LU session. Each node contains a CNMS component that is associated with the node's PU. CNMS communicates with the SSCP via the SSCP-to-PU session. CNMS communicates with CNMA indirectly, via a combination of an SSCP-to-LU session and an SSCP-to-PU session. Management services RUs flow between CNMA and the SSCP. Maintenance service RUs flow between CNMS and the SSCP.

MAINTENANCE SERVICES

Maintenance services include performing traces, recording storage information, executing tests and recording their results, and recording maintenance sta-

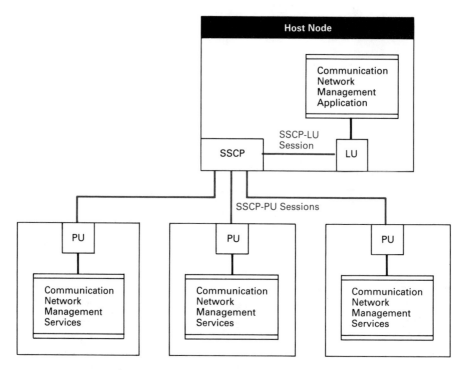

Figure 27.1   Communication Network Management.

tistics. Maintenance services requests can originate within the SSCP or PU, or
they can be contained within a management services request and passed on by
the SSCP to the PU. Maintenance services requests generally occur in sets
wherein one RU requests a test or information and another provides the results
of the test or the requested information. Box 27.1 lists the various maintenance
services RUs. We next examine these RUs, in their related sets.

ACTIVATE TRACE,   An SSCP sends an Activate Trace (ACTTRACE) re-
RECORD TRACE   quest to a PU, requesting that trace data be provided
DATA,   for a specified link. If the link is part of a transmis-
DEACTIVATE   sion group, the Activate Trace RU might specify that
TRACE   trace data be provided for the entire transmission
                         group as well as for a specific link. For a trace to be
activated the link must already have been activated via an Activate Link request,
and there must not be a trace already in progress for the link or transmission
group. An Activate Trace request contains the network address of the link to be
traced and an indicator of whether the entire transmission group should be
traced. It might also contain additional data needed to support the trace.

BOX 27.1   Maintenance RUs

- Activate Trace
- Deactivate Trace
- Record Trace Data
- Display Storage
- Record Storage
- Execute Test
- Record Test Data
- Request Maintenance Statistics
- Record Formatted Maintenance Statistics
- Record Maintenance Statistics
- Request Test Procedure
- Test Mode
- Record Test Results
- Request Echo Test
- Echo Test
- Route Test
- Explicit Route Tested

Data collected while a trace is active are sent from the PU to the SSCP via a Record Trace Data (RECTRD) request. The Record Trace Data RU contains the link address, the trace type, an indication of whether the trace data are in fixed or variable-length segments, and the trace data themselves.

A Deactivate Trace (DACTTRACE) request is sent from the SSCP to the PU to deactivate a trace. The Deactivate Trace RU contains the link address and trace type and, optionally, data needed to support trace deactivation.

DISPLAY STORAGE, A Display Storage (DISPSTOR) request is sent from
RECORD STORAGE the SSCP to a PU, requesting that the PU return the information currently stored in particular storage locations. The Display Storage RU contains the network address of the particular resource whose storage information is to be returned. It also indicates the number of bytes to be returned and the location of the first byte.

A Record Storage (RECSTOR) request is sent from the PU back to the SSCP with the information requested in the Display Storage RU. A Record Storage RU contains the same information as the Display Storage request, plus the information from the specified storage locations.

EXECUTE TEST, RECORD TEST DATA

An Execute Test (EXECTEST) request is sent from the SSCP to the PU, requesting that a particular diagnostic test procedure be performed. The test can be for the PU, for LUs in that node, or for links supported by that PU. The Execute Test RU contains the network address of the resource to be tested, an identifier of the test procedure to be performed, and any data needed to support the test. For testing a link there are different levels of testing that can be performed. Link-level 0 testing requires that the subarea node, link, and peripheral link station be dedicated to the testing. With link-level 1 testing, the subarea node can be shared while testing is being performed. With link-level 2 testing, described later in conjunction with the description of the Request Test Procedure request, only the link station need be dedicated.

A Record Test Data (RECTD) request is sent from the PU to the SSCP to return the status and the results of the test. It contains the target resource address and test procedure identifier as well as the status information and results.

MAINTENANCE STATISTICS RUs

A Request Maintenance Statistics (REQMS) request is sent from the SSCP to a PU to request that maintenance statistics related to a particular resource be returned by the PU. The REQMS RU specifies a particular resource, using either a local or a network address. It also specifies whether the statistics counters should be reset when the statistics are returned. Box 27.2 lists the different types of statistics that can be requested.

BOX 27.2   Maintenance statistics types

- SDLC test command/response statistics
- Summary error data
- Peripheral PU error statistics
- PU/LU-dependent data
- Engineering change levels
- Link-connection subsystem (modem) data

A Record Formatted Maintenance Statistics (RECFMS) request is sent from the PU to the SSCP to return the statistics requested by a REQMS RU. The RECFMS RU echoes the address and type information from the REQMS request and provides the requested statistics or error information. With an RECFMS RU the statistics returned are in a predefined format. The specific format varies with the particular type of statistics.

A RECFMS RU can also be sent unsolicited (not in response to a REQMS request). An unsolicited RECFMS request can be for any of the types listed for the REQMS RU. It can also be used to convey information related to an *alert event*. An alert event is an event that affects the ability of the PU or one of its LUs to perform its functions. An alert event might require intervention to correct a failure. A RECFMS RU contains an indicator as to whether the request is solicited or unsolicited. A series of RECFMS RUs might be sent to provide information. Another indicator in the RECFMS request indicates whether a particular RECFMS RU is the last in the series or whether additional RECFMS RUs follow.

A Record Maintenance Statistics (RECMS) request is sent from the PU to the SSCP to send maintenance statistics that are not in a predefined format. It contains the network address of the resource to which the statistics relate and the statistics themselves.

TEST RUs

A Request Test Procedure (REQTEST) request is sent from a PU or an LU to the SSCP to request that a particular test procedure be executed. A REQTEST RU contains the network name of the resource to be tested as well as the network name of the resource that is to control the testing. It also contains the name of the test procedure to be executed and may contain the ID of the user initiating the request, a password, and user data. If a user ID and password are included, they can be used to verify the authority of the user to access the resource in question.

A Test Mode request is sent from an SSCP to a PU to initiate a particular test procedure. The test procedure may have been requested by a REQTEST RU, but this is not required. The Test Mode RU specifies either the local address or the network address of the resource to be tested and indicates the type of testing to be performed. Currently, the only type of testing defined is link-level 2 testing of an adjacent link station. The Test Mode request also contains information specific to the type of test. For link station testing, this information indicates whether the test is self-terminating or continuous. If it is continuous, another Test Mode RU is sent to terminate the test. For multipoint links, the Test Mode RU also indicates the number of test frames to send to each secondary link station and carries the data to be sent in the test frame.

A Record Test Results (RECTR) request is sent from the PU to the SSCP to return the results of a test. It identifies the resource that was tested and indicates whether the test results were solicited by a Test Mode RU or if the test was unsolicited. A series of RECTR RUs may be required to return the results, so the RECTR request contains an indicator that identifies the last request of a series. The RECTR RU also contains information concerning the status and results of the test.

REQUEST ECHO
TEST, ECHO TEST

A Request Echo Test (REQECHO) request is sent from an LU to the SSCP to request that the SSCP use an echo test to send test data back to the LU. The REQECHO RU contains the data to be sent and a repetition factor that indicates the number of times it is to be sent.

An Echo Test request is used by the SSCP to send the test data to the requesting LU. It contains the test data from the REQECHO RU and is sent the number of times specified by the repetition factor in the REQECHO RU.

ROUTE TEST,
EXPLICIT ROUTE
TESTED

A Route Test request is sent from the SSCP to a PU, requesting that certain explicit routes and/or virtual routes have their status tested. The Route Test RU contains the destination subarea address and either the explicit route numbers or virtual route numbers to be tested. If virtual route numbers are specified, the underlying explicit routes that support these virtual routes are tested. The PU that receives the Route Test request is in the originating subarea node.

Different types of testing can be specified, including testing all explicit routes, testing only operative routes, testing only inoperative routes, and returning the status of the routes as it is known in the node that received the Route Test RU. The Route Test RU also contains the expected maximum length of any explicit route being tested and correlation information that allows the replies received to be correlated to the original Route Test request.

The PU that receives the Route Test request reports the status of the routes as it is known in that node. If testing of routes is specified, the PU generates an NC Explicit Route Test (NC__ER__TEST) request for each explicit route to be tested. The NC__ER__TEST RU is passed from node to node along the route. If a node is encountered where the explicit route is not properly defined or operative, a negative response is sent back to the originating subarea node. If the NC__ER__TEST request reaches the destination subarea node without problem, a positive response is sent back. The NC__ER__TEST RU contains the maximum route length from the Route Test request, a field for calculating the length as the route is tested, the destination subarea address, the explicit route number, the originating subarea address, information on reverse explicit route numbers, maximum PIU size, the network address of the SSCP that originated the Route Test request, and the correlation information from the Route Test.

When the PU receives a reply to an NC__ER__TEST RU, it sends an Explicit Route Tested (ER__TESTED) request back to the SSCP that sent the Route Test RU. If the route test for this route failed, the ER__TESTED RU identifies the node and transmission group where the failure was detected and contains an indicator that identifies the type of failure that occurred. In this case an ER__TESTED RU is also sent to any other SSCPs that have an active SSCP-to-PU session with this PU. An ER__TESTED request contains the calculated explicit route length, the maximum route length from the route test, the originating and destination subarea addresses, the explicit route number, reverse explicit route numbers, maximum PIU size, the originating SSCP address, and the correlation information from the Route Test.

MANAGEMENT SERVICES

Management services are used to support the communication network management application (CNMA) component, which performs functions related to problem determination for the domain of which it is a part. Management services RUs flow between the LU associated with CNMA and the SSCP. Currently, two management services RUs are defined: Forward and Deliver. A Forward request is sent from the LU to the SSCP and contains an embedded maintenance services request. The SSCP extracts the maintenance services request from the RU and sends it to the appropriate PU for processing by CNMS. It also does this with maintenance services requests that it originates. When the PU sends back a maintenance services request containing the results or information requested, the SSCP embeds that maintenance services request in a Deliver request and sends it on to the LU for CNMA to process. Only certain maintenance services requests can be embedded in a Forward or Deliver RU; these are listed in Box 27.3. Figure 27.2 shows an example of a management services control flow. The steps in this control flow are as follows:

1. The CNMA LU sends a Forward request to the SSCP with a Display Storage request embedded within it.

2. The SSCP extracts the Display Storage request and sends it to the PU for CNMS to process.

3. The information from the specified storage locations is sent from the PU to the SSCP in a Record Storage request.

4. The SSCP embeds the Record Storage request in a Deliver RU and sends it to the LU, where CNMA processes the requested information.

As shown in the example, a request can be sent from CNMS to CNMA in reply to a request sent from CNMA to CNMS. This type of request is called a solicited CNM request or a CNM reply. CNMS might also send a request to CNMA without first receiving a request. This is known as an unsolicited CNM

BOX 27.3   Forward and Deliver maintenance statistics

Forward	Deliver
Display Storage	Record Storage
Request Maintenance Statistics	Record Formatted
	Maintenance Statistics
	Record Maintenance Statistics
Test Mode	Record Test Results

request. When a management services request is sent from the LU to the SSCP, the SSCP does not send the LU a response until after it has sent the embedded maintenance services request to the PU and has received a response from the PU. In contrast, when the PU sends a maintenance services request to the SSCP, the SSCP sends a response immediately and does not wait until it has sent the request on to the LU embedded in a Deliver request and received a response from the LU.

FORWARD

A Forward request is sent from the LU to the SSCP, requesting that the SSCP send the embedded maintenance services RU to the appropriate PU. The Forward RU contains flags that indicate whether the embedded RU solicits a reply request and whether it contains a CNM header. A Forward request contains a *destination name,* which is the network name of the PU to which the embedded request should be sent. A Forward RU also contains a *target name,* which is the network name of the network resource tested or affected by the RU, and a type indicator that indicates whether the target network resource is a PU, an LU, a link, or an adjacent link station. One of the functions the SSCP performs is to convert these network names into network addresses.

DELIVER

A Deliver request is sent from the SSCP to the LU in order to pass on to CNMA a maintenance services request from CNMS. The Deliver RU contains a flag indicating whether the embedded RU contains a CNM header, the network name of the PU where the embedded RU originated, the network name of the target network resource to which the embedded RU relates, and a type code for the target network resource. It also contains configuration hierarchy information about the target resource. If the target resource is a peripheral PU, the Deliver RU contains net-

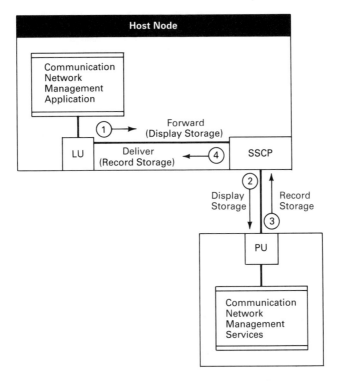

Figure 27.2   Management services control flow.

work names of the subarea node to which it is attached and the link that connects them. If the target resource is an adjacent link station that connects to a subarea node, the configuration hierarchy information includes the network names of the subarea node to which the link station is attached and the link connecting them. If the target resource is a peripheral LU, the configuration hierarchy information includes the network names of the peripheral PU, the subarea node to which it is attached, and the link connecting them.

THE CNM HEADER   Certain maintenance services requests, including Request Maintenance Statistics, Record Formatted Maintenance Statistics, Test Mode, and Record Test Results, contain a CNM header. The CNM header contains either the local or the network address of the target resource, a value called the *procedure-related identifier,* or PRID, and request-specific information. For a request sent from the PU to the SSCP, the CNM header contains flags indicating whether this is a solicited request and whether it is the last in a series of requests. When a maintenance services request is sent as a reply to a previously received maintenance services request from the CNMA, the reply echoes the PRID value from the original request. This allows the CNMA to correlate the reply with the original request. The SSCP can use the PRID field for interleaving requests from multiple CNMAs that are destined for the same PU. The SSCP saves the PRID that was generated by the CNMA and the CNMA's LU address. It then assigns a new PRID to the request and sends it to the PU. When the reply is received, the SSCP-generated PRID is used to retrieve the original PRID and LU address. The original PRID is restored, and the reply is sent to the correct CNMA, based on its LU address.

SUMMARY

There is a Communication Network Management Application (CNMA) component for each domain, which is associated with a host LU, and a Communication Network Management Services (CNMS) component for each node, which is associated with the PU for that node. Management services requests flow between CNMA and the SSCP. Maintenance services requests flow between CNMS and the SSCP. Maintenance services requests are used to perform traces and return trace data, request and return information from specific storage locations, execute tests and return test results, request and return maintenance statistics, request and perform echo tests, and test and return status information on explicit routes. Management services requests are used to route embedded maintenance services requests between CNMA and the SSCP. Embedded maintenance services requests received by the SSCP from CNMA are extracted and sent on to CNMS. Maintenance services requests received by the SSCP from CNMS in reply to an earlier embedded request are embedded by the SSCP in a management services request and sent to CNMA. Maintenance service requests can contain a CNM header that identifies the target resource and contains a procedure-related identifier, or PRID. The PRID is used to correlate replies with requests and to interleave requests from multiple CNMAs destined for the same CNMS.

PART **VI** EPILOG

28 THE FUTURE OF SNA

SNA's history has involved extensive evolution, and a great many features that are available now were not included in the original SNA specifications. The initial releases of SNA supported only simple tree-structured networks, consisting of a single host computer, a channel-attached communications controller, cluster controllers, and terminals. Later releases allowed cluster controllers to be attached to the host, an additional communications controller to be attached through an SDLC link, and switched links to be used. However, the basic network architecture was still tree-structured.

ADVANCED COMMUNICATIONS FUNCTION

A release of SNA known as Advanced Communications Function (ACF) provided for the interconnection of multiple host computers via their communications controllers, allowing the construction of multiple-domain networks. ACF also allowed data to flow during cross-domain sessions without the involvement of both host computers once the session was established.

Other features added in subsequent releases included the following:

- More than two communications controllers associated with a given host computer
- Parallel sessions
- Transmission groups
- Explicit and virtual routes
- 23-bit addressing
- SNA Network Interconnection (SNI)

However, as the capabilities of SNA have grown, the requirements of installations implementing SNA networks have also grown. Installations need to be able to support larger networks, sometimes involving tens of thousands of terminals. The networks need to operate continuously, day and night, seven days a week. SNA networks need to be able to interconnect with other networks, both SNA and non-SNA, throughout the world. And SNA networks must be able to interconnect with the ever-growing networks of personal computers and small systems.

NETWORK ADDRESSING

As networks continue to grow, SNA may well need to expand the *size* of networks it can support. Network addressing has already been increased from 16 bits to 23 bits and may someday be expanded beyond that, to 31 bits or even 48 bits.

ROUTING

As networks grow more complex, *routing* becomes a more critical facility. Possible enhancements related to routing include the following:

- Organization of a domain into clusters for hierarchical routing within the domain

- Dynamic routing, where the set of nodes that make up a route is determined during session initiation rather than being predetermined as part of network definition

- Adaptive routing, where nodes are able to adjust routing while sessions are in progress in response to changing conditions within the network

- Automatic assigning of an alternate route when needed to bypass failed network components.

NETWORK MANAGEMENT

As networks grow more complex, the job of *network management* becomes more complex. Increasing requirements to have networks available without interruption also generate requirements in the area of network management. One possible change is to make network definition easier by building in capabilities for the network to be self-configuring. The ability to make changes to the network configuration dynamically may also be expanded, reducing the need to inactivate the network in order to perform scheduled maintenance. Additional changes may include enhanced alternate routing facilities to bypass failed components and the ability of the network to modify its configuration automatically in the event of failure.

DISTRIBUTED PROCESSING

Early versions of SNA were heavily oriented toward centralized control of the network, with primary responsibility for network operation and control residing in the host computer. As SNA has evolved and the intelligence in other types of network nodes has increased, elements of control have been distributed throughout the network. This trend toward increased emphasis on *distributed processing* is likely to continue in the future. Advanced Program-to-Program Communication, with LU 6.2 and PU 2.1, has been a major advance in this direction. Products that implement these capabilities are just beginning to appear, and the future should find increased emphasis on the use of these facilities, particularly for peer-to-peer communication between low-end processors. APPC allows a program to be accessed using only its program name and an LU name. Future enhancements to SNA may expand on this to allow files to be accessed via their names without specific knowledge of their physical location. Another possible enhancement is to allow lower-level nodes, such as a PU 2.1 node, to handle intermediate routing of messages, as a subarea node does now. SNADS currently provides asynchronous distribution services for documents and messages. As intelligence in nodes increases, these distribution services may be expanded to include network management functions, file transfers, and job networking.

NETWORK INTERCONNECTION

Network interconnection will also be increasingly important. SNI currently provides the ability to interconnect SNA networks. Gateways also exist to non-SNA networks, such as the X.25 packet-switched network gateway and gateways to local area networks such as the PC Network and IBM Token Ring Network. Interconnection to other networks, both large and small, will evolve as the use of these networks grows.

INDEX

A

Abandon connection (ABCONN) request, 352
Acknowledge interchange unit, SNADS, 131
Acknowledgments, SDLC data flow, 177
  individual, 178, 180–81
  multiple frames between, 179, 182–83
  transmission group wrap, 223
Activate connect in (ACTCONNIN) request, 347
Activate explicit route (ACTIVATE_ER) request, 299
Activate link (ACTLINK) request, 332
Activate logical unit (ACTLU) request, 337
Activate physical unit (ACTPU) request, 335
Activate trace (ACTTRACE) request, 360
Activation of SNA resources, 55
Active transmission state, 163
Add link (ADDLINK) request, 332
Add link station (ADDLINKSTA) request, 332
Address(es):
  alias, 146, 147
  link station, 162–63
  network, 22–25
  node, 123–24
  SNADS, 132–33
  translation of, 146–48
Address field, SDLC frame fields, 165, 168
Address split, 24–25
Address structure, 24–25
Advanced Communications Function for Network Control Program (ACF/NCP), 85, 86, 87
Advanced Communications Function for the Telecommunications Access Method (ACF/TCAM), 83, 84, 85, 86–87
Advanced Communications Function for the Virtual Telecommunications Access Method (ACF/VTAM), 83, 85, 86–87
  defining network information to, 88–89
Advanced Communications Function for the Virtual Telecommunications Access Method—Entry (ACF/VTAME), 83, 84
Advanced Program-to-Program Communication (APPC), 11, 16, 95–103

Alias addresses, 146, 147
Alias names, 146, 147
Application layer, 33–34
  OSI model, 73–75, 76–77
Application processing services, DIA services, 125
Application program interface (API), 108–9
Application programs, 9
Application subsystems, 89, 90
Application-to-application services, 57, 58, 76, 264, 273–75
Architected models, 102
Architectures, network, 3–8
  developers of, 4–6
  nature of, 3–4
Asynchronous conversation, 110
Asynchronous transmission, 129

B

Backout, LU, 108
Base set verbs, LU 6.2, 110
Basic conversation, LU 6.2, 109
  verbs used in, 109
Basic information units (BIUs), 45–46, 49, 203
  segmenting, 218–19
  transmission control layer, 233–35
Basic link unit (BLU), 164
Basic transmission units (BTUs), 46–47, 49, 203, 205
Beacon (BCN), loop U-frame commands, 202
Bidder, 250–51, 254
Bind (BIND) request, 297–98
  failure of, 302–3
  negotiable or nonnegotiable, 299–300
Binding, 53
Bit-stuffing technique, 167–68, 172
Block chaining with cipher-text feedback, 243
Blocking, path control services, 61, 211, 220–22
Boundary function, 24
  path control services, 61, 218, 228
Bracket control indicators, 238

Bracket initiation stopped (BIS) response, 255
Bracketing, data flow control services, 60
Brackets, 250
  initiation of, 250–51
  termination of, 251–52
Broadcast address, link station, 162, 163, 168
Brooks, Fred, 4

C

Capacity distribution service level, 138
Cascaded activation, 325
Cascaded gateways, 152–53
Chaining, data flow control services, 60
Chaining control indicators, 237
Chains, 249–50
  types of, 251
Change direction indicator, 238
Character attributes, 272
Character string data stream, 98
  control functions, 268, 269
  SNA, 267
Class of service, 44
Class of service (COS) table, 88
CLEAR, session control commands, 246
Cluster controllers (see Peripheral nodes)
Code selection indicator, 238
Commands, SDLC frames, 167, 174
Commitment control, LU, 107
Commit protocols, synchronization, 274
Common carriers, 4, 5, 6
Communication links, 25–27
Communication network management applications (CNMA), 359, 365
Communication network management header, 367–68
Communication network management services (CNMS), 359
Communication network management structure, 359, 360
Communications controller nodes, 18, 19, 22
Compaction indicator (CPI), 273
Compression indicator (CMI), 273

375

TEAR OUT THIS PAGE TO ORDER OTHER TITLES BY JAMES MARTIN
THE JAMES MARTIN BOOKS

Quantity	Title	Title Code	Price	Total $
———	Action Diagrams: Clearly Structured Program Design	00330–1	$38.50	———
———	Application Development Without Programmers	03894–3	$54.95	———
	A Breakthrough In Making Computers Friendly:			
———	The Macintosh Computer (paper)	08157–0	$25.00	———
———	(case)	08158–8	$31.95	———
———	Communications Satellite Systems	15316–3	$59.95	———
———	Computer Data-Base Organization, 2nd Edition	16542–3	$54.95	———
———	The Computerized Society	16597–7	$26.95	———
———	Computer Networks and Distributed Processing:	16525–8	$54.95	———
	Software, Techniques and Architecture			
———	Design and Strategy of Distributed Data Processing	20165–7	$57.95	———
———	Design of Man-Computer Dialogues	20125–1	$54.95	———
———	Design of Real-Time Computer Systems	20140–0	$54.95	———
———	Diagramming Techniques For Analysts and	20879–3	$49.95	———
	Programmers			
———	An End User's Guide to Data Base	27712–9	$42.95	———
———	Fourth-Generation Languages, Vol. I: Principles	32967–2	$42.95	———
———	Fourth-Generation Languages, Vol. II:	32974–8	$42.95	———
	Representative 4GLs			
———	Fourth-Generation Languages, Vol. III:	32976–3	$42.95	———
	4GLs from IBM			
———	Future Developments in Telecommunications,	34585–0	$56.95	———
	2nd Edition			
———	An Information Systems Manifesto	46476–8	$49.95	———
———	Introduction to Teleprocessing	49981–4	$44.95	———
———	Managing the Data-Base Environment	55058–2	$57.95	———
———	Principles of Data-Base Management	70891–7	$44.95	———
———	Programming Real-Time Computer Systems	73050–7	$46.95	———
———	Recommended Diagramming Standards for Analysts	76737–6	$45.00	———
	& Programmers			
———	Security, Accuracy, and Privacy in Computer	79899–1	$57.95	———
	Systems			
———	SNA: IBM's Networking Solution	81514–2	$44.95	———
———	Software Maintenance: The Problem and Its	82236–1	$49.95	———
	Solutions			
———	Strategic Data Planning Methodologies	85111–3	$43.95	———
———	Structured Techniques for Computing	85518–9	$54.95	———
———	Systems Analysis for Data Transmission	88130–0	$60.00	———
———	System Design From Provably Correct Constructs	88148–2	$49.95	———
———	Technology's Crucible (paper)	90202–3	$15.95	———
———	Telecommunications and the Computer, 2nd Edition	90249–4	$54.95	———
———	Telematic Society: A Challenge for Tomorrow	90246–0	$31.95	———
———	Teleprocessing Network Organization	90245–2	$34.95	———
———	Viewdata and the Information Society	94190–6	$41.95	———
———	VSAM: Access Method Services and Programming	94417–3	$44.95	———
	Techniques			

Total: ———

-discount (if appropriate) ———

New Total: ———

AND TAKE ADVANTAGE OF THESE SPECIAL OFFERS!

When ordering 3 or 4 copies (of the same or different titles) take 10% off the total list price.

When ordering 5 to 20 (of the same or different titles) take 15% off the total list price.

To receive a greater discount when ordering more than 20 copies, call or write:

Special Sales Department
College Marketing
Prentice-Hall
Englewood Cliffs, N.J. 07632
(201)592-2046

SAVE!

If payment accompanies order, plus your state's sales tax where applicable, Prentice-Hall pays postage and handling charges. Same return privilege refund guarantee. Please do not mail cash.

☐ **PAYMENT ENCLOSED**—shipping and handling to be paid by publisher (please include your state's tax where applicable).

☐ **SEND BOOKS ON 15-DAY TRIAL BASIS** & bill me (with small charge for shipping and handling).

Name _____

Address _____

City _____ State _____ Zip _____

I prefer to charge my   ☐ Visa   ☐ MasterCard

Card Number _____ Expiration Date _____

Signature _____

All prices listed are subject to change without notice.
This offer not valid outside U.S.

Mail your order to: Prentice-Hall Book Distribution Center
Route 59 at Brook Hill Drive
West Nyack, NY 10994

Dept. 1   **D-JMAR-NK(4)**

Announcing . . .

TECHNOLOGY'S
CRUCIBLE

by James Martin

Order Your Copy Using This Form and Receive a *SPECIAL 50% DISCOUNT!*

- How will today's high technology and human nature impact tomorrow's quality of life?
- Through a television series set in the year 2019, a narrator asks the question, "Would the course of history have been different if the public in the 1980s had understood the journey on which they had embarked?"
- In *Technology's Crucible,* James Martin, a renowned computer-industry consultant, world-wide lecturer, and best-selling author of over 30 computer text and reference books, describes the forces that are shaping the environment of tomorrow. This book does not forecast the future; it provides a vehicle for helping people think constructively about the future.

QUANTITY	TITLE/AUTHOR	TITLE CODE	PRICE	TOTAL
_____	*Technology's Crucible* (Martin)	90202-3	$15.95	$_____
			−50%	$_____
			New Total	$_____

SAVE! If payment accompanies order, plus your state's sales tax where applicable, Prentice-Hall pays postage and handling charges. Same return privilege refund guaranteed. Please do not mail cash.

☐ PAYMENT ENCLOSED—shipping and handling to be paid by publisher (please include your state's tax where applicable).

☐ SEND BOOKS ON 15-DAY TRIAL BASIS and bill me (with a small charge for shipping and handling).

Name_____

Address_____

City_____ State_____ Zip_____

I prefer to charge my ☐ Visa ☐ MasterCard

Card Number_____ Expiration Date_____

Signature_____

All prices listed are subject to change without notice.
Prices and offer not valid outside the U.S.
For quantity orders and special discounts call either (201)592-2046 or (201) 592-2498

Mail your order to: Prentice-Hall Book Distribution Center
Route 59 at Brook Hill Drive
West Nyack, NY 10994

Dept. 1: D-CAJB-YM(4)

The Conceptual Prism of
Information Systems:

THE JAMES MARTIN BOOKS

Information Systems Management and Strategy	Methodologies for Building Systems	Analysis and Design	CASE
AN INFORMATION SYSTEMS MANIFESTO	STRATEGIC INFORMATION PLANNING METHODOLOGIES (second edition)	STRUCTURED TECHNIQUES: THE BASIS FOR CASE (revised edition)	STRUCTURED TECHNIQUES: THE BASIS FOR CASE (revised edition)
INFORMATION ENGINEERING (Book I: Introduction)	INFORMATION ENGINEERING (Book I: Introduction)	DATABASE ANALYSIS AND DESIGN	DIAGRAMMING STANDARDS FOR CASE
INFORMATION ENGINEERING (Book II: Planning and Analysis)	INFORMATION ENGINEERING (Book II: Planning and Analysis)	DESIGN OF MAN-COMPUTER DIALOGUES	INFORMATION ENGINEERING (Book I: Introduction)
STRATEGIC INFORMATION PLANNING METHODOLOGIES (second edition)	INFORMATION ENGINEERING (Book III: Design and Construction)	DESIGN OF REAL-TIME COMPUTER SYSTEMS	**Languages and Programming**
SOFTWARE MAINTENANCE: THE PROBLEM AND ITS SOLUTIONS	STRUCTURED TECHNIQUES: THE BASIS FOR CASE (revised edition)	DATA COMMUNICATIONS DESIGN TECHNIQUES	APPLICATION DEVELOPMENT WITHOUT PROGRAMMERS
DESIGN AND STRATEGY FOR DISTRIBUTED DATA PROCESSING	**Diagramming Techniques**	DESIGN AND STRATEGY FOR DISTRIBUTED DATA PROCESSING	FOURTH-GENERATION LANGUAGES (Volume I: Principles)
CORPORATE COMMUNICATIONS STRATEGY	DIAGRAMMING TECHNIQUES FOR ANALYSTS AND PROGRAMMERS	SOFTWARE MAINTENANCE: THE PROBLEM AND ITS SOLUTIONS	FOURTH-GENERATION LANGUAGES (Volume II: Representative 4GLs)
Expert Systems	RECOMMENDED DIAGRAMMING STANDARDS FOR ANALYSTS AND PROGRAMMERS	SYSTEM DESIGN FROM PROVABLY CORRECT CONSTRUCTS	FOURTH-GENERATION LANGUAGES (Volume III: 4GLs from IBM)
BUILDING EXPERT SYSTEMS: A TUTORIAL	DIAGRAMMING STANDARDS FOR CASE	INFORMATION ENGINEERING (Book II: Planning and Analysis)	ACTION DIAGRAMS: CLEARLY STRUCTURED SPECIFICATIONS, PROGRAMS, AND PROCEDURES (second edition)
KNOWLEDGE ACQUISITION FOR EXPERT SYSTEMS	ACTION DIAGRAMS: CLEARLY STRUCTURED SPECIFICATIONS, PROGRAMS, AND PROCEDURES (second edition)	INFORMATION ENGINEERING (Book III: Design and Construction)	
		SAA: IBM's SYSTEMS APPLICATION ARCHITECTURE	